# Near the Borderline

*Coming of age (and then some)*
*on the northern frontier*

**David Inglehart**

Copyright © 2024 by David Inglehart

All rights reserved. No part of this book, excepting brief passages for review purposes, may be reproduced in any form or by any electronic or mechanical means without permission in writing from the author. Teachers wishing to photocopy part or all of the work for classroom use, or publishers wishing to include the work in an anthology, should send inquiries to trubadorint@gmail.com.

First Edition

Published in the United States by Troubadour Interactive, LLC
www.troubadourinteractive.com

ISBN 978-1-890642-52-5

Cover photo: Aerial view of the U.S.-Canadian border between Hill Island, Ontario and Wellesley Island, New York. Copyright © Ian Coristine, 1000islandsphotoart.com

*For Donna*

See how the wings, striking against the air, hold the heavy eagle on high, near to the element of fire. And see also how the air, moving over the sea, strikes the bellying sails, causing the loaded, heavy ship to go, so that by these demonstrative and definite reasons you may know that man with his great contrived wings, battling the resistant air and conquering it, can subjugate it and rise above it.

—Leonardo da Vinci

Mood disorders are brain diseases that afflict the integrity of the self—that collection of vital emotions, memories, beliefs, and behaviors that shape each of us as a unique human being. It is because of emotion's central role in both our thinking and our feeling—and because we experience normal shifts in mood every day—that we have such difficulty identifying and accepting a mood disturbance as potentially abnormal. That same difficulty helps explain why people with mood disorders are frequently stigmatized. To put it simply, despite advances in science and medicine, many people are still inclined to view mood disorders as a personal weakness, as bad behavior, rather than a set of illnesses.

—from *The Disordered Mind*, Eric R. Kandel

# Table of Contents

Prologue .................................................................................................. 1
Chapter 1: Northeast Passage ................................................................ 5
Chapter 2: Home Front ........................................................................ 11
Chapter 3: Brothers from Other Mothers ............................................ 19
Chapter 4: Brave New Neighborhood .................................................. 27
Chapter 5: Mission Improbable ............................................................ 33
Chapter 6: Aerial View from Cloud Nine ............................................. 45
Chapter 7: Awakenings .......................................................................... 53
Chapter 8: Gone for a Sailor ................................................................. 69
Chapter 9: When Donkeys Fly .............................................................. 79
Chapter 10: A Not-So-Grand Tour ....................................................... 93
Chapter 11: Sugar Mountain Farewell ................................................ 111
Chapter 12: The Story Behind the Stories ......................................... 117
Chapter 13: Westward Ho, the Rag-wings! ........................................ 131
Chapter 14: Asylum in Academe ......................................................... 157
Chapter 15: Going Off-Road ................................................................ 171
Chapter 16: North Country Narcosis ................................................. 183
Chapter 17: Re-entry ........................................................................... 207
Chapter 18: Family of Choice .............................................................. 217
Chapter 19: Three Days of the Canada Goose ................................... 225
Chapter 20: A Near Thing ................................................................... 241
Chapter 21: Any Landing You Walk Away From ................................ 249
Chapter 22: Survivor Bias ................................................................... 257
Chapter 23: Secrets of the Borderline ................................................ 265

# Prologue

As a boy growing up in the Thousand Islands, I had a favorite spot along the shore in front of my family's summer cottage. It was a ledge on a granite outcropping where I could sit and stare at a body of water whose namesake, Saint Lawrence, no one ever bothered to mention; for those familiar with the area, it was simply the River. Our cottage overlooked a narrow channel on the U.S.-Canadian border, and from my chosen perch I spent many idle moments gazing out across the water, half-expecting a visible borderline to appear on the surface like a highway lane-marker.

How could borderlines be so conspicuous on maps, I wondered, yet have no counterpart in the real world? After all, a border was something to be reckoned with. To cross a border, even a state line, meant going from one system of laws to another, and crossing an international border was more consequential still, routinely involving changes in language, customs, and currencies. Indeed, having one in my front yard seemed a great privilege, if for no other reason than the opportunity to cross it unannounced on a regular basis. I had only to swim fifty yards from shore to enter Canadian waters, and familiarity with the practice tended to breed, if not contempt, a certain dismissive pride. I was technically flouting international law and getting away scot-free.

Even so, I found it vexing that something as important as the border should have no visible manifestation. Somewhere out in the channel that served as my swimming hole lay a duly agreed-upon boundary established in the aftermath of a history-altering war, yet nowhere along its thirty-mile course through the Islands was the border's actual location indicated by so much as a single makeshift buoy. And yet, upon crossing this imaginary threshold, boaters from both countries were legally required to make their way to a custom station on the appropriate mainland to report in. This system made no sense to me, and more perplexing still was the fact that those charged with enforcing such expectations had scant means to patrol the far-flung waterways of the River, let alone apprehend such offenders as they might encounter.

Reporting in by car, on the other hand, was far less random a proposition. Upon entering a customs pavilion on the cross-island highway, motorists were shunted into one of several lanes for questioning by waiting agents in a process as unavoidable as it was simple, like placing an order at a fast-food drive-through. Indeed, the relative convenience of reporting in by land always struck me as an insult to the boating class, representing a species of conveyance discrimination. Moreover, the discrepancy between the two methods tended to invite abuses, for as I well knew, scofflaws could easily swim across the border at any number of places, entering upon foreign soil with little or no chance of detection. Those intent on more serious cross-border mischief had only to avail themselves of a boat and find suitably isolated locations to launch and land on opposite shores, preferably under cover of darkness. Who was going to stop them?

In time of course, such inconsistencies tended to blend in with a litany of other governmental regulations, and I got over my resentment, learning to appreciate the role the border played in defining the region's unique character. Like the freighters that plied the St. Lawrence Seaway, it helped establish the area's popularity as a tourist destination and lent a certain international cachet to the various riverside communities. This, and the long-standing comity and goodwill that existed between the two neighbor-nations, helped account for why residents on both sides of the line complied more or less happily with the border's otherwise annoying impositions. Accordingly, we Americans flew the stars and stripes from the transoms of our boats, just as Canadians did their maple-leaf ensigns, and the same went for our respective island homes, where national flags were routinely on display, helping newcomers identify where they were among the river's otherwise baffling network of waterways. However casually, these flags served as the markers I had found wanting as a boy, roughly sketching the borderline and helping establish its reputation as the longest undefended international boundary on earth.

*Prologue*

Suffice it that by the end of my high school years I had acquired a deep backlog of memories of the River, and in the process had come to consider myself a card-carrying denizen of the borderlands. So it was that, when the time came to decide where to go to college, my thoughts returned to my private viewing place by the shore and the way the summer clouds drifted in unison with the river's current, forming a single tableau of water and sky making its way inexorably northeast. Serving me as a compass bearing, such memories had the effect of pointing me to a school in far-off Maine, a state that appealed to me in part because it shared a long border with Canada. Only after I'd been accepted did more practical considerations occur to me, things like travel times and related arrangements, or the fact that I knew next to nothing about the Pine Tree State. Even so, such uncertainties seemed the stuff of which adventures were made, and I was keen to learn about them for myself.

*Near the Borderline*

# Chapter 1

# Northeast Passage

It had been an eventful year from the very start. In January, the Supreme Court ruled on a case known as Roe v. Wade, establishing a woman's right to decide for herself whether or not to carry a fetus to term. And before the month was out, a group of inept burglars pled guilty to breaking into a D.C. office building called the Watergate, spawning a series of investigations that would bring an end to the Nixon presidency.

In other, less prominent, news, I turned 21 and come September was on my way back to college at the outset of my senior year. Ever since acquiring a car of my own car—a '67 Chevy Impala—I had always traveled to and from school along the route my father took when dropping me off as an entering freshman three years earlier, on which occasion we skirted south of the Adirondacks, taking the interstates east to Massachusetts, then north into Maine. Now, having officially reached adulthood, I decided to break with tradition. The faster route along the four-lanes had been my father's way, but I was bound to find another, and chose instead a more leisurely course through the mountains. Though the choice would add at least an hour to the trip, I thought to spend the time enjoying the late-summer scenery.

The day began under a dense layer of cloud, however, and as the first leg of the journey transited a long stretch of flat and featureless cow country, I soon had second thoughts about the plan. After an hour and a half on the road and with at least eight more to go, I'd seen my fill of broken-down farms and dystopian rural landscapes, when suddenly a weather-beaten wooden church loomed into view along the roadside, a crooked message board out front displaying the words "To know all is to forgive all."

It was the last straw bale, as it were.

—To know all? I scoffed inwardly. —As if religion hadn't obstructed the pursuit of knowledge for untold centuries, the better to peddle its tedious catalog of superstitious fables! (I was now a college senior, with claims to universal knowledge of my own.)

If nothing else, my fit of pique on the theme of forgiveness served to dispel another ten miles of dreary terrain, and soon enough the flatlands gave way to low hills, the sky grew brighter, and the offending proverb faded from my thoughts.

By the time I reached the shore of Lake Champlain, the sun was shining in a clear blue sky and, following the road signs east, I started across the outlet of the lake on a mile-long, two-lane bridge of doubtful construction. Causeway was more like it: a narrow strip of asphalt perched six feet above the water on irregular wooden pilings and flanked by rusty pipework railings such as might have been sourced in a local plumbing supply. Even so, the views to be had from the middle of the span were the more impressive for the peril of the crossing. A mile to the north lay the Canadian border, while to the south, densely forested mountain ranges ramped skyward, framing the scene in sunny swathes of greenery. In between, the long body of the lake stretched to the southern horizon, serving the geographical function of a distinct regional boundary. Once across the bridge, you were in New England.

The highway came ashore on a narrow peninsula and proceeded south across a chain of islands to the Vermont mainland, where it veered eastward again to begin a long ramble through mountain ranges Green, White, and Blue, before settling down at last on the rolling uplands of central Maine. Between the top of Champlain and the Kennebec River lay some 250 frost-mangled miles, yet by now I no longer cared about making good time or being the least bit sensible. I was blazing a new trail, forging my own destiny, and as I made my way through the high country on that green and golden day an idea began to form in the limpid pool of my mind.

*Northeast Passage*

    This idea had everything to do with events of earlier that year, when a friend from high school and I went in on the purchase of a Rogallo-type ski-kite, a primitive flying machine designed to be towed aloft behind a boat and released at altitude, enabling the pilot to glide back to the surface in free flight. Discovered in the pages of a water-skiing magazine, the kite instantly appealed to our penchant for showy self-promotion, and, intent on introducing the new sport to our summer haunts in the Thousand Islands, we placed an order with the manufacturer sometime over spring break.

    Our friendship dated back to eleventh grade at Watertown High, where a mutual connection to the River provided us with no end of shared talking points. Over the ensuing summers of high school and college, when not working various jobs in and around the riverside community of Alexandria Bay, we spent much of our time on the water, skiing or otherwise hacking around in boats, compiling a trove of experiences that leant themselves to just the sort of minimal-cue partnership conducive to ski-kiting.

    The new toy arrived via freight carrier from California pending our return from college, and was delivered to a place on the U.S. mainland overlooking the river's main shipping channel. We took possession during the first week of May, arriving by tow-boat with a plan to ski and/or fly it some seven miles downriver to my family's place on Wellesley Island. Tearing open the elongated shipping carton to reveal the kite's shiny aluminum tubing and colorful Dacron sail, we feverishly assembled the airframe on a nearby beach, scanned a few simplistic instructions ("Don't go for the moon on your first flight") and played paper-scissors-rock to see who would go first. Having "won," I donned a makeshift plastic hockey helmet, strapped myself into the kite's primitive harness, and prepared to commit aviation.

    Given the seasonably chilly water and considerable distance to be traveled, my ambitions at this point were decidedly sub-lunar. Awkward enough to lift and balance on land, the kite required considerable effort to carry on one's shoulders while skiing, and during the long, downwind leg of the journey I negotiated the unquiet waters of the river's main channel on a pair of stubby trick-skis, the kite poised ominously above my head, fitfully pitching and yawing with every adverse breeze. After some fifteen minutes of this, fatigued from the effort and the cold, I had all but decided that my first flight was going to have to wait.

Just then, however, the boat turned into the wind for the last mile of the trip, at which point an oncoming breeze filled the sail, the kite's heavy frame lifted from my shoulders, and the harness began tugging me skyward. After watching me make a few tentative hops, Sam—a nickname derived from the parlance of Eddie Haskell, of "Leave it to Beaver" fame—throttled up, and I went airborne in a steady rush.

It was a moment of sublime discovery. The thing actually flew, and, more encouraging still, proved readily maneuverable by means of shifting one's weight relative to a central control bar. After ascending to the dizzying height of some ten feet above the water, I made a series of turns before descending to the surface, deploying the towline release mechanism, and skiing to a stop on the beach in front of the family cottage, shivering with cold yet utterly elated.

Moments later, we switched places and Sam followed suit, taking to the air with wide-eyed wonder. So began a summer-long fixation in which we flew at every opportunity, racking up countless hours of airtime and adding more and more towline until we were able to "top out" at altitudes over 500 feet, from which heights we "cut loose," releasing the towline and gliding back to the surface with the fearless aplomb of comic-book superheroes.

It had indeed been an eventful summer, and now as I proceeded back to school the thought occurred to me that, using snow skis and a larger, gliding version of the tow-kite, I might continue my flying career from the slopes of any number of ski resorts throughout the region. The previous winter, a west-coast flyer had made a series of ski-launched flights from a mountain resort in Washington State, a feat I'd read about in the pages of a glossy magazine. The new sport remained virtually unknown in the East, however, and, determined to "be the change I wished to see in the world," I began to consider how such a thing might be accomplished.

The business of landing, for example, seemed to warrant some forethought. Over water, it had scarcely been an issue, the broad channels of the River providing plenty of room for maneuver and a botched touchdown threatening little more than a vigorous dunking. The narrow confines of a ski trail, on the other hand, presented all sorts of annoying obstacles—trees, lift towers, cables, skiers—any one of which were apt to be less than forgiving in the event of collision. Then there was the glider itself, which, even when disassembled and folded upon itself, formed a long and cumbersome package requiring some means of transport uphill.

If the scheme itself remained sketchy, however, the question of where best to attempt it was never in doubt. An hour and a half north of school, Sugarloaf Mountain boasted one of the highest vertical drops and best facilities in the East, and its particular topography—a near-perfect cone with ski trails funneling down to a shallow, open slope in front of the main lodge—seemed custom-made for my purpose. As big as a football field, the open area at the base of the trails was uncluttered by trees, power lines or other obstructions, and was known, suggestively enough, as the Landing. While many details remained to be worked out, by the time I arrived back at school my idle road-reveries had morphed into a glorious quest with a momentum of its own.

Over the course of the ensuing fall, the project grew into an obsession, rendering even the ribald distractions of college life a bit tiresome by comparison. Sometime in early November, having decided upon specifications of airframe size and sail color, I submitted an order for a new glider along with a check for the princely sum of $650. Scheduled for delivery in six weeks, its arrival promised to coincide nicely with the start of the coming ski season. With any luck, my new dream-machine would be waiting for me upon my return home for Christmas break.

*Near the Borderline*

Chapter 2

# Home Front

During the summer of 1967, the Queen of England paid an official visit to Canada aboard the royal yacht, *H.M.S Britannia*, on the occasion of Dominion Day, the Canadian equivalent of the Fourth of July. Bound for Toronto via the St. Lawrence Seaway, the great ship arrived in front of Alexandria Bay one sun-drenched afternoon, and I remember standing on the well-kept lawn of family friends whose summer home overlooked the American channel, watching as it motored slowly past amid a picture-postcard Thousand Islands tableau: blue water, green islands, cerulean sky, and a pageant of boats. Tour boats, cruisers, launches and runabouts—boats of every description crowded the narrow waterway, forming a vast flotilla over which *Britannia* loomed like a colossus, its decks as high as those of the lofty freighters that routinely plied the seaway on their way to and from the ports of the Great Lakes.

There was nothing of the merchantman about *Britannia*, however; she was all showboat. On her decks, impeccably uniformed crewmen could be seen standing at their posts, heedless of the adoring masses below, who bobbed about in the wake-riled waters like so many courtiers genuflecting in the presence of Her Majesty. Along the ship's superstructure, an array of masts and spars flaunted brightly colored pennants, while above the stern an immense Union Jack the size of a highway billboard waved languidly in the breeze.

Then 15, I was wonderstruck, and deeply shocked to think that such a magnificent vessel was the property of one rather frumpy-looking, middle-aged woman. Knowing little about the English monarchy of much of anything else, I could scarcely imagine the basis for such personal preeminence, and the idea of it struck me as a violation of basic principles of fairness and propriety. It was one thing for Her Majesty to own a lot of castles and lord it over everyone on account of her breeding. This I could accept; it didn't touch me. That such audacity should extend to the world of boats, however, approached too near my own pretensions, for I knew boats, or imagined I did. Boats and the status they conveyed represented a large part of my understanding of human society. I had grown up around boats. Boats were a part of my heritage. I was a boat-snob.

    In this, I was joined and largely inspired by two male cousins of similar age, whose father, my uncle, owned a number of classic wooden inboards, the pride of the collection a 28-foot Gar Wood launch with immaculately-varnished mahogany decks, hard-topped main cabin, and two-seat cockpit aft. Beneath a wide, chromium-trimmed hatch lay a large-bore, eight-cylinder Chrysler Marine engine with high-performance, hemispherical powerhead and twin four-barrel carburetors. When idling, it produced an ominous rumble interrupted by the throat-clearing spew of coolant water, which spurted from the dual exhaust pipes to a distance of several yards. At full throttle, it produced a continuous thunder modulated by the high-pitched whine of whirling machinery.

    Built in the 1930s, the model had long since gone out of production, giving it a certain mystique and accounting for its considerable value. One of the last survivors of a dying breed, it had earned a name and reputation much like that of a celebrated elder personage. Indeed, we could scarcely have been more respectful had it been the reincarnation of our storied grandfather, its original owner, who had grown up on the river during its heyday as a summer resort. Many were the hours we spent lounging in the comfort of its deep, leather-appointed seats, engine hatches propped open, gazing affectionately at "the hemi."

    That we should have admired that boat so much is somewhat baffling in hindsight. Loud it certainly was, and, for its size, exceptionally fast, but there were many louder, faster boats on the River, and its hard-topped cabin gave it a staid and domesticated look, the look of a boat best suited to transporting well-dressed ladies to afternoon teas—its actual purpose in days gone by. In addition, it had a nasty habit of broaching at high speed in a following sea, a characteristic that led to moments of abject terror when, without warning, the hull would plow into a rising swell, list perilously to port, and—given the engine's prodigious torque—very nearly roll over, threatening to trap its occupants inside a foundering vessel. Our admiration had little to do with either practicality or safety, however; the boat's timeless charm lay in its ability to turn heads and inspire envy. It was its aura of exclusivity we cherished.

And then there was *Britannia*. Watching as it made its way through a clutter of lesser vessels, the largest of which would scarcely have served as its tender, I was forced to confront my own shabby elitism. Here was the biggest, most luxurious pleasure boat in the world, its impossible grandeur eclipsing all sense of scale, such that I could never again entertain the slightest degree of boat-pride without thinking of its belittling magnificence and going red-faced with humiliation. More worldly observers might enjoy the spectacle of its passing, but I was not of an age to appreciate the import of the moment, and Her Majesty was no queen of mine. When I considered that in the course of her passage through my home waters, she didn't trouble herself to appear on deck, never deigning to wave so much as a hanky at the many hundreds who had gathered to see her, my resentment verged on outrage.

In time my chastened boat-pride would devolve upon a more modest vessel within my uncle's collection. For everyday use, such as the three-mile trip to our place on Wellesley, he drove a less ostentatious, yet equally stylish, Gar Wood runabout with a raked windshield and modern V-six engine. He and my cousins would come visiting on a regular basis, and I would await their arrival at the end of our dock, gazing intently downriver in an effort to spot the boat's distinctive profile as it appeared from behind a distant Canadian island and made its way upriver, crossing the border as it came.

Technically, such traffic was required to check in with U. S. Customs before landing in the States, but as this would have involved a lengthy detour to the Bay, the practice was routinely ignored. In the case of return trips, Canadian authorities in nearby Rockport tended to command more respect, if only because the custom dock directly overlooked that section of the river. Even so, border security was far from rigorous on either side in those days. Much as they had during the region's early history, when the Embargo Act of 1807 first gave rise to an illicit cross-border trade in tea and rum, the islands presented a kind of middle ground between American and Canadian shores, effectively isolated by the river's many channels and inlets.

The area's reputation for smuggling was revived during Prohibition, when a growing demand for contraband liquor gave rise to a local fetish for sleeker and faster boats with which to elude the authorities. By that time, the region had long since attracted growing numbers of summer people, including various Gilded Age tycoons whose palatial estates, featured in various scenic boat cruises, helped make tourism a mainstay of the local economy. This in turn led to the construction of numerous large, wooden hotels throughout the islands, many of which would eventually burn down, leaving behind micro-communities of Victorian-era cottages in their immediate vicinity.

Such was the case with the Westminster Hotel, located near the foot of Wellesley. When it was lost to fire in 1914, the hotel grounds would lie vacant, including a remote piece of property that my grandfather would eventually purchase for the site of his summer home. Though the cottage he built on the site was avant-garde in comparison to those in the vicinity, it was by no means luxurious, consisting of a single-story dwelling erected upon a simple concrete slab. Located on the site of the hotel's former linen-processing facilities, the place was known as Laundry Point.

It was one of my earliest memories of the River. I was five years old and in the company of my older brother. We were standing down by the shore, skipping stones, and after making a selection from the beach's trove of likely projectiles, I sent it spinning out across the water, watching as it hopped along the surface and settled into the depths. I had just turned back toward the beach to look for another when I was suddenly struck in the forehead by an unseen object. Momentarily stunned, I soon became aware that I was bleeding profusely from a wound directly above my right eye, a discovery that sent me wailing in distress up to the house in search of medical attention.

*Home Front*

Taken to an emergency room on the mainland, I was stitched up and eventually returned home, where, after conferring with my brother, my mother concluded that he had lost control of his skipping stone and inadvertently hit me with it. This seemed a plausible enough explanation, except that I clearly recalled having been some thirty feet away and perpendicular to his line of fire at the time of the incident. It was either a wildly erratic throw or something darker was at work; I couldn't be sure which, and such doubts would only grow stronger in the years to come.

By the time he was in middle school, my brother had begun to show signs of developmental difficulties. While otherwise bright and well-formed, something was wanting in the general area of sandbox skills, the basic ability to share stuff and get along with others. As his default companion for much of our childhood, I confronted the problem on a regular basis—an inflexibility of temperament that frequently managed to defeat the whole point of playing. Over time I came to accept it as simply part of his character, a trait that made it hard for him to get along with others. Unlike the rest of his siblings, who routinely invited schoolmates over to our house and went visiting in return, he showed little inclination to make friends of his own and often demonstrated a general hostility to the presence of strangers in the house.

As time went on, he grew increasingly moody, his customary social reticence giving way to violent outbursts that threatened injury to himself as well as others. While such episodes inevitably involved all of his siblings, I was on the receiving end of much of it, if only because I was closest to him in age and least inclined to defer to his older-brother status. Despite periods of relative harmony, the resentments associated with his unknown malady would eventually get the better of him, he would visit his frustrations on me, and we would let slip the dogs of fratricide, engaging in epic fights that ranged widely about the house and yard.

For all of his aggression within the family, however, he tended to be shy to the point of paralysis in public, where confrontations sent him into a state of debilitating emotional turmoil. This became a major hurdle in high school, where he became the target of regular harassment from would-be toughs who homed in on his social awkwardness, intent on harassing him for no other reason than they were able do so with minimal risk of retaliation. Here too, I tended to have a front-row seat on the problem, for while the other siblings went away to private schools, my brother and I carried on in the public system, where the student body was less refined and adult supervision tended to be spotty at best.

In one instance, I happened upon him in a school hallway where he stood partly surrounded by several low-functioning hecklers intent on tormenting him. Recognizing his predicament, I walked over and engaged him in conversation as a means of lending support. On a strictly physical basis, the gesture was symbolic at best; standing a mere five feet tall (I had yet to "get my growth"), I was not exactly an intimidating presence. Nevertheless, the idea that someone might willingly establish a connection with the object of their intimidation gave his tormentors pause, and soon enough the surrounding boneheads broke up and departed. My involvement, however, only seemed to make matters worse, for in bearing witness to his humiliation I managed to implicate myself in his cumulative anger over such incidents.

Shortly thereafter, I happened to be home from school recovering from abdominal surgery. A week earlier, while the parents were away on a ski trip, I suffered an attack of acute appendicitis that forced me to seek help at the house next door. As our neighbor was a doctor, I hobbled Quasimodo-like across the intervening sidewalk, rang the doorbell and was soon admitted by his wife, who had me lie down on a sofa while she called her husband at his office. Minutes later he arrived and, once informed of my complaint, made a point of pressing firmly with his fingertips against my lower right side. When I showed no sign of distress, he removed the pressure just as deliberately, at which point I doubled up as if I'd been stabbed. It was all the confirmation he needed, and, helping me to his car, he took me straight to the hospital, where the offending organ was summarily removed with permission obtained from my grandmother. Meanwhile, my parents were contacted and, cutting short their vacation, arrived the next day to take me home.

I spent the following week hobbling around the house on crutches and happened to be in the front entry one afternoon, picking up the mail, when my brother arrived home, clearly seething over some fresh outrage at school. Storming in the front door, he started in on me without prologue or provocation, giving me a brief thrashing before continuing on his way. Though I managed to fend him off sufficiently to avoid tearing my stitches, the incident was revealing—to me, at least—of something seriously amiss with his moral compass and basic self-control.

Even so, he never seemed to fight in anger so much as frustration. It was nothing personal, really, just a habit he had acquired to ward off a more desperate response. And I was a convenient sparring partner, someone he could take his anger out on in what was readily construed as a standard case of sibling rivalry. I disagreed with this analysis, but was hardly in a position to say so, and on some level, knowing what I knew of his difficulties at school, I didn't really blame him. He was my brother, after all, and our fights were a kind of ritual to be performed when no one was around. In any case, they were performed in earnest, many lasting as long as a half-hour and ending only with the complete exhaustion of the respective combatants.

Persisting throughout my middle and high school years, this species of domestic abuse inevitably took its toll. Among other things, it gave me a certain tolerance for disruption and uncertainty, and the more such fighting became normalized, the more I came to see myself as a roughhewn sort of character with a comfort level, if not appetite, for risk. Soon I began performing random acts of rebellion of my own, for no other reason, it seemed, than to assert my inalienable right to do so.

My first foray in this direction took place at age sixteen, when I snuck a beer from our refrigerator and retired to the seeming seclusion of our back yard to drink it, little suspecting that the same doctor's wife who had summoned help during my abdominal emergency had a clear view of my ill-considered subterfuge. Moreover, she had the temerity to tell my mother about it, which I could only interpret as a betrayal of her former kindness. Meanwhile, my mother, in her non-confrontational way, eventually asked me why I'd felt it necessary to sneak outside to drink some beer, when I might have simply asked her for some—a response that, however sensible, scarcely served to discourage further episodes.

Thus, one night several months later, I moved on to the hard stuff, downing a short glass of scotch from my father's supply and heading out the back door. It was your standard adolescent revolt, scarcely worth recalling except for the fact that my destination that night was a chaperoned teen-age dance at the nearby First Presbyterian Church, where, visibly drunk and reeking of booze, I made quite an impression on those of my friends in attendance. Though I'd never been a regular at the church, prior to this I'd generally been perceived as something of a straight-arrow.

    Not anymore.

## Chapter 3

# Brothers from Other Mothers

I don't recall when I first became aware of the practice of smoking marijuana, but by the time I was a senior in high school there was no escaping its influence on the prevailing zeitgeist. The previous summer had seen the alarming gathering of wayward youth known as Woodstock, as well as the grisly Manson murders in far-off California, neither of which events recommended the drug culture to my high-school friends and me. Nor had it been discovered by the local "hoods," those socially-disadvantaged classmates who generally modeled all unsavory behaviors for the rest of us—known as "clicks." Unlike other taboos, however, pot-smoking tended to be a top-down rather than bottom-up phenomenon, and was widely perceived as a mark of sophistication among college students of the day.

That's how I discovered it, anyway, smoking for the first time within a week of my arrival at college, on which occasion I was taken under the tutelage of a couple of dorm-mates—a sophomore from nearby Portland, who supplied the stuff, and a fellow freshman from Providence with considerable experience in the smoking arts—both of whom were glad of the chance to initiate an admitted neophyte in the ways of the mysterious weed.

We prepared for the ritual by taking the standard precautions: locking the door and placing a rolled-up towel along the threshold to avoid detection by passersby in the hall. Next, we huddled furtively around my desk, where our supplier rolled a bulky joint from the contents of a plastic baggy, lit it up, and passed it to me with a certain nonchalant largesse. Taking a windy drag in my turn, I passed it along, and so we continued, passing and puffing, until the merest stub was all that remained, by which time my instructors had slipped into a heavy-lidded haze and began looking at me for signs of similar incapacity.

I fear I was a disappointment to them. Like many first timers, I didn't get high, partly as a consequence of not knowing what to expect. Anticipating some sort of dramatic transformation, I seemed to miss the mood of the thing and sat waiting impatiently for the effects to kick in. Meanwhile, my companions were growing goofier by the minute, and, as if to prove how impaired he'd become, the Portland native decided to perform what I gathered was some sort of pot-smoker's version of a sobriety test.

"Watch this!" he announced.

Moving to an open area in the middle of the room, he bent over, placed the palm of one hand on the floor, and shuffled around it in a tight circle three times as fast as he could, at which point he stood up, took a deep breath, and held it.

What happened next occurred so seamlessly as to appear intentional. Passing out on his feet, he tipped over like a felled tree and landed flat on his back, his head hitting the floor with a sickening thud. This, I decided, was going a bit too far in the name of entertainment, and as I continued to watch, he began twitching spasmodically, his head bouncing off the floor like a tightly-dribbled basketball.

Now genuinely alarmed, I turned to the experienced smoker next to me for guidance, only to find him staring open-mouthed and glassy-eyed at our fallen comrade.

"Whoa, man!" he drawled, "—Holy shit! Holy shit!"

At this point, lurching into action, I went to the assistance of the still-convulsing figure before me and, placing my hands on his shoulders, held him firmly against the floor (not a recommended procedure in such cases), whereupon his spasms ceased and he remained motionless for what seemed a long time. Eventually coming to, he opened his eyes and looked straight up at me.

"What happened?" he asked, oblivious of his recent peril.

"Jesus, man!" exclaimed the Rhode Islander, more aggrieved than concerned, "you were really fucked-up! You passed out and went all, like, catatonic!"

At this, the victim slowly sat up and looked at me for confirmation, to which I responded with a dubious sort of frown, as if to say it hadn't been as bad as all that. On second thought, anxious to avoid any further surprises, I made bold to offer some advice.

"That thing you do, twirling around and then standing up? Don't do that again, okay?"

"Yeah," he agreed, rubbing the back of his head. "It worked, though, huh?"

"Oh, yeah—like a charm."

"You crazy bastard!" continued the other. "I was freaking out over here!"

Next, the two of them started complaining of hunger and decided to go in search of something to eat, and when I begged off, they looked at me suspiciously and inquired about my state of mind.

"I feel pretty weird, alright," I said, "which is why I better stay here—in case I freak out or something."

They allowed as how I was probably right.

"Don't worry," announced the Whirling Dervish in parting, "you'll get the hang of it."

That I was able to keep a straight face at this point will attest to the quasi-religious nature of pot-smoking in those days. As for my then state of mind, I began to experience a certain residual paranoia at the thought that involvement in a drug-related death would probably have constituted grounds for dismissal. Apart from this, however, I was not aware of any particular change in mood, and remained perplexed by the whole marijuana craze. Despite my best efforts, pot's unique form of lunacy seemed to have eluded me, and I decided the stuff was vastly overrated. Overall, I'd gotten more light-headed and had considerably more fun smoking cigarettes with my cousins back when I was twelve.

The next morning, as if to reinforce my disillusionment with the whole experience, I no sooner awoke from sleep than the room began to spin violently, forcing me to retreat into darkness. Moments later, I opened my eyes again, and again the room spun crazily, driving me back once more into self-imposed blindness. Now fully conscious, for a few terrifying seconds I wondered if my vision, or indeed my brain, had become permanently skewed, but when I opened my eyes a third time the room swung to a stop, and as far as I could tell I was back to normal.

Attributing the strange dizziness to pot's insidious after-effects, I experienced a pang of remorse, yet the thought never occurred to me to swear off the stuff or avoid those who smoked it. Instead, I came to accept its ritual significance—the sense in which it represented an act of communion uniting the adherents of a new faith, the central tenet of which was that the world was hopelessly fucked-up and only by defying accepted norms could one begin to appreciate the extent of its confusion. Thus, as my newfound friends had assured me, I got the hang of it, and eventually became a habitual smoker.

Later that first year, I joined the college swim team, where I soon found myself in the unenviable position of mainstay in the distance events. Too skinny for a sprinter, my métier was the mere doggedness required for the 500, 1,000 and 1,650-yard freestyle. While the latter was reserved for the regionals, I was obliged to swim both shorter events during all regular meets, which tended to dampen my enthusiasm for the thrill of athletic competition. How I resented the sheer labor of it.

Only the fellowship of my teammates made it tolerable, and during the ensuing spring term a number of us decided to pledge a fraternity, if only as a means to avoid the annual room draw by which our living circumstances would be left to chance. For my part, the idea of joining a frat further promised to model a more benevolent and companionable notion of brotherhood than I'd been accustomed to, and thus I talked up the idea with several friends within and beyond the swim team. By joining as a group, I argued, we might avoid the more unsavory aspects of initiation.

As it turned out, we needn't have worried much on that score; it so happened that the house we opted to join was comprised for the most part of pot-addled slackers who scarcely bothered to recruit us, let alone subject us to anything as strenuous as hazing. After several years of declining enrollments, the existing members were in no position to discourage our interest, nor, to their credit, were they the least bit inclined to do so. Instead, they took the position that their unkempt appearance and practiced indifference provided all the inducement we could possibly require—and how right they were, for we quickly came to embrace their dysfunctional cynicism, aspiring with all our hearts to their lack of aspiration.

Such perverse allegiance was attributable in part to a larger malaise in the world beyond college, where the war in Vietnam continued to consume lives and resources with a steady appetite, not the least of its ironies being a draft lottery in which birthdates became the basis for determining who would be called to military service, a system with the wonderfully insensitive effect of associating the occasion of one's birth with the real possibility of his meeting an untimely death. A political sleight-of-hand, the lottery only heightened the sense of randomness and illogic by which, absent a clear mandate in support of the war, large numbers of unlucky young men continued to be delivered to a far-off, foreign shore, where all manner of evil things were apt to befall them and the people they met with.

Meanwhile, college attendance continued to exempt one from service, and thus my new brothers and I pursued our academic careers according to an unspoken deal designed to placate the more powerful elements of the body politic. It was as shameful a bargain as could easily be imagined, and, having begun our freshman year in the aftermath of a nationwide student strike, we had missed the chance to be involved in any meaningful protest against the conflict, which left us in a kind of ideological limbo. As a result, our opinions on the war, insofar as we presumed to have any, remained mired in a deep ambivalence.

If the country's predicament in Vietnam was beyond the reach of our indignation, however, the figure of Richard Nixon was not, and in many ways the Nixon presidency represented a greater evil than the war itself. In part this was due to mere convenience, other targets of opportunity having left the field, and in part to a profoundly mysterious quality about Nixon. For reasons unknown to political or behavioral science, the man had a knack for provoking the pent-up rage of an entire generation. Something about his dark physiognomy and disingenuous expression made him a perfect symbol of the political subterfuge that had caught us in its web of guilt, and many of us would learn to hate him with a fury bordering on hysteria.

Throughout the latter stages of the 1972 presidential election, we followed the nightly newscasts with a degree of participatory zeal seldom seen outside professional wrestling arenas. Draping ourselves in semi-recumbent ease upon a collection of decrepit chairs and sofas in the fraternity's basement rooms, we gazed up at a large, wall-mounted television like so many zombies awaiting the motivating influence of a full moon. And sure enough, as soon as the president appeared, something within us came to life; we jeered, fumed, carried on obscene conversations with his image, threw things at the set, all traces of pot-induced serenity a distant memory. It was as if, like characters in an aliens-among-us horror movie, we possessed a special clairvoyance the rest of the population lacked, and in shouting at the TV we sought to alert those others to the strange indentations on the neck or the elongated finger that marked Nixon as a monster. "Don't you see?" our imprecations seemed to say, "He's one of them!"

It soon became apparent, however, that a substantial majority of the voting public didn't see, and moreover didn't appreciate the insights of a bunch of whiny, self-indulgent college kids. Winning reelection by a comfortable margin, Nixon embarked upon his second term in what could only be construed as a wholesale rejection of our political judgment and intelligence. To this we responded with all the maturity and self-restraint we could muster—we began taking stronger, more psychoactive drugs, among them a variety of pills identifiable by color-coded names such as Orange Sunshine and Purple Haze, names to which we attached mystical significance. While the popularity of such substances had diminished considerably in recent years, with a growing sense of nostalgia for the Good Old Days of the previous decade we thought to bring them back, as if by so doing we might reveal the insidious link between those who had reelected Nixon and the similarly ill-informed, reactionary forces that opposed recreational drug use.

These experiences were indeed revealing, for nothing about the mellow euphoria of pot had quite prepared us for the active derangement of LSD. It was not that the drug inspired particularly outlandish behavior, but rather that under its influence the most innocuous events or encounters were apt to seem bizarre or disturbing. Whereas pot tended to suppress a lot of traditional male behavior (including sperm production), the hyperconsciousness of acid tended to throw them into stark and startling relief, such that on more than one occasion while under the influence we found ourselves reverting to the petty rivalries of boyhood, posing dares and asserting claims to dominance we would otherwise have considered flagrantly uncool. In the context of the larger challenge posed by the drug itself, however, such behavior made perfect sense. Like the ability to hold one's liquor, this challenge involved "keeping one's shit together" under the disconcerting effects of a neurological toxin, and according to the unwritten rules of maleness, asserting the integrity of one's shit inevitably called for a certain amount of one-upmanship.

Other such adventures involved a substance I first discovered one evening upon returning to the fraternity in the company of a girlfriend. Hailed by a group of partiers in the main living room, we stopped to investigate and were invited to sample some sort of amazing new weed. While my companion sensibly declined, I felt a certain obligation to determine whether the vaunted compound was worthy of my refined, pot-smoker's palate, and after taking a generous hit from a small hash pipe I awaited the effects with a wine-taster's careful deliberation.

"Interesting bouquet," I mused, "—what is it?"

"Parsley flakes saturated with animal tranquilizer," came the reply.

This put me in mind of certain episodes of the television series "Wild Kingdom," in which drug-darted rhinos, wildebeests and other large ruminants were seen to stagger pitifully about the African plains before collapsing in a heap. Indeed, after taking another hit, I considered lying down for a while myself, and if somebody had wanted to staple a tag to my ear or fit me out with a radio transmitter, well, where was the harm?

At this point my companion and I were sitting next to each other on the floor, and for no apparent reason she nudged me with her shoulder, a gesture that sent me crashing to the carpet with all the violence of a concerted shove. For a moment I lay there awaiting an explanation, but she only laughed, calling attention to my apparent helplessness and suggesting that she could out-wrestle me. This, I decided, was idle boasting, and after taking a moment to plan my strategy (a cross-body tackle followed by a leg lift for the pin), I exploded into action. Or tried to. Getting sluggishly to my knees, I lunged at her, but with amazing swiftness she slipped away and I ended up sprawled on the carpet again. The next thing I knew she had forced me onto my back and was straddling my chest, pinning my arms above my head. At this point, hopelessly outmatched, I succumbed to successive waves of laughter emanating from somewhere deep in my gut, a laughter so pure and mindless that it seemed to carry me off in a torrent of hilarity.

For all of its debilitating physical effects, however, the drug proved a great dispeller of social unease and didn't seem to interfere with the kind of wrestling that went on in private. Even so, Angel Dust, the vaguely sinister name by which it was known, was thought to be hazardous to one's intelligence, on which account I swore off the stuff. As it turned out, an even stranger sort of euphoria was about to overtake me, and it wasn't long before the advent of my flying career would suggest a whole new paradigm for getting high.

# Chapter 4

# Brave New Neighborhood

That November I decided to forego the long trip home for Thanksgiving, arranging to stay with a fraternity friend in the off-campus apartment of a mutual acquaintance. By this time, I had quit the swim team in order to free up my schedule for flying, and having confirmed that my new glider would arrive on schedule, I thought to spend the week-long vacation gathering myself for the glorious day, now nearly at hand, when I would grace the skies above Sugarloaf with breathtaking feats of derring-do. With the vacation upon us, my new roommate and I threw our gear into the Impala and drove to a two-bedroom walk-up in nearby Waterville, where we settled in for a week-long hiatus from obligations of any kind.

Later that evening, intent on celebrating our new freedom with some heroic drinking, we drove to a pub normally frequented by the college crowd, where we sat quaffing beer at the bar. Though the school break had left the place nearly empty, in time three young women arrived and made their way to a nearby table. We studied them more or less discreetly for a while, and on a sudden whim I walked over and asked if they would like some company. It was a slow night, I didn't appear to be—and indeed was not—a predatory pick-up artist, and after a brief exchange of glances they consented, at which point I waved my friend over, we introduced ourselves, and were soon caught up in conversation.

They were local girls—"townies" in the privileged parlance of college—and had formerly worked in a local shirt factory, an experience they proceeded to describe in some detail, chattering excitedly about the various dodges they used to break up the monotony of the daily routine. One of them—I'll call her Sara—had attracted my notice from across the room. She was young and pretty in an unpretentious sort of way, with a smile that was by turns sardonic and full of girlish glee, creating an effect reminiscent of certain miniature dioramas in which the image changes according to the play of light. I found myself looking at her the way one examines those little pictures, seeking the precise angle of transition.

Meanwhile, one of her friends made a point of asking her about someone named Tasha, at which point I chimed in: "Who's that?"

"She's Sara's little girl," said the friend, "—How old now?"

"Eight months," reported Sara with muted pride.

"Really?" I said. "—That's... great."

I was improvising, half expecting it was a joke, but the look with which she confronted the revelation of her motherhood removed all doubt. For a moment she closed her eyes in apparent defensiveness, but when she opened them again her expression was full of self-possession, if not defiance, for it went without saying that she was unmarried and unattached. I had seen that in her gaze as well.

We kept talking as before, but I could hardly avoid certain unspoken implications. Here was someone in whom I'd taken an unmistakable interest, and it remained to be seen what I intended to do about it in view of what could only be considered a daunting complication. Under the circumstances, I might easily have demurred, turned my attention elsewhere, fled the scene, yet something in the perfect equanimity of her expression seemed to defy such a response, turning my otherwise reasonable reservations into a kind of spinelessness.

The two of us started talking, at first within the hearing of the group, but increasingly between ourselves, the voices of the others fading into the background. She and her daughter lived on the outskirts of town with her mother and stepfather, a younger sister and brother, "a temporary situation" as she framed it. Previously, she'd been living in a farmhouse in the country with a number of friends from high school. Together they formed a commune of sorts in which everyone chipped in to cover expenses and provide moral support.

For Sara, they'd been the best of times; between her job in town and the work of maintaining the farm, life was full of adventure and the future bright with possibility. Then, during the spring of the group's second year, she discovered that she was pregnant and the brightness faded. Among her housemates, there was talk of a surgical solution, but she wouldn't agree to it, and over the course of the ensuing summer the household started to come apart. She and a girlfriend stayed on into the fall, and then, two months before the baby was due, she moved back home. The transition hadn't been easy, but things were getting back on track for her. She had made plans to enroll in a job-training program at a local hospital come spring.

In college circles, her situation tended to be portrayed in unambiguously doleful terms—a fate to be avoided at all costs. As I listened, however, I couldn't seem to appreciate the tragedy of it anymore. The consequences seemed so benign, and the 'victim' so unbowed. No doubt this reaction had much to do with my own situation, in which the carefree world of college was beginning to fade from view, to be replaced by a new theater of operations in which the stakes were higher and one was obliged to take a stand. In any case, this new awareness came home to me with a resounding jolt that was scarcely to be resented for all of its shock; she seemed at once the bravest and most intriguing girl I'd ever met.

Inspired by her example, I regaled her with accounts of my kite-flying exploits and let her in on my plans to fly from Sugarloaf, as if such a feat bore comparison with Lindbergh's crossing of the Atlantic. At one point in our increasingly private exchange, one of her friends cut in on us, making fun of our obliviousness in order to return us to the general conversation.

"Hello-o!" she laughed. "Don't mind us."

The interruption was only temporary, however, for the thought that our paths were not likely to cross again proved a spur to my advances. So it was that later, with closing time at hand, I invited Sara back to the apartment, offering to take her home from there, and with a nod she consented. It remained for us to tell the others of our plans, and while she huddled briefly with her friends, I explained to mine, at which point the impromptu party broke up amid knowing smirks and glimmers in the eyes of the various companions.

Out in the parking lot, the night was clear and moonlit as Sara's two girlfriends called out their good-byes before getting into a much-used compact. Waving in return, we piled into the Impala and started for the apartment, making small talk along the way.

Upon our arrival, my fraternity friend obligingly retired for the night and Sara and I made our way to a living room sofa, where, with the lights out and moonglow entering through the windows, we settled in and got better acquainted.

"I read somewhere how in olden times people used to think women could get pregnant just by exposing their bellies to a full moon," I told her in a cryptic sort of way.

"Yeah, right," she responded. "Sounds like a theory someone dreamed up to get out of trouble—blame it on the moon. Anyway, you don't have to worry, I'm on the pill."

"Who said I was worried?"

"Shouldn't you be?"

"Yes," I admitted, "but it wouldn't have been polite to say so."

"I see."

We carried on from there to my new and as-yet unfamiliar sleeping quarters, where, in the process of opening a balky door, I managed to hit myself with it. Though it struck me in the face, the blow was a glancing one, and, following a brief pantomime of feigned injury for her amusement, I was determined to ignore it. Not long thereafter, however, I experienced a strange sensation in my nose and realized I was leaking hot blood directly in her face.

"Christ, I'm bleeding!" I announced.

The admission led to a quick shifting of gears and considerable commotion as I struggled to the side of the bed, applying pressure to my wounded proboscis with one hand and groping for the light switch with the other. Meanwhile, Sara became no less animated, and, quickly arranging herself, departed the room in some haste.

Switching on the light, I was relieved to find no sign of blood on the bed, putting me in hopes that she had been spared any great torrents of gore. Moments later, the bleeding staunched, I too collected myself and went in search of her, comforted by the knowledge that she couldn't have gone far without her blue jeans.

I found her in a nearby bathroom, standing in front of the sink in partially-buttoned shirt and panties, breathing somewhat deliberately.

"You okay?" I asked.

"I felt a little queasy there."

Dampening a washcloth, I checked the mirror above the sink and cleaned traces of blood from my upper lip, then looked her over for evidence of more. A single drop had landed on her cheek and trailed ear-ward like an errant tear, and with a wry smile she let me wipe it off.

The crisis past, we made our way back to the bedroom, where I promised not to bleed on her anymore if she would promise not to puke. It was a deal, and we laughed about it, but were careful with each other just the same.

Later, in the car on the way to her house, I followed directions to a modest two-story dwelling on a country road not far from the college, and after pulling into the driveway, asked if I might give her a call sometime.

"I suppose so," she said coyly, giving me her stepfather's name for the listing.

We'd been playing it cool, treating the evening's encounter as no big deal, but for some reason both of us were grinning during the good-night kiss. Then she slid across the seat and was gone, and I drove back through the sleeping town feeling by turns smugly contented and strangely unsettled by the suddenness of events.

For the next couple of days, I was unsure about following through with the call. After all, if I were to see her again there were bound to be implications. It was crazy to think about getting involved, but I kept thinking about it just the same. I figured I would wait another week or so, then see if she wanted to go to a movie or something. It would be doing the right thing, a kindness of sorts, but who was I kidding? –kindness wasn't the half of it.

Finally, three days after our initial meeting and unable to stand the strain of the decision any longer, I called her up and asked if she would like to come over to the apartment the following afternoon, a Sunday, to watch a football game on TV. She asked if one of her friends from the night at the pub might come along, which suited me fine, for the occasion promised to serve an ulterior purpose; I needed to know if she were really as intriguing as I had found her on our first meeting, or if in the light of day the spell would be broken and she would be revealed as an ordinary girl in an awkward situation.

    At the appointed hour she and her friend arrived, and with my roommate on hand the four of us sat watching the weekend spectacle on a small black-and-white set in the living room, where Sara sat Indian-fashion on the sofa next to me, taking occasional sips from a shared bottle of beer. Every so often, I glanced over at her, waiting for the scales to fall from my eyes, but nothing had changed. She was still a mystery to me, and for reasons that would remain a mystery to us both, we seemed to be compatible.

# Chapter 5

# Mission Improbable

Upon the arrival of Christmas break, I sped home via the interstates to collect my new glider. By previous arrangement, my friend Sam had taken delivery, and when I showed up on his doorstep the morning after my return the two of us quickly set to work assembling the airframe on his snow-covered driveway. Absent the heavy steel frame and bulky floats of the tow-kite, it weighed a mere 35 pounds and its gleaming, aluminum-alloy tubing and bright gold sail made it nothing less than a thing of beauty. Taking turns, we hoisted it to our shoulders and charged down the driveway, filling the sail with air and letting it float up in simulation of take-off. Compared to the towing rig, the new wing seemed enormous, and we marveled at its nimbleness and prodigious lifting power, awed by the uncertain prospect of controlling it in flight.

Eager to put it to the test, we loaded it onto the Impala and drove to Snow Ridge, the nearest ski area of any size, where we paid a visit to the business office upon our arrival, thinking to explain our intentions to the management—a mere formality as we supposed. For some reason, however, the man in charge wasn't thrilled by the prospect of a couple of would-be aeronauts careening downhill in an untested flying machine amid crowds of unsuspecting skiers. While refusing to authorize the use of the regular trails for such a thing, he nonetheless revealed a certain morbid curiosity about the sport, suggesting that we might give it a try—without official approval, of course—on a small, partially-groomed slope immediately outside the bounds of the ski area.

*Near the Borderline*

    Despite the snub, we grudgingly complied, and were soon lugging glider and gear to the base of the hill in question, a mere knoll whose crest was little more than thirty feet above a long, flat outrun. It wasn't clear that we would even be able to get airborne from such a slope, and we scoffed at the prospect of so paltry a challenge compared to our high-flying summer exploits. Even so, the prospect of flying an untested wing over land as opposed to water posed a new challenge, and we started uphill keen to prove ourselves to a doubting public.

    Arriving at the top, we assembled the airframe and, donning skis and helmet, I strapped myself into the harness, hoisted the glider to my shoulders, and stood awaiting sufficient motivation to start downhill.

    "Looks higher from here," I observed.

    "It is a good day to die," intoned Sam, gazing somberly at the horizon in the manner of Old Lodge Skins, the antic Indian chief from the movie, *Little Big Man*.

    "Lighten up, willya?"

    "Very well. It is a good day to be badly injured...."

    Seizing upon the only avenue of escape, I let the skis run, built up speed and went airborne, reaching a height of some six feet above the snow before descending to a landing on the flats below. The flight had been little more than a hop, but everything had gone according to plan and I was well satisfied with the glider's handling. I took a few more turns, then Sam had a try, borrowing my gear and flying down to a stand-up landing in his first outing on snow skis.

    Later, with no chance to put the glider to a more demanding test, we celebrated the morning's limited success in a nearby bar. Though relegated to the equivalent of a bunny slope, we'd shown the skeptics what was what. (In fact, our efforts had gone entirely unnoticed.) From then on, we told ourselves, the ski area might beg us to fly from its slopes, but we would refuse, holding out for cash in amounts that increased with every fresh swig of beer.

    A week later, with Christmas over and New Year's in the offing, I packed glider and gear and started back to school two days early, crossing the snowy wastes of northern New York to begin another long journey through the mountains. It is one thing to make that trip under summerlike conditions, however, and quite another to attempt it in late December. Having grown up in snow country, I knew this well enough, and my refusal to consider the safer, more expedient alternative of the interstates suggests the degree to which I'd abandoned all reasonable restraint in pursuit of my self-appointed destiny. I was a trailblazer, I told myself, a bold and visionary pioneer about to make aviation history.

As to the visionary part, not so much. Within an hour of my departure, snow started drifting out of the sky in large, innocent-looking flakes that crumpled on contact with the road and blew away in the whirlwind of the car's passing. Before long, however, the flakes grew smaller and multiplied, slanting against the windshield with growing intensity and smothering the horizon in their profusion. Soon the entire landscape was transformed into a windswept tundra upon which the highway itself was steadily disappearing. Even so, I kept going, making my way from one desolate north country hamlet to another.

Noon had come and gone by the time I reached the narrow bridge across the outlet of Lake Champlain, the precariousness of which was now magnified several times over by the onslaught of wind, wave and accumulating snow. There was small consolation to be had upon reaching the Vermont shore, either, for the eastern sky was growing increasingly dark and ominous. With little more than two hours of daylight remaining, I had only just begun my journey through the northern Appalachians, and soon enough darkness would join the list of accumulating hazards. Still, I kept going. The storm would let up before long, I fantasized, never bothering to consider that the constant headwind buffeting my windshield could mean only one thing—I was heading ever deeper into a classic Nor'easter.

Somewhere beyond Montpelier I came up behind a state snowplow and followed it all the way to St. Johnsbury, letting its flashing emergency beacon lead me through whiteout conditions. Meanwhile, here and there along the roadside, the cabs and tail sections of various abandoned vehicles poked out of the deepening piles of snow, ominous portents of the fate that awaited me if I didn't abandon my quest and ride out the storm in some safe haven. Still, I kept going.

*Near the Borderline*

    By the time I crossed the upper Connecticut, the day was fading fast, but the snow not a whit, and I started across the Presidential Range in the wake of another heaven-sent snowplow. Full darkness arrived somewhere in the passes, where the wind tugged at the Impala and its elongated cargo like a raging incubus born of the storm and the night. At this point, the world outside was reduced to the narrow corridor created by my headlight beams, within which the snow swirled in ever more furious blasts. Somewhere out in that wild and terrible night, Mount Washington loomed in the darkness, tearing a hole in the sky, and when at last the car began a long and steady descent, I realized that I had entered the broad valley on its northern slope. Though still far from a safe haven, I was "over the hump," and when, shortly thereafter, I crossed the Maine state line, it seemed the worst was over.

    Even as the storm diminished, however, Route 2 remained little more than a set of snowmobile tracks through the woods, and it was after eight o'clock when I finally reached Farmington, where a few lingering flakes were visible in the well-lit vicinity of a roadside motel. The owners, an older couple, were preparing to close for the night when I entered the reception area and began filling out a registration form, haggard with road-weariness.

"How'd you get here?" asked the wife.

"Route Two," I reported. "—Took me all day, but I made it."

"Route Two's been closed since this morning," the husband said, as if to belie my story.

"Really? —Nobody told me."

"Have you had any dinner?" asked the wife.

    Later, after disposing of a Cheeseburger Special in the motel's modest dining area, I made my way across the snow-choked parking lot to a spartan, pine-paneled room, where I threw my kit onto a chair, scuffed off my boots, and fell onto the bed.

    Flipping on the TV, I tuned in the nightly weather report from the top of Mount Washington, a broadcast that had become something of a nightly ritual at the fraternity, if only for the opportunity to make fun of a certain disheveled weatherman with outsized eyewear. Stationed alone on the mountaintop for weeks at a time, the strange-looking fellow had a habit of making hopelessly mundane observations followed by unaccountable bouts of self-conscious chuckling. We considered him frankly insane and couldn't imagine how he'd been given access to the public airwaves. After my own lonely vigil behind the wheel and with the next day's hare-brained scheme in prospect, I now found myself laughing more in appreciation than ridicule. The guy was clearly "living inside his head," but it seemed a cheerful sort of place, and I couldn't fault him for it, especially as his forecast was everything I could have hoped for: clear skies and perfectly windless conditions.

Indeed, early the next morning I peered out a heavily frosted window to find over a foot of fresh powder glinting with startling clarity against a cloudless, deep blue sky. In the breathless quiescence of dawn, the storm seemed to have taken with it all traces of atmospheric turmoil, leaving in its wake an elemental calm.

Wasting no time, I got dressed, gathered my gear and prepared to complete the final leg of my journey, intent on ascending the snowy slopes of Sugarloaf and launching myself into that glorious blue vault of sky. Returning to the motel office to drop off my key, I lingered over a complimentary breakfast of donuts and coffee in the dining area, where the wife of the previous evening and a woman I took to be her daughter were interested to know what the strange package on top of my car might be.

"It's a hang-glider," I said, an expression that only deepened their curiosity. "—A wing made of Dacron and aluminum tubing. I'm on my way up to Sugarloaf to fly off the mountain with it."

They responded with a mixture of skepticism and alarm, their smiles taking on a stricken quality, as if my plans only confirmed suspicions engendered by the previous night's account of my adventures on Route 2. Even so, they wished me luck, and, taking an extra donut for the road, I made my departure.

Heading north on a freshly plowed highway, I was soon in open country, where isolated farmhouses peered out upon trackless, snow-covered fields, their chimneys sending plumes of smoke straight up through the still morning air. Before long a jumble of foothills morphed into lofty peaks, and, passing through the village of Kingfield, I followed the course of the Carrabassett River through an ever-deepening valley, where brief flashes of open water appeared within the stream's snowbound course. Meanwhile, hidden from view behind a series of concealing ridges, the ski area remained invisible, coming into view only as I rounded a dramatic curve in the highway a mile from its base. At this point, the mountain loomed up in its entirety with spectacular suddenness, its network of ski trails leading to a treeless summit, where a dazzling white snowcap shone like a beacon above a deep-green sea.

Upon arrival, I retrieved the glider from the roof of the car and, carrying it on one shoulder with skis slung over the other, headed for the open slope in front of the lodge. Outside the entrance to the gondola terminal, I leaned the glider against the wall of the building and deposited my skis nearby. Next came the crucial matter of clearing my intentions with the management, and taking instruction from my earlier experience with ski-area officialdom, I steeled myself for the all-important encounter. If the question of my credentials came up, I was prepared to cite my recent exploits at the hill near home, where I'd accumulated a total of perhaps thirty seconds of flying time.

Arriving in the main office, I was ushered into the manager's presence and had no sooner launched into an explanation of my intentions than he cut me off:

"Yeah, your buddy was in here a couple weeks ago. Told me all about it. Sounds like a lot of fun."

Surprised as well as baffled by the reference, I went with the moment: "So, I assume we're all set as far as approval."

"Well, like I told what's his name... Paul, I'm prepared to let you guys go ahead on a conditional basis, but it's up to you to prove that this kind of thing can be done safely. I mean, we can't have you crashing into people out on the bunny slope. You'll have to sign a waiver to keep the lawyers happy, and after that we'll see how it goes."

"You won't be disappointed," I assured him.

Ushering me into an outer office, he requested a form from his secretary, and while we waited for the paperwork, he wondered aloud, "So how do you plan to get these things uphill?"

"—On the gondolas," I told him. "The attendants can fit them in between the skis and the bubble."

At this he gave me a dubious sort of look. "Does Charlie know about this?"

"Yeah," I lied. "Paul talked to him about it."

In truth, the gondola scheme was something I'd arrived at through pure speculation. I had no idea if it would work, or who Charlie might be, not to mention Paul, whose identity was an even greater mystery. Nevertheless, use of the lifts was vital to my plan, and I was on a roll.

Moments later, ecstatic at having succeeded on a grand scale where I had earlier failed on a small one, I started for the main lodge, the ground seeming to race beneath my feet. After buying a lift pass, I returned to the gondola terminal to collect glider and skis and, making my way inside, maneuvered my long and cumbersome burden beneath the massive bull-wheel around which the lift-cable sped. Setting it down on the loading floor in front of the attendant's station, I looked up to see a burly character in pack boots and heavy overalls appear as if out of the roar of the machinery itself.

"What the hell have we got here!" he shouted above the ceaseless din.

"It's a glider," I shouted back. "I've got permission from the main office..."

"Glider?" returned the attendant—none other than the redoubtable Charlie—with a mixture of outrage and incredulity.

"A hang-glider. I'll be flying it down from mid-station."

"And how do you propose to get it up there?"

"On a gondola. It can slide right in between the skis and the bubble."

"Jesus H. Christ!" the other sang out in disgust. "This is a ski lift, not a damn merry-go-round!"

"I just got the manager's approval," I protested. "—Signed a waiver and everything."

For a moment he seemed prepared to tell me what I could do with said waiver, but with a large group of skiers beginning to file in behind me he relented and, fuming inwardly, motioned me to get into a waiting gondola.

For all of his belligerence, he clearly grasped what I had in mind, and, once aboard, I watched as he placed a ski in each of the brackets on either side of the gondola door, then hoisted the glider up and wedged it between the skis and the fiberglass shell. After a bit of jostling to test its stability, he stepped back and stood shaking his head with a grudging expression as I called out my thanks. Next, pulling back on the release lever, he sent the gondola rolling down the access rail to where it swung onto the moving cable and started uphill.

With the roar of the terminal receding behind me, I rode through the morning calm in something of a daze. For months I had anticipated this moment, and only now could I appreciate how sketchy and unlikely my planning had been. Yet everything had worked just as I had hoped, indeed far better than I had any right to expect. Now the lift carried me up and up, its low hum punctuated by the periodic clatter of the passing tower-trucks as I scanned the treetops for any sign of an untoward breeze. Miraculously, all was stillness.

Half-way up the mountain, I rolled into the mid-station and called out my intention to get off, explaining to the bewildered attendant the need to remove the glider before the door could be opened. Another round of explanations—yes, Charlie knew all about it—and soon I was out on the slope, where, with skis on and glider balanced precariously on a shoulder, I started down a trail running laterally across the mountain, eventually coming to a stop above a steep pitch running straight downhill. Here, well away from the towers and cables of the lift, I set the glider down on the snow, took off my skis and began setting up the airframe: attaching control bar and flying wires, then flipping the assembly over to unfurl and secure the wing-tubes. Minutes later a final pre-flight inspection confirmed that everything was in order.

Meanwhile, the odd feeling that things were happening all by themselves had ceased. By this time, several skiers had stopped along the sides of the trail below and stood peering up at me. Beyond them, across a wide gulf of air, the landing area appeared no bigger than a playing card. If all went well, shortly after takeoff I would be hundreds of feet above the ground, and while I had been that high under tow, this was different somehow. Skiing out into that void was going to take some initiative. For the hundredth time, I visualized rising well above the trees and, once over the open slope, making a series of turns preparatory to landing. While I believed it could be done, I didn't know for a certainty, and suddenly the difference between believing and knowing yawned like a bottomless chasm in my mind.

Next, with skis back on, I tipped the glider onto its nose, strapped myself to the harness and, with airframe resting on my shoulders, stood facing downhill, my skis spread and edged in a deep snowplow. At this point a low murmur passed through the spectators below, who suddenly seemed to recognize that my intentions were somehow connected to aviation. All that was required at this point was to relax my grip on the snow and let the skis run down the fall line.

"Go for it!" someone called out with vicarious valor.

It was as good a cue as any, and, responding dutifully, I started downhill, quickly building speed until the airframe lifted skyward and, giving my weight to the harness, I took to the air.

No sooner had I left the slope, however, than the glider began to wallow and lose altitude, descending with increasing speed until I dropped back onto the slope and, turning uphill, skidded to a stop. Something had gone wrong. I was supposed to be flying, yet here I was back on the trail. Several spectators groaned in disappointment.

Quickly trying again, I started downhill as before, building speed, advancing the control bar, going airborne, and once again sinking down, slipping out of the sky to land back on the slope. I was screwing up, making a fool of myself, when it suddenly occurred to me that in the excitement of the moment I had reverted to the familiar instincts of a tow-kite pilot, pushing out on the control bar in anticipation of a steady ascent, a maneuver which, in an unpowered glider, had quickly stalled the wing.

Starting downhill once more, I felt the sail fill and the bar drift forward, at which point, I tugged back slightly in response and felt a familiar sensation communicate itself through the airframe—the subtle, self-sustaining inertia of flight. Now the mountain fell away as I sailed out above the treetops, the valley opening out before me in a broad aerial panorama. Even so, the two failed take-off attempts had carried me below my intended launch-point, and it soon became apparent that my flight path was not going to carry me as far as the open slope. Instead, descending back within the narrow confines of the trail, I touched down on relatively flat terrain, and brought the airframe to rest on my shoulders. I was safely back on the ground, but instead of landing in front of the lodge, I was obliged to ski the rest of the way down like a common mortal. Indeed, apart from the small number of witnesses on the trailside, no one seemed to have noticed my flight at all. This was intolerable, and, arriving back in the vicinity of the gondola terminal, I packed up the airframe and was soon on my way back uphill, determined to make a spectacle of myself.

The next flight proved a considerable improvement on the first. Carried far above the open slope, I made a series of turns, bleeding off altitude to make a final approach in sync with the downhill traffic, landing as planned in front of the lodge amid scores of skiers who scarcely knew what to make of my sudden appearance among them. I was ecstatic, nearly as incredulous as they were, and, skiing down to the vicinity of the gondy terminal, I dismantled the glider and immediately started back uphill.

By the time I had completed two more flights, it was past noon, and with a breeze building, I called it a day, skiing the glider to an open area near the lodge, where I stood dismantling it as a number of skiers stopped to get a look and ask where I had learned to fly it. I wanted to say, 'Why, right here, just now' but resisted the urge lest word of my neophyte status get back to the management.

"Out west," I told them. Strictly speaking, the claim wasn't untruthful.

Later, the curious few having drifted away, I stood intently rolling up the sail when a voice broke in on me:

"—You beat me by two weeks!"

The speaker, a round-faced, mustachioed fellow with a shock of black hair above a pair of aviator sunglasses, was ambling over from the direction of a slope-side pub, crossing the snow with a stiff-legged, ski-boot-encumbered gait, a steaming cup of chowder in his hand.

"How do you mean?"

"I've got three just like it on order," said the stranger, gesturing toward the glider.

"You must be Paul," I said, recalling the manager's mysterious reference.

"A-yuh."

Glad to have solved the riddle of his identity, I introduced myself and we began comparing notes. Without meaning to, we had already furthered each other's interests considerably, and when I told him of my conversation in the office—how I had benefited from his advance work and used his name to wrangle my way onto the gondola—he laughed appreciatively. As it happened, my use of the lift was an idea he hadn't considered, and he listened intently as I explained the technique by which gliders could be transported on individual gondola cars.

Recognizing that we had much to talk about, he suggested that we drive down to his place, where he had some hang-gliding literature to show me. After loading the car with glider and gear, I followed him as he started down the access road in a much-used Jeep. Soon we were sitting in the ill-lit main room of a rundown A-frame, where I pored over a pile of promotional materials while he related something of his flying history. He and a friend had spent the summer building a makeshift glider out of bamboo and polyethylene, and flying it from various hills on the Maine coast, eventually arriving at the notion of flying from the mountain about the same time I had, though their plans had been somewhat more ambitious. Placing an order for three new gliders from the manufacturer in California, Paul had established himself as a dealer in hopes of starting a flying school.

That we would become friends and join forces seemed all but inevitable. By the time we had finished enthusing about the prospects of the new sport, the sun was low in the sky, and, glad to have made so fortuitous a connection at the mountain, I prepared to resume my extended journey back to school. At this point, the previous day's storm-battered odyssey on Route 2 seemed a distant memory, and, standing in the driveway of his place, I gazed up at the mountain one last time, reveling in the day's events. The ground that had seemed to race beneath my feet earlier in the day was once again in motion; I would allow it to carry me until such time as I could get back up there and cast myself free again.

*Near the Borderline*

Chapter 6

# Aerial View from Cloud Nine

Shortly after returning to school, I checked in with Sara. With our acquaintance now over a month old, it seemed only fitting that I meet her family. Thus, in the course of taking her to a movie, I paid a visit to her house on the country road, where she made introductions to her mom and stepdad, her younger brother and sister, and her daughter. Though the occasion threatened to expose her world in all its familial intimacy, she carried it off with her usual aplomb, and soon I was sitting on a sofa with Tasha crawling about on my lap. The one person in the room without a trace of nervousness, the soon-to-be toddler gave me a thorough visual examination—bright eyes wide with curiosity—before patting me about the face and otherwise invading my personal space. I wasn't offended in the least.

In truth, such encounters served to rebuke my genius for self-absorption. For once, it seemed, I'd met someone in Sara whom I couldn't talk myself around or over, for she possessed talking points of her own and held the power to reshape my thinking more than I hers. The recent Supreme Court case, Roe v. Wade, decided a year earlier, was still much in the news, making her situation seem all the more courageous, for I couldn't help thinking that, had her status as a mom been effectively mandated by law, in all likelihood I wouldn't have felt the same way; only then would she have been a victim. Instead, the conspicuous bravery of her choice continued to bring me up short, forcing me to acknowledge a wider world of experience. Even so, the two of us never spoke about such things. Her situation was argument enough, and I came to approve her decision without question or discussion, having arrived at a perception of truth beyond the reach of reason or politics.

To be sure, this transformation, and our relationship itself, proved more than a little awkward in the context of life at the fraternity, the inevitable scene of our trysts. The brotherhood could hardly be expected to approve. Getting involved with significant others was one thing—the larger purpose of college for some—but a local girl with a kid of her own... this was beyond the pale. I was throwing off the curve, setting a bad example for the younger guys. Nobody said anything, but I could hardly avoid a general sense of alienation. In truth, apart from a place to live, I had little use for the organization anymore, and so long as I retained sufficient good will to avoid overt ostracism, I was content.

Meanwhile, there was my gliding career to consider. By this time, I had re-organized my entire schedule to accommodate it, not infrequently foregoing classes in favor of the more experiential learning to be had at the mountain. Maintaining a close vigil on the weather forecasts, I planned accordingly, and when the portents were right, I would be up at first light, retrieving the glider from the fraternity basement and lashing it to the roof of the Impala. Throwing the rest of my gear on the back seat, I was soon racing across the Maine countryside in the pre-dawn twilight, intent on performing the sacrament of flight.

One day it went like this:

A clear blue, breathless morning, the sun winking up along the route north, revealing the whole of the snowbound landscape in all of its crystalline clarity. Crossing the Kennebec at Norridgewock, I follow the river north to the Carrabassett, then up into the high country.

Finding no sign of Paul at the A-frame, I continue to the mountain, and soon, geared up and ticketed, am on my way uphill, determined to make my first-ever flight from the summit. Rolling into the mid-station, I call out to the attendant: "Send me up!" to which he responds with a whoop of encouragement.

Now the lift cable rakes steeply upward, and as I ride through the morning stillness the familiar scenes of the lower mountain fall away, the trees becoming stunted, icebound, the sky opening up until nothing remains but a patch of frozen tundra beneath a cloudless sky and the clarion call of an archetypal dream.

Once outside the terminal, I ski a short distance down the summit ridge to a point where a double-diamond trail begins its abrupt descent of the mountain's northern headwall. Coming to a stop on a flat stretch of terrain some twenty yards from the drop-off, I step out of my skis and begin setting up the glider, at which point some half-dozen male skiers about my age appear on the trail above and eventually ski to a stop nearby. Forming a rough semi-circle around my position, they lean on their poles, studying the glider.

"What is it? —some kind of tent?" asks one.

"It's a glider," I reply.

"What do you mean?"

"—A hang-glider. I'll be flying down from here."

"Flying off the mountain?"

"That's the plan."

"Right!" scoffs another, looking to his friends for support. For some reason he seems to take the idea personally. "No way, man. —No fucking way!"

"This I gotta see!" says another.

"Be my guest. Just leave me a clear path to the top of the trail."

"Sure, buddy," he calls over his shoulder, "—IT'S YOUR FUNERAL!"

The rest follow, laughing heartily, but before going, a final skeptic makes a blunt observation: "You're out of your mind, you know that, right?"

It's just an expression, but as this will be my first attempt from the mountaintop, I experience a flicker of doubt on the subject. Even so, the sound of blowhard laughter emanating from the others on the slope immediately below provides an incentive of its own, and after a thorough check of the glider, I step into my skis, strap into the harness, and bring the airframe to my shoulders.

For a moment, I consider side-slipping down to the lip of the headwall and launching from there, but partly to avoid any further sniping from the waiting bystanders, I decide to let the skis run from where I stand, which requires me to tuck the control bar tightly to my waist to ensure a clean take-off. Quickly building speed, I hear the sail flap loudly in the resulting breeze, and, as I reach the edge of the drop-off, the sail inflates with a sudden snap as the glider leaps skyward amid shouts of alarm from the on-lookers. Now, carried well above the slope by an excess of momentum, I tug back slightly on the bar and feel the wing slip into a glide. Glancing back at the receding trail, I take some satisfaction in noting that several spectators lie sprawled out in the snow, having lost their footing in a rush to get out of harm's way.

Heading straight out from the summit ridge, I am soon high above the valley in a place of unmatched solitude. Some ten miles to the north, the series of peaks comprising the Bigelow Range seem curiously foreshortened. A towering presence from the valley floor, the mountain escarpment is now easily surmounted by the eye, and beyond it I glimpse the frozen expanse of Flagstaff Lake and the boggy Dead River country of local legend. Here, two centuries past, the Arnold expedition—flinty woodsmen from as far away as the wilds of Pennsylvania and Virginia—slogged toward Quebec, intent upon the conquest of Canada. I think of them and seem to recognize the scope of their ambition.

Through an immensity of space I float, my remoteness from the ground eliminating all sense of motion until I am aware only of the slight, upward drift of the horizon, the steady inertia of the airframe, and the low whistling of the wires. I'm not flying so much as acutely being, my consciousness expanding in every direction until it seems I am locked in some inexplicable stasis, frozen in place and watching as the universe passes slowly around me. Far away, elsewhere in the swirling unrest of the atmosphere, tempests rage, yet I have been granted this moment's calm.

In time the muted hum and clatter of the ski lifts rise up from the trails below, breaking the spell, and I swing the glider in a series of turns high above the open slope, bleeding off altitude before setting up for a final approach. As the slope grows closer, my consciousness quickens, and, touching down, I am back on my skis, moving once again to the rhythms of a clock-bound world.

Later, after two more flights from the summit and a number of ski runs thrown in for good measure, I packed up and started back to school, stopping at a small gas station/store in Kingfield for something to eat. While standing at the check-out counter, I looked up to see a distinctive character enter the place and walk directly up to me.

"You're the kite-flyer," he declared, as if I might be unaware of it.

"Yes."

"Good."

Stationing himself near the door as if to prevent my escape, he waited for me to complete my transaction before following me outside.

"Saw the glider on your car from across the street. —Name's Jake," he said, locking thumbs with me in a hip handshake.

Wearing an American-flag-motif parka and well-worn bell-bottoms, he sported a paisley red bandanna atop a thicket of shoulder-length hair. Having recently become one of Paul's first customers, he was anxious to begin flying from the mountain as soon as possible. Indeed, there was that in his expression that wouldn't countenance any doubt on the subject, and when I assured him that I would be glad of his company, he radiated good fellowship and insisted that I accompany him to his nearby apartment. Though the purpose of the visit was not immediately clear, the sheer intensity of the invitation was difficult to resist, and, dropping off my purchases in the car, I followed him across the street to a large wooden tenement.

Two flights up a narrow stairway, we arrived in a seemingly empty room, where bright sunlight streamed through a series of curtainless windows upon a deeply scuffed wooden floor. Temporarily blinded by the light, I was about to ask him when he was planning to move in, when a jumble of objects in a corner resolved itself into a sitting area of sorts. Motioning me toward an amorphous, bean-bag chair, he sat on a bare mattress opposite, and, digging into a pile of stuff in a corner, produced a baggy and began rolling a joint. In the manner of aboriginal Americans cementing a new friendship, we were to smoke on it.

*Near the Borderline*

  A former seaman in the Navy, he'd been stationed at various bases throughout the Pacific, including a stint in southern California, where he witnessed a number of hang-glider freaks flying from some sand dunes near Long Beach. Since then, having returned home to Maine and learned of the new sport's arrival at the mountain, he'd wasted no time in becoming a convert.
  "So, what do you do for dollars?" I asked, at which he held up the joint and smiled broadly.
  "Best home-grown in the valley."
  He had a point there, for the next thing I knew the two of us were sprawled out upon what passed with him for furniture, having entered that state of pot-induced oblivion in which it becomes possible to stare at nothing in particular—a light fixture, one's shoelace—without a trace of boredom or social unease. Somewhere along the way, we had devoured the contents of a large box of dry cereal, which now lay empty on the floor between us. Meanwhile, the apartment had grown noticeably cooler (the great thing about a third-floor room, according to Jake, was that hot air rises, but it was only a theory). Suddenly recalling plans to check in with Sara, I struggled out of the bean-bag and got to my feet. Thanking my host for his hospitality, I promised to look him up on my next visit, and made for the door.
  "If my truck ain't out front, look for me at the mountain," he called out in response.
  On the way back across the street, I took note of a VW van parked nearby and connected the dots: of course, the classic hippy-mobile. Anyway, it was good to know that Paul's dealership business was taking hold, and with daylight rapidly draining out of the sky I continued my journey back to school pleasantly attuned to the celestial afterglow.
  By the time I arrived back at the fraternity, darkness had fallen, and after stowing glider and gear, I called Sara, only to learn that she wasn't home. At this point, I hadn't been in touch with her for several days and, making a mental note to catch up with her, I proceeded into town intent on taking part in the Saturday night foosball wars.
  The best table-soccer venue in town was attached to a popular nightspot in the basement of an old railroad depot, where an ample

bar overlooked a large dance floor with a bandstand on one side and a dozen or so tables on the other. Arriving around nine, I stopped for a beer at the bar before making my way to the adjoining game room, where I hunted up a partner from among a crowd of spectators and was soon busy manning my favored post in the backfield. Life was good, and after holding the table through several games, my makeshift partner and I were finally beaten by a couple of shit-heel amateurs with an impossible run of luck (abusive epithets, after all, were an integral part of the sport).

    Eventually returning to the bar, I ordered another beer and stood gazing across the ill-lit dance floor to where a DJ was overseeing a playlist of familiar rock tunes while in the middle distance a mass of shadowy figures sat at the tables, their forms and faces briefly illuminated by the intermittent flash of a strobe light. So it was that while gazing at the strange, stop-action effect of the strobe I recognized a familiar face from out of the surrounding darkness. There, seated next to a shaggy companion at a table cluttered with the accumulated glassware of a larger group, was Sara.

    This gave me pause. While forbearing any unwarranted conclusions, I couldn't deny a measure of concern about my place in her affections. My first impulse was to avoid being seen in return, but this thought was quickly followed by a determination to remain at least long enough to finish my beer, and, eventually draining the bottle, I sent a final, querulous look in her direction before wading back through the crowd and out the door.

    Arriving back at the fraternity about midnight, I waded through the lingering revelers and accumulated trash of yet another weekend blowout, and, making my way up to my room, was soon fast asleep. I hadn't been out long, however, before I was awakened by the sound of someone surreptitiously entering the room and approaching my bed. At first, I assumed the unannounced visitor was a refugee from the recent party looking for a place to crash, but it turned out to be Sara. Later, she explained that she'd been invited to an impromptu reunion with some of her high school friends, but meanwhile she slipped out of her clothes, crawled in beside me, and neither one of us said a word.

*Near the Borderline*

# Chapter 7

# Awakenings

At some point during the weeks leading up to my college graduation, I attended an event known as Career Night in one of the school's lecture halls. For those about to transition from humble seekers of knowledge to productive members of society, the occasion promised to lend a sense of closure to the efforts of the previous four years and start us on a path to gainful employment. At some institutions, such events feature actual job interviews in which corporate head-hunters entice prospective employees to join their ranks with lucrative compensation packages. Our career office was more discreet than all that, with a program consisting of some five or six speakers from the surrounding community who had been invited to talk about the particulars of making a living within their chosen fields.

Among them was an artist/painter who lived "off the grid" somewhere out in the Maine pucker-brush, where he practiced his craft, chopped wood, and generally made do without modern conveniences. Sporting the decidedly casual look of a confirmed bohemian (well-worn sweater, faded jeans and work boots), he made a case for pursuing a career outside the more traditional professions, if not outside traditional society altogether. From a purely objective standpoint, it wasn't a very compelling argument, featuring as it did tales of physical hardship set against a backdrop of foul weather and artistic angst, yet there was something about his straightforward, unembroidered account that commanded my respect. Unlike his comparatively well-heeled co-presenters, he conveyed none of the oily glibness of the occupational insider, presenting himself rather as a humble traveler from a far-off land some few miles away. In the words of the poet, he had taken "the road less traveled by" and it had made "all the difference."

Upon a closer reading of those lines in later years, I would come to appreciate the sense in which they convey the possibility of regret over missed opportunities and shattered dreams every bit as readily as they do a sense of satisfaction for a life well lived. At the time, however, the 'difference' in the artist's choice of career seemed to me emblematic of all the self-sufficiency and rugged individualism to which I aspired. Thus, despite his efforts to demystify the role of artist and present his life in practical, unglamorous terms, I was nonetheless inspired by his experience, departing the seminar full of the ill-informed, lunatic ambitions of youth, and secretly determined to make my own glorious journey down a road to self-realization and occupational dysfunction.

In truth, I had already begun such a journey some time before this, though not so much from any artistic ambitions as from a decidedly unfavorable impression of the traditional workplace. My first paying job was as a busboy in the dining room of a resort hotel just down the road from my summer address on the island, where, at age 17, I worked two meal services a day, five days a week.

Apart from the novelty of receiving a regular paycheck, the experience proved a considerable disappointment. Its heyday having long since come and gone, the hotel had been in decline for years, and along with it the morale of the staff. This was especially true of the dining room, which was then under the purview of a maître d' in his early 40s. Every evening, prior to the commencement of dinner, he strode through the dining room, briskly and imperiously clapping his hands above his head, and calling out, "It's show time, boys and girls!" The waitresses routinely rolled their eyes and made fun of him. For my part, as a newcomer to the working world I reserved judgement, performing my duties with what I took to be a commendable degree of job-worthiness.

Admittedly, I wasn't the best judge of such things, and didn't pretend to be employee-of-the-month material. Even so, it came as something of a shock to discover that the maître d' was somehow unhappy with me or my performance, an unhappiness made all the more unsettling by the oblique way in which his dissatisfaction was conveyed. Rather than speak to me directly about the matter, he took to making derogatory references in various conversations within my hearing. Precisely what this name-calling consisted of I don't recall, and such was the context that I could never be entirely sure that I was the one, or the only one, to whom he was referring. And yet, there was no mistaking the dismissiveness with which he treated me. At first, I assumed his strange animosity had something to do with my appearance, of which I tended to be rather careless, or with my general ignorance of the finer points of dining-room etiquette. As he never corrected me in such matters, I could only assume his animus was merely personal, and, knowing what the waitresses thought of him, I didn't take it very seriously.

By failing to respond, however, I only seemed to provoke him to more insidious tactics, and in time he seemed intent on making my working life miserable. I recall with particular resentment certain weekday mornings when the regular breakfast routine was abandoned in favor of a buffet, on which occasions the bulk of the dining-room staff would be given the morning off, the only necessity being to keep the buffet tables supplied with whatever happened to be on the menu. For some reason, this duty routinely fell to me, and while there was nothing particularly onerous about the work, the maître d' made it so by insisting that I oversee the tables from a post outside the dining room and indeed outside the hotel itself. Standing on a stone patio on the other side of a glass door, I was to return inside only if required to restock the table.

This was hardly a problem in mild weather, when it was a pleasure to be outdoors with unobstructed views of the river and a nearby swimming pool. The pointlessness of the arrangement assumed abusive proportions, however, on those raw, rain-sodden mornings—all too familiar during summers on the St. Lawrence—when wind and temperature produced chill factors in the low 50s. On such occasions, clad in a uniform of short-sleeved white shirt, clip-on bow tie, black chinos and thin, cotton jerkin, I was required to stand outside the door, scarcely out of the rain, while inches away, on the other side of a single pane of glass, lay the warm, dry interior of the dining room. The deliberate indignity of this duty was unmistakable. I couldn't possibly do anyone any good standing out there, and the reason he gave for the practice—that I not intrude upon the privacy of the guests—was simply absurd. More often than not the dining room was completely empty, as was the greater part of the hotel. Nevertheless, every fifteen minutes or so he would pass an interior doorway and glance out to be sure I was at my post. Why I didn't simply refuse, I can't say. Had it meant the loss of the job, I would have been delighted to be shut of the place. Nevertheless, I simply endured, unwilling to admit that he, or the weather itself, had any power to affect me.

Insofar as it is possible to convey a sense of perfect comfort while suffering the onset of hypothermia, I think I gave a reasonably good performance. Even so, the wind fairly howled across that patio, inevitably forcing me inside on the pretext of a trip to the bathroom or in search of some unnecessary item for the table. I was never able to stay long, however, before he would seek me out, repeat his asinine rationale and order me back outside. It was all a game, of course, whose object was to compel me to seek his favor, and while I never did so, on more than one occasion I left work shivering uncontrollably, my hands so stiff with cold that I had trouble shedding my hated uniform in favor of a wool shirt and sweater, wanting nothing so much as to find a crackling, hardwood fire and warm myself before it.

As it happened, I outlasted him. Arriving at work one day in the latter part of August, I found the waitresses in an uproar and soon learned that the maître d' was gone, having absconded in the night with a considerable sum of cash. Representing the collective gratuity from a large convention group, the money was to have been divided among the entire dining-room staff, and had been anticipated for some time. When the details of the theft came out, several of the waitresses made free with a number of choice remarks concerning his personal life. For my part, I weighed the monetary loss against the joyful prospect of never seeing him again, and was well satisfied with the bargain.

Far from encouraging my further pursuit of gainful employment, the job had the effect of eroding my faith in humanity in general, as on the memorable night earlier that summer, when I abandoned my post in the middle of a busy dinner service to mingle with a group of the hotel's more sentient patrons in front of a TV set in the lobby, where the Apollo 11 moon-landing was being broadcast live. Caring not a whit what the management might say about my absence, I was all the more incensed upon my return to find the dining room half-full of patrons who had chosen to forego so momentous an event for the sake of what passed for cuisine in that hopelessly pretentious place.

The next summer I sought to broaden my experience in the service sector, taking a job as dock attendant at a large marina in Alexandria Bay, where my duties included pumping gas and otherwise serving the needs of the boating community. If nothing else, the job provided a welcome contrast to dining-room work, and, clad in the marina's logo-emblazoned shirt and cap, I was glad to be outside on a regular basis and engaged in what I considered more seemly and substantial duties.

To be sure, there were aspects of the job I didn't care for, chief among them being the task of emptying the holding tanks of those vessels with on-board toilet facilities, an operation involving a pump apparatus with long and cumbersome hoses for conveying waste materials to an in-ground tank on shore. A balky piece of machinery, the device never seemed to function properly and, what was worse, I was obliged to operate it in full view of the marina's patrons, which tended to highlight my lowly status. Despite the rugged-handyman mystique I sought to bring to it, the nature of such work was not apt to impress the likely young women who frequented the place, whose attention I otherwise sought to attract. Of lesser concern was the good opinion of those boat owners whose vessels I was required to service, the more discreet of whom made a point of running errands or otherwise making themselves scarce during the operation, a courtesy that enabled me to perform my duties with a minimum of personal contact. Those who remained on board generally displayed signs of unease in my presence, in response to which I learned to affect a breezy self-absorption as I attended to the job, affixing the main suction hose to its proper fitting and withdrawing ashore to man the pump.

It was never a good idea to remain in the proximity of a tank in the process of being serviced. Things could go wrong. Not infrequently, the hose would become obstructed by effluent materials, resulting in a build-up of pressure. This in turn placed considerable strain on the coupling mechanism connecting the hose to the onboard tank, and if and when the coupling failed, the hose was apt to fly off and gyrate wildly, spewing partially-treated sewage over decks, docks, and anyone foolish enough to be in the vicinity. When such mishaps occurred, I strove to remain calm. The first step was to turn off the pump, after which, a cheerful whistle tune on my lips, I made my way to a nearby water hose and proceeded to wash the results of the spill into the river, all the while seeking to convey a tolerant understanding of a complex piece of machinery. "This is its normal function," my affect seemed to say, an assertion that proved only too true.

During the summer of my sophomore year, I moved on to a job as lifeguard at a state park beach on Wellesley. Having picked up my life-saving certificate at the end of the college swim season, I thought to spend the summer basking in the sun, performing the occasional, miraculous rescue, and otherwise beguiling crowds of adoring, bikini-clad maidens. Instead, I found myself committed to long hours of mindless inactivity punctuated by moments of sheer, unadulterated boredom. Apart from monitoring hordes of oblivious bathers, the job's only real duty lay in enforcing a few rules of beach etiquette via bullhorn from the lordly eminence of life-guard stands perched some six feet above the sand.

As tedious as such duties inevitably became, this aspect of the job initially appealed to my well-developed sense of self-importance, and I took a certain satisfaction in acquainting myself with the nuances of crowd control. Whenever obliged to address the beach-going public, I learned to pitch my voice somewhere between the solicitousness of a concerned parent and the insistent authority of an arresting officer. For the most part, announcements thus carefully modulated produced a magical acquiescence, whereas any tonal departure in one direction or the other was apt to engender resistance in the mutinous hordes of beach denizens under my supervision. Every day saw various infractions of one sort or another, forcing us lifeguards to repeat a familiar litany of warnings. There were the usual proscriptions against unsafe conduct in and around the water: head-dunking, chicken-fighting and the like. Other concerns had to do with basic issues of hygiene, calling upon us to keep a wary eye out for dog-owners, who had to be reminded of their pets' instinctual urges and the beach's resemblance to a giant litter box.

And then there were special cases, like that involving a certain brazen couple whose synchronized swimming routine—staged directly in front of my stand amid crowds of splashing, shouting bathers—turned out to be a more or less restrained performance of the sex act. The mechanics involved were not difficult to imagine (a slight displacement of their suits, and voila!), but their lack of discretion left me quite speechless. Eventually returning ashore flushed from their exertions and fully aware of my having found them out, they treated me to a good deal of lascivious grinning and winking, to which I responded with a mixture of wonder and dismay. Seeking to maintain a supervisory presence, I made a series of mute gestures, first toward the scene of their coupling and then vaguely in the direction of the crowded beach, thinking to convey something of the indelicacy of their conduct. At this, they only grinned more broadly and proceeded on their way.

Left to ponder the situation on my own, I tried to conceive a more effective response to such incorrigible randiness, but the only thing that came to mind was a ludicrous announcement via bullhorn: YOUR ATTENTION, PLEASE—NO FUCKING ALLOWED IN THE SWIMMING AREA. THANK YOU! Even here, however, I found myself on uncertain ground, for the Red Cross Manual—unimpeachable source of all life guarding knowledge and precedent—proved oddly silent on the subject of public mating. Thus, it seemed I had been caught out, trapped in a dilemma that pitted my duties as lifeguard against the irrepressible forces of life itself. For days afterward, I struggled to maintain a sense of occupational integrity, but it was no use. Increasingly hard-pressed to take the job seriously, I grew sadly careless of my duties, confining my oversight obligations to near-death experiences only.

Such was the range and substance of my work experience at the time of graduation: not a very impressive resume, to be sure, but what did I care? I was about to become a college graduate. Before me lay endless vistas of opportunity, where I had but to knock and doors would fling open, ushering me along a well-marked path to professional success and untold riches. I never actually believed this, of course, but the subversive power of so compelling a fantasy must not be underestimated. One doesn't suffer through sixteen years of continuous schooling without a certain amount of psychic damage. Consciously or unconsciously, rightly or wrongly, expectations are raised, expectations which must inevitably be reconciled with reality in a process bound to be every bit as humbling as that by which one succumbed to so specious a notion in the first place.

    This post-college disillusionment began during the commencement ceremony itself, an event held on the campus' central concourse under clear skies and warm breezes, conditions made to order for a gloriously uplifting occasion. My fraternity cronies and I were having none of it, however; to a man we were wary, somewhat glum, staggering through our final initiation rite with feelings akin to dread, spooked by the sight of our unhip medieval gowns and keenly aware of the doom of conformity that awaited us in the world beyond that in which we had sheltered with such idiosyncratic abandon for the previous four years. Through no fault of the school or its faculty, the times themselves had taught us a deep and abiding suspicion of the world we were about to enter, and thus the traditional optimism of the occasion was lost on us. Thinking to lighten the mood, some of us decided to get high before lining up for the opening procession, but the effect was not nearly as droll as we had hoped, the prospect of receiving our diplomas under the influence—however appropriate to the state in which we had earned them—tending to exacerbate the usual feelings of paranoia.

    The commencement speaker that day was noted ornithologist, Roger Tory Peterson, whose best-selling book, *A Field Guide to the Birds of North America*, was a regular source of study in my younger days, when I learned to distinguish the various species of raptors and waterfowl that frequented the fields and marshes of the River. Even such fond associations as these could not dispel the mounting sense of disquiet on the national scene, however, where the House Judiciary Committee was even then preparing to convene impeachment hearings. By this time, the Watergate burglary and the machinations by which it had been disavowed by the Nixon White House were well known to everyone, having been the focus of increasingly intensive reporting for much of the previous two years. Then too, the Vietnam War, though officially ended as a matter of public policy, continued to weigh heavily on the public consciousness, with another year to go before the fall of Saigon. Given the import of such pending developments, it seemed strange that our college experience should end with a speech on the subject of birdlife, and those with a conspiratorial bent were inclined to suspect school officials of deliberately trying to change the subject.

When it came to escapism, however, we could hardly presume to judge, and as we dutifully filed up to receive the scraps of parchment symbolic of our entry into adulthood, the recognition that we would no longer be able to hold ourselves aloof from the world of our elders evoked a final sense of loss. Following the ceremony, we milled about, negotiating the difficult terrain that lay between the intimacy of family members and the more immediate knowledge of those with whom we had spent many an hour in a state of shit-faced delirium. The time had come, if only symbolically, to say goodbye to both.

Earlier that week, with exams over and my departure imminent, I spent time with Sara. With her birthday in the offing, I wanted to get her a present, and thus, one bright spring afternoon we drove to a small dress shop on the outskirts of Augusta, where she modeled a number of outfits for my approval, and was well pleased with the final choice. Later, on the way home, she talked about the state-sponsored training program she was about to begin, declaring her intention, once settled into her new job, to rent an apartment in town. We talked over the possibility of my returning to Maine later in the summer to help her with the move and possibly move in with her. It was just an idea, one of many potential plans running through my head during those baffling times, but I was open to suggestion about it and couldn't deny the appeal of seeing her in her new dress again.

Once back at the River, I took up where I'd left off the previous summer, resuming my life-guarding duties, tow-kiting at every opportunity, and frequenting the bars of Alexandria Bay on a nightly basis. This lasted about six weeks, by which time Sara had started working at the hospital where she did her training. In addition, she had carried through with plans to rent an apartment within walking distance of work, and solicited my help with the move. Accordingly, about mid-summer, after giving notice at work, I prepared to drive back to Maine. Where things might lead from there was anyone's guess.

Thus began another day-long odyssey on Route 2, a journey once again full of fond hopes for the future. Whatever arrangement the two of us might come to, the need to find a steady job, if not a career, loomed large in my thoughts, and as the familiar scenes of the northern highway slid past my car windows, I half-expected to discover my occupational destiny in much the same way I had arrived at the idea of a gliding career a year earlier. On the present occasion, however, lowering skies darkened my mood, and as I looked out over a seemingly endless expanse of woods and fields, my job prospects seemed meager at best.

Dusk was falling, along with persistent rain, by the time I reached my old college haunts and followed Sara's directions to a modest two-story house on a tree-lined street in Waterville. Climbing a narrow flight of stairs at the rear of the house, I arrived in a back entryway cluttered with various boxes, and for a moment stood wondering what had brought me to so unfamiliar a place on such a dismal night. Moments later Sara opened the door and I stopped wondering. Dressed in flannel shirt and blue jeans, her hair done up in work-a-day fashion, she welcomed me inside, and after saying our hellos, we stood grinning at each other, both a bit nervous, she on account of the new place and what I might think of it, and I on account of her concern for my opinion.

Though I had arrived too late to be of much immediate help with the move, she seemed glad of my presence just the same, and, showing me around, led the way to a small room she had converted to a nursery, where Tasha was standing in her crib, enthusing loudly about the day's ongoing adventures. When I offered to free her from her padded prison, however, she wasn't quite ready to renew our acquaintance, preferring to study me anew from the familiar perch of her mother's hip. Following a brief tour of the place, we had something to eat, and later a couple of Sara's friends stopped by for an informal housewarming. Later still, the friends having gone home and the baby asleep in her crib, we made our way to the bedroom, where a mattress lay on the floor amid various boxes of her belongings. There was still a lot of straightening up to be done, but nothing that couldn't be put it off in favor of the more compelling matter of our reunion.

The next morning, we awoke to a series of babbled inquiries from the next room, and moments later Sara carried Tasha in and placed her on the bed between us. Freshly changed and dressed in her Sunday best overalls, she sat quietly for a moment before suddenly grabbing each of us by the cheek and treating the flesh of our faces like so much Play-doh. Letting go only after we both cried out for mercy, she set off on a crawling tour of her new home with a triumphant cackle.

After breakfast, we did some tidying up, then drove into town in search of a dresser and bedframe with Tasha in tow. It was the first time the three of us had been out together in public, and I found myself strangely self-conscious on account of the baby's presence. Winding up in a small, used-furniture shop, we found a likely dresser readily enough, but the only thing in the way of a bedstead was a set of unadorned box springs, which the proprietor—a rheumy-eyed fellow with a week's growth of stubble—privately assured me was still up to the job, vigorously jouncing the springs by way of illustration.

"See what I'm sayin'?" he asked with a smirk.

"Yeah, I get it, and no thanks," (I was trying to play the family man, dammit!).

Settling up, I loaded the dresser into the car, and we proceeded to a grocery store for supplies.

Later, back at the apartment, Sara made sandwiches while I lugged the dresser up the back stairs and installed it in the bedroom. After lunch, she hung up some curtains and filled the new dresser with the contents of several boxes of clothes, whereupon we paused to admire our handiwork. With the windows open and a warm summer breeze flagging the curtains, the room took on a new charm, and suddenly Sara decided it was time for the baby's nap. Putting her into her crib, we waited until she was down and quiet, then went back to bed ourselves.

All in all, it was a pleasant sort of reunion. Now possessed of a job, apartment, and live-in partner, Sara fairly glowed with a newfound sense of independence. As for me, I basked in the glow, proud of her for her accomplishments and of myself for playing a part in them. At the same time, however, I was acutely aware that my presence in that household carried with it an implicit expectation, and under the circumstances finding a job seemed the least of my concerns. Thus, on weekdays, with Sara at work and her younger sister serving as babysitter, I set out to find suitably dignified and remunerative employment, thinking—or at least trying to imagine—that at some point I might become a family man in earnest. To what degree I believed in this possibility, I can't say. At the time, I believed in it as much as I believed in anything, but this didn't necessarily imply deep conviction. The thing is, I wanted to believe, which in itself seemed such a huge shift in perspective that I was carried along as if by momentum alone.

Meanwhile, the immediate problem of getting a job seemed manageable enough. After all, I had a history of regular employment, and previous experience hadn't burdened me with unreasonably high standards when it came to the kind of work I was prepared to do. On the other hand, the situation seemed to militate for something more substantial than the seasonal jobs to which I was accustomed, which left me in a sadly familiar quandary. Despite or because of my four-year apprenticeship in academe, I still had very little idea what sort of career I ought to pursue, much less how to proceed once I made the discovery.

Even so, I forged ahead, seeking first to stake a claim upon the field of journalism. A visit to the offices of the local newspaper turned up no openings, however, and in an interview with the managing editor I was informed that, barring the untimely death of a member of the existing staff, I should not expect to hear from him.

This led me in another direction altogether. Thinking to find work first and worry about a likely career later, I made my way to the personnel office of a sizeable factory engaged in the manufacture of some industrial widget. They too were not hiring, however, and I went away feeling a mixture of disappointment and relief.

Next, in response to a newspaper ad, I showed up at a local department store, where it turned out they were looking for a shoe salesman. Even more than factory work, selling shoes was not something I could easily imagine myself doing, yet I felt compelled to say that I would think it over, never doubting that the job was mine for the asking. To my profound humiliation, however, the supervisor responded with the time-honored phrase, "Don't call us, we'll call you," by which I came to understand that he was even less enthusiastic about my application than I was.

Despite these setbacks, I was determined to keep looking. Surely something would turn up, and meanwhile I continued to take a vicarious satisfaction in Sara's new outlook. She, at least, was moving forward, and despite the sketchiness of my employment prospects, it seemed our relations couldn't have been better. If nothing else, our new sleeping arrangement represented a big improvement over the room-hopping trysts we had managed in the fraternity house, and waking up in her company did not exactly darken my outlook on the day.

Before long, however, I began to wake up to other realities as well, recognizing by slow degrees that the future I had allowed myself to imagine was inherently flawed. Newly liberated from the constraints of the academic calendar, with aspirations that swung wildly across all points of the occupational and recreational compass, I was in no position to undertake a settled life. After all, there was my gliding career to consider. With admirable self-restraint, I'd managed to put it on hold for several weeks, but the lure of my favorite pastime had scarcely diminished. Like a siren's song it called out to me, and the temptation would only grow stronger with time.

Recent communication with Paul revealed that he and Jake had been flying regularly throughout the summer and were organizing a regional fly-in for the end of September. Then too, there was the prospect of the coming ski season to think about. The idea of spending the winter anywhere but at the mountain seemed inconceivable, yet such plans now gave rise to a disturbing moral dilemma, for it began to dawn on me that if I were not prepared to stay with Sara and be her helpmate, conscience dictated that I get out of her way so she might find someone who would.

The moment of crisis arrived one otherwise idyllic mid-summer evening, when, with her sister on hand to baby-sit, Sara and I walked the few blocks to a neighborhood store for the makings of dinner. Following an afternoon of oppressive heat, the day was finally growing cooler, and along the tree-lined street a welcome breeze was fragrant with the scent of flowers and new-mown lawns. Grateful for the chance to be off by ourselves, we took our time, ambling along the sidewalk with an easy intimacy, looking forward to the weekend and an anticipated camping trip.

Having gathered what we needed at the store, we were retracing our steps through the neighborhood when, in a moment of sudden clarity, I realized that my visit—for that is what it had been all along—was coming to an end. It was as if the vision of the future I had been struggling to conceive, finding fulfillment in a brief moment of contentment, had suddenly burned itself out, leaving me with the dazed and disappointed feeling of waking abruptly from a pleasant dream. Sooner or later, I was going to have to come clean with Sara, and every passing moment would only make it more difficult.

Even so, I couldn't bring myself to mar the occasion of our evening stroll, nor could I summon the necessary resolve upon our return to the apartment, nor after supper, by which time the burden of my confession was becoming nearly intolerable. When Tasha's bedtime routine put me off further, I was obliged to wait until we had gone to bed ourselves—not the most favorable of moments, perhaps, and yet the thought occurred to me that only by speaking the necessary words at such a time and place would I ever be able to summon the will to carry them out. Accordingly, I started talking into the darkness above our heads, as if thinking aloud. My inability to find work was a key point, and I made it the cornerstone of my position. Without a job or the prospect of one, I was weeks away from going broke and needed to plan accordingly. The only consolation I could offer was the hope of finding work at the mountain come ski season, which hardly promised to suit her circumstances.

In any case, the next morning, with the promised camping trip still in the offing, we pretended nothing had changed between us, thinking only to escape another day of sweltering heat. After putting the apartment in order and collecting our gear, we cinched Tasha into her car seat and started on our way, the windows rolled down and a welcome breeze whipping through the car. Despite its awkward implications with respect to my confession, our destination was a foregone conclusion; following the familiar route north, I headed to Sugarloaf in hopes of running into one or both of my flying cronies.

A scan of likely places failed the turn them up, however, and the ski area itself was all-but-abandoned upon our arrival, leaving me strangely disconcerted. As we drove through the empty parking lots to the vicinity of the lodge, it seemed the distinction I had always drawn between the settled life of the town and the compelling wildness of the mountains was not as dramatic and inviolable as I had always imagined. Here we were, baby and all, entering upon the mythic realm of my vaunted feats of aviation (absence from the sport had only heightened my delusional tendencies), and as the snowless and somehow diminished vistas of the ski slopes rose before us, I began to suspect that the imaginary wall I had erected between the two worlds was nothing more than a dodge by which to escape the inconvenient realities of life.

Stepping out into the cool mountain air, we fitted Tasha into a carrying pack and I hoisted her onto my back, where she tugged happily on my ears as we made our way past the lodge and ascended the open slope. Continuing uphill, we arrived at last in a swath of alpine meadow very near the spot from which I had made my first abortive take-offs some eight months earlier. Here we stopped to rest, letting Tasha totter around in the tall, summer grass while the two of us sat watching the play of sunshine and cloud-shadow upon the valley floor. Though it had hardly been a considered plan, I suspect that in returning to that spot I hoped in some implicit way to explain something to her, yet as we sat gazing out over the valley the explanation seemed less and less valid, and after a series of awkward silences we eventually started back down.

Getting on the road again, we continued north, skirting the Bigelow Range and eventually coming upon a small campground on the western shore of Flagstaff Lake—the very scene, as it happened, of the Arnold expedition's existential crisis in the fall of 1775. After six weeks of paddling up the Kennebec, then carrying their leaky bateau overland to the boggy meanders of the Dead River, the exhausted army was scarcely halfway to its destination, and with the first snows of the season upon them, the chances of their making it out of the wilderness alive, let alone seizing the fortress at Quebec, were growing dimmer by the moment. While leading elements of the expedition searched for the trail north, the rest of the army lay scattered along the length of the Dead River swamps, and it was at this point that a unit of Connecticut men surreptitiously abandoned the campaign and started back to the coast, taking with them a portion of the army's dwindling supplies. For their desertion, they would be roundly condemned as traitors by their commander, whose name would itself become a byword for treason and dishonor.

By morning, a dense overcast had settled over the lake, obscuring the mountains and threatening rain. We lingered for a while in hopes conditions might improve, but it was not to be, and, bowing to the inevitable, we repacked our things and started back to town in a steady drizzle. Along the way the rain started coming down in earnest, and whereas the outbound journey had allowed us a certain respite from the implications of my recent decision, the return trip only made the situation seem the more inescapable. That evening, when I confirmed my intention to return to the River, she responded with a grudging acceptance.

The next morning, while she took care of Tasha and got ready for work, I went out to pick up some supplies at the local market and was standing in the checkout line when a dull pain suddenly gripped my chest with the immediacy of some kind of attack. Nothing seemed to come of it, however, and back at the apartment I dropped off the items, we said our good-byes, and I hit the road.

# Chapter 8

# Gone for a Sailor

The months that followed recur in my memory with the sketchiness of a movie marred by inept camera work. Like a fly in a bottle, baffled to the point of madness by the illusion of freedom, I raced about seemingly at random, crashing into invisible walls and continuing in new directions. Returning to the River, I scared up my lifeguard job and worked the remaining three weeks of the season, putting together some money against my next foray into the world. This time my purpose would be clearer and more exclusively recreational.

Earlier that summer, my friend Sam and I had gone in on a new tow-kite, but due in part to my hiatus in Maine we found few opportunities to fly it. And now, with the summer nearing an end, I converted it to a glider with a plan to try to sell it at the upcoming fly-in at Sugarloaf, scheduled for the latter part September. Thus, I loaded it atop the car along with my standard glider and started east again, this time taking the southern route along the interstates and making a detour to Newport, Rhode Island, where the America's Cup races were about to begin. The challenge matches earlier in the summer promised a hard-fought series between Americans in *Courageous* and an Australian crew in *Southern Cross*, and I had arranged to witness the event in the company of a cousin with whom I'd done a lot of sailing at the River.

Arriving in Newport on a balmy, late-summer afternoon, the two of us rendezvoused in the Black Dog, the harbor's dockside bar of record, where we dined on beer and pretzel logs before making a tour of the piers. While I'd always been a freshwater enthusiast when it came to the boating world, I quickly came to appreciate the charms of the ocean-going scene and the well-heeled world associated with it. Vying with each other to discover the sleekest, most expensive yacht in the harbor, we made a careful study of the local fleet, balancing luxury against speed and seaworthiness, and passing the rest of the evening defending our choices.

The next day, after spending the night in a run-down boarding house, we decided to go in search of *Courageous*, which we learned was being kept under lock and key at a secure boatyard to safeguard the design secrets of its radical winged keel. While the yard in question was not hard to find, a chain-link fence topped by barbed wire discouraged our initial efforts to get so much as a peek at the fabled craft. Even so, no one seemed to be around, and in hopes of finding a way through the fence, we split up and started in opposite directions, thinking to sneak into the compound without attracting notice.

After walking the length of the barrier, I came to a point where two docks in close proximity to each other abutted the shore on either side of the fence, and a carefully-choreographed leap from one dock to the other landed me inside. Thinking to pass myself off as a local dockhand, I made my way toward the center of the yard, and sure enough, there was *Courageous*, supported by yacht stands in the middle of an open lot, its keel carefully concealed from view by a large canvas tarp. Meanwhile, a portable stairway stood along its aft quarter, allowing access to the deck, and in front of the stairs velvet ropes had been strung between a series of free-standing posts, forming a barrier of the sort found in movie theaters and hotel lobbies, though its purpose in the present case was something of a mystery.

Half expecting to see my cousin appear from the other end of the yard, I ambled over to the vicinity of the stairway and was contemplating my next move when a pair of limousines arrived in a nearby parking area. Moments later, a group of young men tumbled out and wasted no time making their way to the stairway, where I stood in sudden fear of being discovered for the rank interloper I was. The newcomers paid no attention to me, however, hopping over the rope barrier and starting up the stairs without so much as a glance in my direction. Following in their wake was a dignified older woman wearing large sunglasses that obscured much of her face. Arriving at the makeshift barrier, she paused, at which point, seizing upon the chance to make myself useful, I unclipped the velvet rope and drew it aside to let her pass. Acknowledging the courtesy, she looked up and thanked me, enabling me to get a better look at her face, which seemed oddly familiar. Some ten seconds elapsed, however, before I put together who it was, and from that day to this I have sworn to all who will listen that I "met" Jacqueline Onassis.

No sooner had I tumbled to her identity, however, than a hitherto unseen man-in-charge appeared on the deck above and began glowering at me. Suddenly fearing arrest on a charge of impersonating a rich person, I withdrew along the route of my unauthorized entry, and was soon back at the gate, where my cousin stood awaiting my return, having been unable to find a way inside. When I told him what had happened, he listened wistfully to my alleged sighting, which was later confirmed by a newspaper report to the effect that members of the Kennedy clan had received an exclusive tour of the compound prior to the start of the series. While I never got to see the top-secret keel, it seemed I had stumbled into a "Zelig" moment.

Having arranged to watch the races from the deck of a Coast Guard cutter, we spent the next several days making regular excursions to Block Island Sound, where, surrounded by a vast flotilla of spectator craft, we followed the progress of the sleek, 12-meter sloops amid non-stop talk of sailing strategy. On lay-days, of which there were several, we drove to nearby New Bedford, where we spent time polishing the teak and bright work on a 42-foot ketch whose captain we had met in the Black Dog. Preparing to make the fall run to Florida, he was looking for someone to crew the journey as well, and for a while I considered signing on, thinking to be down and back within a month. As this would have put me out of the fly-in at Sugarloaf, however, I decided against it, and after staying through the final race, in which the American crew retained their eponymous cup, I parted company with my cousin and drifted northward, back to Maine.

Along the way, I made a brief stop in Concord, Massachusetts, where my aunt taught school and my uncle was an administrator at

Middlesex Academy. Deciding to pay them a visit on the spur of the moment, I arrived on the Middlesex campus late in the afternoon and, asking directions from a group of students, made my way to my uncle's office in a stately stone building. Despite my unannounced arrival, after checking with my aunt, he extended an invitation to dinner and an overnight stay, and shortly thereafter I joined the two of them at their well-appointed house, a perquisite of his job at the academy. Over dinner, I remarked upon their enviably refined and efficient sort of life, at which point my aunt inquired about my plans.

"You mean, in the way of a career?" I stammered.

"Yes, what are your career plans."

"Well, I'm not sure. I mean, I really haven't settled on anything."

"I'll tell you what: I'm going to work tomorrow, about eight, and you're welcome to join me if you like. It might give you some ideas."

"Oh, I don't know," I said. "I should probably get up to the mountain and help out with preparations and such."

"Well, think about it. If you'd like to spend the morning visiting my classroom, I'd be happy to have you."

"I'll think about it."

The next morning, I was only the more anxious to be on my way, however, and when I confirmed my intention to continue the seemingly aimless journey that had landed me on her doorstep, my aunt sent me on my way with a pointed observation: "Good luck at the mountain. But remember, you can't fly kites forever, even if you are flying in them."

It was the closest thing to admonishment on the subject I'd ever received. My father—whose role as an adviser had ended, it seemed, with his parting words during the outset of my college career—had never ventured upon such territory in so forthright a manner, though I felt sure he shared her opinion. In any case, though touched by her offer I was frankly horrified by the thought of standing in front of a classroom full of impressionable young minds. Jumping off mountains seemed considerably safer and less stressful by comparison.

Arriving at Sugarloaf a few days before the scheduled fly-in, I found Paul at his run-down A-frame in the valley, and was quickly updated on the summer's flying activities. Making use of his jeep, he and Jake had been hauling their gliders uphill along a tote road and foot-launching from a steep pitch on the upper mountain, a practice that attracted a number of other glider freaks from New Hampshire. Based on such wider interest, Paul approached the ski area manager about the possibility of reopening the gondola lift for an informal fly-in, and the idea was duly accepted. On the appointed weekend some two dozen flyers from as far away as Connecticut showed up, taking advantage of ideal conditions to launch from the summit and float far over the valley on warm, upwelling air currents. The event attracted a number of spectators, and hopes were high that the sequel would be an even bigger hit than its predecessor.

 Later, Paul and I linked up with Jake and the three of us made tentative plans for the near future. With the management clearly open to the promotional possibilities of our flying exploits, we were keener than ever to become a regular attraction during the ski season, in anticipation of which we resolved to pool our slender resources and rent a likely place for the winter.

 As it turned out, the September fly-in was "blown out," with conditions too windy to fly even from the lower mountain. Even so, some half-dozen pilots showed up, providing me with likely customers for my extra kite, which I assembled for display purposes in the ample interior of the lodge. While none of the visiting flyers happened to be in the market for a new ship, one of them put me in touch with a friend of his from Boston, and when I spoke to the friend by phone, he suggested that I bring the glider to a downtown address for a showing.

 Thus, I soon found myself in the middle of Beantown, some few blocks from the Prudential Center, where I was assembled the airframe on a traffic island in the middle of Boylston Street, a steady stream of cars and buses whizzing past on either side. Struggling to keep the wing from being swept away with every violent gust, I staggered about like some crack-pot aviator from an early newsreel.

 Even so, I made the sale, and ended up wondering if I might be able to get a living hawking gliders to passersby on the street. In any case, with another month remaining before the start of the ski season, I departed the city for the River once again, thinking to collect skis and gear for a concerted move to Sugarloaf sometime around

Thanksgiving. Anything in the way of a career plan was still a long way off, but for the time being I was content to interpret movement alone, no matter how aimless, for progress toward life's higher goals.

    By this time, fall was advancing on the north country, and I ended up spending much of the ensuing month at the family's townhouse in Watertown. Since going away to college four years earlier, I'd spent little time there, and my return was not exactly providential, especially as my brother's situation had changed very little in the meantime. Despite having maintained good grades throughout his high school years, in the months preceding graduation he had run into difficulty completing the final coursework. For some reason, he couldn't or wouldn't do it, despite which, on the basis of his good record and reputation, school officials had eventually granted him a diploma, enabling him to attend college that fall.

    The sudden lapse in his work ethic proved an ill omen, however, for at the end of his first semester of college, he dropped out, returning home around Christmas time. Clearly something was amiss, but nothing was said about it, and, with no apparent plans or prospects, he settled back into his old room as if the entire episode were of little consequence. Baffled as much as concerned, our parents made every effort to give him space to find a way forward, but with the passage of time his situation had only seemed to become more intractable.

    For the time being, however, the volatility that had led to our many fights in the past seemed in abeyance. No longer obliged to endure the tribulations of high school together, we got along well enough, and in the course of my stay I recalled more pleasant memories of growing up in the town.

    There was the time when, as a fifth grader, I took it into my head to restore an old bicycle that had been a favorite from years past. With my resurrected ride, I took to the streets accompanied by a madcap gang of fellow daredevils. Dubbing ourselves the Hell-bikers, we prowled the neighborhoods looking for trouble, venturing as far as Public Square, a four-block downtown area where various alleyways led down to a railroad station, offering the closest thing we could find in the way of urban atmospherics.

*Gone for a Sailor*

  Shortly thereafter the skateboard craze hit town and I was right on top of it—after a fashion. These were the days of the first manufactured boards, thin and flexible, with specialized trucks accommodating wide, composite wheels. By this time, however, I had become sold on the virtues of do-it-yourself restoration and decided to make my own board out of a pine plank and one of my sister's clamp-on roller skates. While I managed to trim the corners of the plank somewhat, the resulting vehicle was bulky and all-but-impossible to turn, which was probably just as well, because its metal wheels were prone to skidding at the slightest provocation. Indeed, my new creation proved to be the Corvair of skateboards—unsafe at any speed. Nevertheless, I was proud of it, and promptly bragged to my friends that I could ride it the length of the most challenging skateboard terrain known to Sherman Elementary School: the dreaded Chestnut Street Hill.

  Alarmingly, several of my biking pals took me seriously, and a few days later a small group of spectators accompanied me to the top of the hill to bear witness, threatening to scatter in the event I got hurt. When the time came, I was every bit as skeptical about my chances as they were, but with reputation on the line there was no going back. A few tentative strides started me rolling along a gradual in-run, and soon I was racing down the face of the hill at breakneck speed, the metal wheels of my homemade death-mobile shrieking across the asphalt with such intensity that the soles of my feet grew numb from the vibration. Even so, I was holding my line, and if not for a narrow strip of new pavement running across my path, I might have made it all the way to the bottom. Instead, anticipating the hazard, I angled my way toward the roadside, where a dense hedge bordered a nearby lawn. Upon hitting the curb, I parted company with the board to mingle with the shrubbery, which proved a mixed blessing, arresting my headlong trajectory yet tumbling me onto the sidewalk with a number of bloody scratches on arms and abdomen.

  Meanwhile, at the top of the hill, my would-be fan club waited until I struggled woozily to my feet before descending to check out my wounds. Bearing up manfully against the pain, I thought to have proven myself, but the next day the consensus of opinion at school seemed to hold that I was more foolhardy than courageous, and I hadn't been sufficiently injured to warrant even the lesser attention paid to all medical curiosities. My act clearly needed work.

Now, when I considered the trend of my post-college career, it seemed I hadn't come very far from those days, having traded one new craze for another and moved on to more expensive toys. Still, my plans to spend the winter at Sugarloaf promised to fulfill my fondest ambitions, and in early November, having collected the bulk of my belongings, I started east again, arriving back at the mountain determined to find a job before the advent of the ski season. Since my departure in September, Paul and Jake had moved into a three-bedroom rental several miles from the ski area, and after laying claim to the remaining room I ponied up my share of the rent and added my glider to a makeshift rack situated under the eaves. Next, I embarked upon a concerted search for employment, and within a week had landed a job in a pub at the base of the slopes. Now the only thing we all required was sufficient snow to open the mountain for skiing, an event the three of us awaited with fond hopes for another season of high-flying self-promotion.

In my case, however, something more was required as well, for try as I might throughout the preceding months, I had been unable to put Sara out of my mind. Ever since my departure in August, I had neither written nor called her, yet the dull pain in my chest had scarcely diminished, and, having established a place at the mountain, the opportunity to check in with her, if only to confirm that she was okay, now presented itself. As awkward as such an encounter threatened to be, in the end I was prepared to endure any amount of recrimination to see her again.

Thus, one crisp fall day I drove downstate and made my way to the tree-lined street where I had spent part of the summer. Climbing the back stairs to the apartment, I knocked on the door, but there was no answer, and indeed no sign of recent habitation. This came as a shock. While I had tried to imagine any number of scenarios, the possibility that she might no longer live there had scarcely occurred to me, and, finding the door unlocked, I walked through the now-desolate rooms in a quandary every bit as deep as the one I had left under. As much as I'd convinced myself of her self-sufficiency, I couldn't help thinking that all she had done to make the place livable had been done at least in part with the expectation that I might choose to stay with her. Instead, I breezed in for a visit and abruptly left, continuing on my half-assed way to nowhere in particular. Suddenly my long silence seemed a unforgivable transgression.

Luckily, she was on duty at the hospital, and, asking after her at the front desk, I waited in the reception area, searching the carpet for something to say. The months of silence now seemed a monstrous and unaccountable transgression, and I half expected she would simply refuse to appear. Moments later, however, I looked up to find her standing in front of me, looking a bit severe in her uniform, though not entirely disappointed to see me.

"I stopped by the apartment but there was no sign of you," I began.

"I'm living in the country now."

"Really, what's it like?"

"It's nice. There are lots of fields and a pond just down the road."

"I'm sharing a cabin near the mountain with my gliding buddies," I admitted.

"How's it working out?"

"Pretty good, I guess. –Be a whole lot better if I could start seeing you again."

"Would it?" she asked with unmistakable emphasis.

The dilemma I had run away from several months previously was staring me in the face again, and there was no sense trying to deny its complications for me.

"I don't know... maybe," I ventured. For all of my recent contrition, it was as much of a commitment as I could honestly make, and honesty, it seemed, was the only virtue remaining to me. "—So, what do you say?"

"I don't know... maybe."

*Near the Borderline*

# Chapter 9

# When Donkeys Fly

Following a series of snowfalls during the week of Thanksgiving, the ski area officially opened for business and life suddenly moved to a new rhythm. Now, every morning in the pre-dawn twilight an incoming tide of traffic advanced along the state highway and up the approach road, streaming into the ski area parking lots to deliver a steady influx of day-trippers to the base lodge, where they milled about, organizing tickets and gear, before heading outside, fully accessorized and bundled to the eyebrows. Making their way to a variety of lifts, they stood in line amid the hum and clatter of the machinery, awaiting their turn to start uphill.

Throughout the forenoon the flood continued, until the lodge and its environs were awash and along the ski trails of the upper mountain, animated specks could be seen filtering their way downhill. By midday the still-burgeoning crowds surrounding the base lodge had spread into outlying shops and restaurants, and the microcosm of the village buzzed with activity. Then, about three o'clock, the tide started to turn, and the trails of the upper mountain beginning to show fewer and fewer signs of life as the downhill traffic gradually drained onto the open slope, pooling in front of the lodge and seeping into the parking lots. Now the pubs and eateries at the base of the slopes created a temporary backwater as patrons stood three-deep at the bars and swirled about in restless eddies within their cramped interiors. In time the day-trippers receded back down the valley, the condo-dwellers retired to their trailside apartments, and the lodge itself grew quiet, awaiting the next day, when the cycle would begin again.

Meanwhile, in the roadside cabin some three miles north of the main entrance, the day began with a preliminary check of conditions, a procedure accomplished by the less-than-scientific yet remarkably accurate method of peering out the windows and examining the tops of the surrounding pines. If the upper boughs were in motion, even slightly, the air above the mountain was bound to be too unstable for our fragile style of flight, in which case there was little enthusiasm for early rising. If, on the other hand, even the slimmest chance of getting airborne seemed possible, the cry would go forth, "Looks flyable!" and the three of us, along with any overnight guests, were soon up and about, tumbling into the main room, pulling on clothes and gear, grabbing something in the way of breakfast, and heading out the door to start cars and dig them out of any overnight accumulations.

Upon arrival at the lodge, the first order of business was to make a phone call to the summit station for definitive word on the wind. Provided gust differentials were not too high, baseline wind speeds up to ten miles an hour were considered manageable, and once such parameters were confirmed, it was on to the gondola terminal, where, in token of the management's growing endorsement of our activities, a special flatcar otherwise reserved for maintenance purposes was available for our use. Additional perquisites included free season passes and access to an ample storage room for the gliders in the basement of the lodge, all of which benefits were granted on the basis of "promotional considerations." While the actual value of our activities remained open to interpretation, if tireless enthusiasm for the "work" of flying counted for anything, we were a bargain.

Further stream-lining our operations was a decided preference for foot-launching as opposed to ski-launching, a refinement that freed us from the burden of heavy boots and skis, improving the performance of the gliders. Thus unencumbered, we had only to carry the airframes from the storage room to the gondola, where we circumvented the lines of waiting skiers, proceeding directly to a corner of the terminal where the flat-car awaited on a separate track. Clambering aboard, we waited for the attendant to send us on our way, and were soon standing up on the open platform, riding uphill with the smug self-assurance of high-wire artists as the clatter and hubbub of the lower slopes fell away and the valley spread out before us like the hidden realm of Shangri-La.

If the upper mountain was open and flyable, we transited the mid-station and continued uphill, arriving at last at the bunker-like summit terminal, where we grabbed our gliders and made our way out of the building along a narrow path leading to the absolute summit. Trudging up through the snowfields, we watched the terminal dropped from sight within a protective swale, the whine of the lift machinery giving way to the sounds of our labored breathing as we ascended the last, steep pitch of the summit knoll, kicking footholds into the hardpack as we went. Here the slope leveled out in a field of partially-exposed boulders overlooking the mountain's northeast face, where a crude launch platform consisting of two-by-twelve pine planks awaited, a wind telltale mounted on a small mast to one side.

Setting the gliders down, we made last-minute assessments of the wind, holding our arms out wing-like in the breeze and making practice runs down the in-run to a point where the ground dropped away in a precipitous scree-field. Thus assured, we scrambled to assemble the airframes, our impatience to be airborne tempered by an obsessive concern to secure all fastenings. Then, one after another we carried our gliders to top of the runway, strapped ourselves in, and stood waiting for the universe to coalesce in a moment of decision. This could take a while, as the wind was often subject to unpredictable cycles, sometimes blowing downhill, dissipating, and going quiet... only to turn and gather strength—at which point, the telltale beginning to flutter in the building breeze, we raced to meet it, bolting down the makeshift launch platform to float out over a jumble of rocks and stunted firs, on our way.

Where to? –part of the fun lay in not knowing. If the wind was right, we might follow a crest running westward from the summit in search of ridge lift. In the opposite direction a lesser peak loomed in the middle distance, its slopes appearing curiously flat and foreshortened from above. And there was always the option of flying straight out, watching the mountain drop away until, at altitudes over a thousand feet, a strange feeling of stasis took over, one's movement relative to the surrounding peaks becoming all but imperceptible in the wide gulf of air. Whatever our flight path, we inevitably arrived over the landing field with altitude to spare, enabling us to fly in formation, call out to each other, engage in mock dogfights or carve long, sweeping turns before lining up for landing. Skimming the treetops on final approach, we negotiated ski-borne traffic on the open slope and touched down at last amid whoops of exhilaration.

So it went for as long as conditions allowed, which was seldom very long. In the time it took us to reach the top of the mountain again, things were apt to change, with the result that no two flights were ever quite the same. If the summit became unflyable, we might still catch a ride from the lower mountain, and on occasions when the wind came from around the shoulder of the peak, there were places along the westernmost trails where it was possible to take off and gain sufficient altitude to make a downwind turn to the landing field. Even advancing weather systems could be accommodated, as on one memorable day when we launched from the summit in bright sunshine only to descend within a thick stratus cloud about mid-mountain and, after a brief, unsettling period of effective blindness, fly out beneath it in the midst of a steady snowfall.

It was a rare day when conditions remained stable throughout the afternoon, and in any case by three o'clock I was routinely obliged to be at work in the pub. Though the job recalled something of my less-than-halcyon days as a bus boy, the time passed quickly, and in exchange for emblazoning the name of the pub on the sail of my glider, the owner of the place—an affable mountain man and backwoods philosopher who did much of the cooking—consented to pay me extra every day I flew. I was not exactly on a fast-track career-wise but getting paid to fly seemed an occupational coup, and I was well-satisfied with the arrangement.

No sooner had life in the cabin settled into a pattern, however, than according to the terms of our lease we were obliged to move out, enabling the owner to make use of the place during the week of the Christmas holidays. Having made few preparations for this contingency, we were days away from finding ourselves out in the snow when Jake came up with an alternate abode in nearby Stratton, some three miles up the highway from the cabin. Recalling his previous apartment, I might have known the accommodations were going to be no-frills at best, and so they were: three bare rooms off a narrow hallway, a small Franklin stove for heat, and a dingy, effectively unusable kitchen area. Nevertheless, for the time being we were prepared to put up with very little, and as both Paul and Jake spent much of the holiday week visiting family downstate, I had the place mostly to myself.

And yet, not entirely. At some point shortly before Christmas, a friend of Jake's named Rick showed up, traveling in a van with his girlfriend, and for lack of any likelier connection the two of them ended up spending much of their time parked in front of my temporary address. A professional football player from a Canadian-league team, Rick was thinking of taking up hang-gliding and possibly staying through the ski season. This was okay by me, though it was going to take a sizeable glider to carry his 250-pound linebacker's bulk aloft. Moreover, he seemed temperamentally ill-suited to our particular pastime, which he insisted on viewing entirely in terms of a reckless sort of daring. That he was sufficiently reckless to try it was clear from accounts of his exploits on the ball field, and the scars he showed in proof of such claims left little room for doubt. Yet mere recklessness, it seemed to me, was not high on the list of a hang-glider pilot's most valuable attributes, and in fact the more I saw of him the more I began to suspect that, in addition to being ill-suited to the new sport, he was quite possibly ill-suited to life outside an institution.

Even so, his enthusiasm for the sport was such that we got along well enough, and the presence of his girlfriend—a wild-eyed, buxom babe, herself of formidable proportions—seemed to have a calming effect on his otherwise volatile personality. They came and went about the place mainly to use the facilities, and might have moved in altogether as far as I was concerned, though inside temperatures seldom broke 50 degrees, and they doubtless generated sufficient heat of their own in their mobile bedroom. In any case, they remained throughout the holiday week, and upon returning late from the pub on New Year's Eve, I discovered the van in its wonted place out front, a light glowing from within, where the two of them could be heard singing and carrying on despite the night's bitter cold. Entering my all-but-empty apartment, I started a fire in the stove, placed my sleeping bag within its immediate vicinity, and, dressed in two-layer union suit and woolen shirt for nightclothes, crawled in for a chilly night's sleep.

Or part of one, anyway. Several hours later in the pre-dawn twilight, I was awakened by a loud crash and the thunderous tattoo of running footsteps. At once wide awake, I caught sight of Rick's girlfriend racing down the hall with Rick close on her heels. Dodging through the doorway on the far side of the room where I lay in front of the stove, she managed to evade her pursuer, and, without breaking stride, sprinted back toward the front door, coming close to trampling me in her progress and crying out "HELP, GODDAMMIT, HE'S AFTER ME!" It was all the conversation she had time for, and moments later she was gone, back into the hallway and out the door.

Struggling to my feet, I looked out a window to see her running full tilt in her stockinged feet across the snowy parking lot in front of the place, wearing blue jeans and a sweater and hugging a pair of boots to her middle. I was sorry to see her go, too, for just then Rick, who had crashed into the end of the hallway with a painful-sounding thud, began bellowing like a gelded bull-calf, and with a growing sense of dread I turned to see him stagger into the room and come to a stop in front of me. Naked from the waist up, a pair of unsightly long underwear below, he was desperately drunk, his hair wildly disheveled and his flushed, bleary-eyed features so full of witless rage as to appear demonic. It was not a pleasant sight under any circumstances, and coming as it did hard upon my departure from dreamland I half-considered climbing back into my sleeping bag and awaiting a likelier vision with which to begin the new year. I could no more have turned my back on him in his present state, however, than if he were a ravening bear or other wild animal, and instinctively I stood my ground.

"Hey man," I breezed, "—what's happening?"

He scowled, trying to bring me into focus, the effort of which rocked him back on his heels. Leaning against a nearby wall, he stood for a moment looking thoroughly perplexed, and it was then I noticed the empty, half-gallon bottle of Jack Daniels he was holding in his hand, his fingers wrapped around its neck as if it were the hammer of Thor. Even as I took note of it, however, his grip slackened and the bottle tumbled to the floor, where it bounced heavily but didn't break. The sound seemed to rouse him, however, and I was relieved to see a light go on somewhere behind his eyes. It wasn't a very bright light, to be sure, but then, under the best of circumstances the candlepower to be found there was not exactly blinding, and I was grateful for the glimmer that now appeared.

"Sh'axt frit!" he uttered by way of explanation.

Interpreting him to say 'she asked for it,' I attempted to defuse the situation: "Some party, huh?"

"Yah, helvanite, ay? –Helvanite!"

Feigning a sleepy sort of wakefulness, I pretended to stretch. "Well, guess I'll be heading up to the mountain, see if it's flyable."

"'Kay, man. Seeya."

Staggering back into the hall, he made his way out the door and across the frozen ground in his bare feet, weaving gingerly as he went. Following at a safe distance as far as the door, I watched him climb into the back of the van, then returned to my bedside in front of the stove, where the fire had long since gone out, leaving no hint of warmth. Meanwhile, the girlfriend was doubtless in need of assistance and, getting dressed, I went in search of her, stopping first near the van to confirm that Rick was duly passed out inside. Sidling up to a window, I peered in to see a shock of straw-colored hair sticking out from under a blanket and was satisfied.

Driving the short distance to the middle of the village, I saw no sign of the girlfriend, and wondered if she had headed north along the highway leading to the Canadian border at Coburn Gore. Heading in that direction I drove for a mile or so, hoping to find her hitching on the roadside, but she was nowhere to be found. For all I knew, she had already hopped a ride on a logging truck and was already headed home. If not, she had to be bound for the mountain, and, turning around, I started back, keeping an eye out for her. As it turned out, however, I never saw either one of them again.

Meanwhile, the holidays over, Jake and Paul returned, and we took up residence again in our original quarters. By this time, I'd patched things up with Sara sufficiently to visit her on a more or less regular basis, driving down to her place in the country every so often when she had time off. Our relationship remained sketchy at best, however, and during one such visit I became aware that I was not the only one with claims upon her affections. By this time, she had acquired a car of her own, and, meeting her in town, I followed her back to her house, a modest bungalow off a rural highway south of Waterville. Arriving at dusk, we pulled into the dirt driveway to find a truck parked out front and lights on inside the house, a discovery that caused Sara some distress. As the two of us made our way up the front path with Tasha in tow, the door of the house flung open and a long-haired fellow came out, carrying various belongings and not in the mood for polite introductions.

The thought occurred to me that I had made his acquaintance once in a bar, though his connection to Sara had never been clear. Now the two of them exchanged a few curt remarks, and as we passed each other in the semi-darkness I played dumb about the whole thing, pretending that his presence there was some strange coincidence. The pose proved difficult to carry off, however, as one of the belongings he was carrying away was a shotgun, the muzzle of which he allowed to linger in my general direction for several seconds. It was no way to handle a firearm, and I would have told him so if it weren't for a sudden desire to spare his feelings.

Soon he was gone, tires spinning as he left the driveway, and we settled in for the evening. The episode left a bitter aftertaste, however, and once again I faced a familiar dilemma, only compounded by the now-certain knowledge that I was intruding upon Sara's relationships with other potential partners. Then too, when I considered the implications for Tasha, I felt worse still. Now nearly two, she had grown into an energetic elf who could scamper about and talk in mostly intelligible sentences. In a thousand little ways she was becoming her own person, and on the evenings of my occasional visits, while Sara was occupied in the kitchen or elsewhere, the two of us spent time playing with her toys or reading stories. Even as I sought to renew our acquaintance, however, I was plagued by guilt, for as much as I might contrive to excuse my conduct with her mother, there was no getting around the moral authority of a child, whose trust and affection represented arguments much louder than any rationalization I could possibly devise. And yet, the next morning I would be on my way without so much as a 'Thank you, ma'am,' leaving behind a situation that had grown every bit as complicated as I had every reason to expect it would. Soon enough, however, with the road slipping beneath the hood of the car—the same road I had driven during my college days—I was on the way back to the mountains and focused on flying again.

The least I could do was reciprocate her hospitality, and sometime during the latter part of January I arranged for my days off to coincide with hers and invited her to drive up to the cabin for a visit. She seemed glad of the offer, and so it was that one mid-winter morning, with both Paul and Jake downstate on errands, I spent some time straightening up the place in anticipation of her stay, eager to play Lord of the Manor and treat her and Tasha to a fun-filled weekend.

Upon their arrival, I ushered them inside and got them settled, making a game of constructing an improvised bed for Tasha. Next, we fixed some sandwiches and had lunch, after which, running out of likely attractions in the cabin, I came up with the brilliant idea of driving up to the mountain, where the two of them could witness my flying exploits with their very own eyes.

"Why not?" said Sara with a shrug (a tepid enough response, but where flying was concerned, I didn't require much encouragement), and soon we were on our way.

Outside, the day remained heavily overcast, and during the brief drive down the valley I fretted about the wind. At times, the tops of the pines along the highway were swaying noticeably, but upon arriving at the mountain I was encouraged to find the flags in front of the lodge fluttering only slightly and pointing straight uphill—a good sign. In any case, I would only be flying from mid-station.

Inside the lodge, I found a place for my guests to sit in front of some large picture windows facing the slopes.

"I'll be taking off from mid-mountain," I explained. "Probably take me another fifteen minutes or so."

Collecting glider and gear, I headed for the gondola feeling somewhat distracted by the presence of my guests. Sensing something was amiss, I made an equipment check after loading everything onto the freight car. It was all there, nothing missing, and on the way uphill I studied the trees for any adverse signs. While the uppermost branches were clearly in motion, the direction was all uphill, and despite a few unsettling gusts the indications were mostly favorable as I rolled into the mid-station.

"Where're your buddies?" called out the attendant.

"Away on business," I told him, bringing an imaginary joint to my lips, at which he laughed knowingly.

Once out on the slope, I hoisted the glider to my shoulder and started hiking across the mountain some fifty yards to a likely take-off site, where I no sooner arrived than the nagging sense of having forgotten something suddenly came clear: I had forgotten to call the summit for a reading on the wind, and now the chance to confirm this important piece of information had effectively passed. As unsettling as the omission was, the immediate indicators were still positive. Though the treetops were clearly in motion, the direction was straight uphill, and in the absence of any definitive decision I started setting up the airframe, knowing well enough that, once assembled, the glider would present its own argument for take-off.

Indeed, no sooner had I unfolded the wings than the sail came to life, obliging me to scramble from one fastening to the next, all the while struggling to keep the airframe within my grasp. Now, with the wing subject to regular buffeting, there was no time to stop and think, and, following an abbreviated preflight check, I buckled in and squared off to the wind. Even at a neutral angle of attack, however, the glider was difficult to manage, and for once, instead of waiting for an oncoming breeze, I waited for the wind to die sufficiently to make a controlled launch. When it did, I made the merest suggestion of a take-off run, whereupon I was summarily yanked off the ground, above the trees, and then, with frightening violence, straight up.

Crushed into the harness, my legs trailing awkwardly from the force of the climb, I shot skyward, my mind racing as I watched the mountain drop away at a dizzying rate. Something was very wrong. With the bar drawn tight to my waist and my upper body thrust forward, I tried to counteract the violence of the lift, but my efforts had no effect whatsoever, and I continued to be swept upward like a leaf in a whirlwind. Up and up I went, until, at a point level with the summit itself, the harness lines went slack, the glider pitched radically forward and the sail went slack. No longer flying, I seemed rather to be falling upward, carried along by the momentum of my dizzying ascent, and in a sudden flash of insight I hit upon the reason. Though indications on the ground had given me no clue, the wind was not northerly at all, but hard out of the south, and blowing with such force that what I'd assumed was its true direction was in fact the backdraft of a powerful rotor created as air swept over the summit and curled back against the lee slope. Drawn upward to the apex of the updraft, I had risen into the true wind, which struck the glider from behind, tumbling me out of the sky.

Now as I clung nonsensically to the control bar, I watched the ground loom upward with fatal suddenness, and, without any means of control, I simply awaited the one hard jolt that would put out the lights, feeling a strange sense of embarrassment at the awkward situation I was about to create. Even as I reconciled myself to this eventuality, however, the glider inexplicably righted itself and the sail re-inflated with the sound of a shotgun blast, jerking me like a rag-doll in the harness and sending me upward once more with the same terrifying violence. Now fully aware of what awaited me at the top of the rotor, I scrambled to take advantage of the unexpected reprieve, reaching through the control bar and pulling myself forward along the flying wires. Under any other circumstances, the glider would have pitched headlong toward the ground; now it scarcely held its own against the up-rushing air. While I managed to penetrate the lift sufficiently to prevent another trip to the top of the rotor, I received a thorough thrashing in the process, obliging me to scramble around like a spider, one moment through the bar, another angling laterally to counteract a radical roll.

Eventually descending within the calmer air below the rotor, I glanced longingly at the slope below, where a number of skiers waved cheerfully up at me, apparently interpreting my desperate efforts to cheat death as a bit of stunt flying performed for their amusement. As much as I resented their ignorance, I longed to be standing by their side, suddenly envious of the simple joys of bipedalism. Such was my residual terror that even after entering the relatively quiet air above the landing area I was loath to relax my death-grip on the control bar in preparation for landing. Dropping down below the tree-tops, I touched down at last and was no sooner on my feet again than I unbuckled the harness, tossed the glider to the side of the slope and sat down on the snow, if only to be that much closer to the ground. I'd been miraculously lucky, yet the thought was hardly a cause for rejoicing. Recalling the events leading up to the flight, I tried to exonerate myself in some way, but it was no use; in the end I had simply failed to establish the true direction and speed of the wind, an oversight so fundamental as to be completely inexcusable.

I was still sitting there, mulling things over, when Sara appeared, making her way across the open slope from the vicinity of the lodge, leading Tasha by the hand.

"You're not going to believe it," she said. "While you were up there, this one decided to go exploring and nearly fell through a railing. Scared me half to death and I ended up missing everything but the landing."

"That's okay," I said, laughing ruefully, "—wasn't much of a flight."

"Are you okay? You sound kinda funny."

"I'm okay."

"So, how'd it go?"

"I screwed up," I confessed. "—Nearly bought the farm."

At this point, Tasha came over to see what was the matter and stood facing me at eye level.

"Guess you got in trouble," I said, to which she nodded, frowning. "–Join the club. You want to go sledding?"

"Yah!" she shouted, jumping at the thought.

Getting uncertainly to my feet, I set about disassembling the glider.

"The wind wasn't right, huh?" continued Sara.

"Nope."

"But you said the flags looked good."

"The wind here in the valley is blowing in the opposite of what it's actually doing up above. It's gotta be blowin' 25 up there. We're just seeing the back-draft."

"I don't get it."

"The real wind is out of the south, coming over the top of the mountain and curling back against this side. I'm gonna do what I should've done when we first got here. Check the reading from the summit."

When I did, the reality was even worse than expected: gusts to 31 mph, direction SSW. I'd flown the lee side of the mountain in what amounted to gale force winds.

Struggling to put the episode behind me, I packed up the glider and returned it unceremoniously to the storage room, after which we drove down to the public skating rink in the lower village. With the place all to ourselves, Sara skated while I pulled Tasha around on a plastic sled, swinging her in a tight arc, then letting go to send her skidding half the length of the ice, shrieking with glee. My guests, at least were having a good time, yet I couldn't help thinking what their day might have been like if not for my fluky recovery from an otherwise terminal dive. For once, I contemplated giving up my flying habit, collecting my stuff, and following Sara back to her place in the country—if she would have me—where I would take whatever work I could find and we would spend our days skating and sledding together. Of course, this was just an idle dream.

Later, after an early dinner at the Red Stallion, the valley's infamous restaurant/bar/music-hall, we returned to the cabin, where we built a fire and watched TV. As much as I tried to forget about it, however, the memory of the morning's near-disaster kept flooding into my thoughts, forcing me to make excuses to myself and leaving me distracted. With the arrival of Tasha's bedtime, we tucked her in, then sat up talking—or trying to. Though we had always been able to ramble on about nothing in particular, the day's events seemed to leave the subject of our future hanging in the air, and we found ourselves hard-pressed to find a way forward. The awkward truth was we didn't have a future to talk about, and for once we both seemed to recognize it. In the morning, they would return home and I would return to my flying habit.

As for that, my former confidence in the air would be a long time returning. While I had always been aware of the hazards of the sport, prior to my recent transgression I'd contrived to dismiss a wide range of such dangers by lumping them under the category of "pilot error," thereby assuring myself that the sport's otherwise lethal potentialities were entirely avoidable. Now I began to suspect that my dismissive attitude toward such blunders was mere bravado, and that pilot error represented the most enduring and intractable threat of all.

If my enthusiasm for flying had dimmed, however, it was not yet extinguished, and sometime about the first week of February a stunning piece of news arrived that would go far to restoring it altogether. Arriving by mail in the form of a glossy brochure was the announcement of a major gliding competition to be held in the

*Near the Borderline*

Bavarian Alps in the middle of March. Sponsored by Swissair, the event was billed as the First World Hang-gliding Championships. While Jake was content to forego the opportunity, Paul and I were determined to take part, and quickly made plans to scare up the $800 travel expenses required. In addition to money, there were issues of sponsorship to consider, and when a Massachusetts manufacturer offered to supply us with new gliders and cover shipping expenses to and from Austria, we decided to switch our allegiance from the California company for whom we were both dealers.

    It was going to be the first trip overseas for both of us, and with less than a month to prepare, we scrambled to get passports and hit up a few of the slope-side businesses for some extra cash. With the ski season in full swing, there was still flying to be had, and the prospect of participating in the upcoming competition promised to add new luster to our growing presence at the mountain.

# Chapter 10

# A Not-So-Grand Tour

On the day of our departure for Austria, Paul and I drove to a Boston suburb, where we joined several other New England pilots and continued to New York in a van provided by our sponsor. At the airport, some forty more flyers—mostly Californians—were waiting at the Swissair gate, all instantly recognizable by their decidedly casual attire and accessories. Joining in, we mingled with our fellow pilots, and, upon boarding, were glad to find the flight far from full, enabling us to sit together in a large group about mid-plane. Once aloft, we had dinner and drinks, and with the main cabin mostly to ourselves there was every opportunity to stretch out across the rows of seats and sleep in a level of comfort rarely afforded on such trips. Instead, the night passed in nearly continuous conversation.

    Dawn found us talked-out and groggy as we approached the mountain-ringed airport at Zurich, and after a white-knuckle descent through severe turbulence we dropped onto the runway with a collective sigh of relief. Next, a brief connecting flight took us to Munich, where we caught a bus to Kufstein, Austria, and continued through increasingly rugged terrain to the Bavarian village of Kossen. Disembarking in a central square, we grabbed our gear and had time for a short, bleary-eyed look at the towering massif of the Unterberghorn, our new flying site, before retiring to our respective pensions, drawing the shades, and going straight to sleep.

    That evening, partly refreshed from long afternoon naps, we made our appearance at an opening banquet in the main hall of the village, where some three hundred pilots of various nationalities were gathered. Taking our places at a series of tables in the banquet hall, we listened to some welcoming remarks, after which a bevy of waitresses in traditional costumes served us various courses of Austrian specialties. Later, the same waitresses treated us to a performance of traditional music and dance, which was all very nice, but with the contest looming, their audience was more interested in sizing up the competition. Later, many in the American contingent congregated in one of the local pubs, where we compared notes about the requirements of the competition and various strategies for success, after which we were ready to hibernate, the effects of jet-lag having caught up with us in earnest.

The next day we didn't roll out until mid-morning, by which time our European counterparts had gotten the start of us. Already a steady stream of gliders could be seen drifting down over the slopes of the Unterberghorn, and we were eager to learn the idiosyncrasies of the site. With a total of ten days in which to complete the event, there were to be two days of warm-ups followed by two rounds of competition, with lay days interspersed as needed. After a quick breakfast, we caught a shuttle to the mountain, where our gliders awaited us in a storage area at the base of the slopes. Hiking them up to a chairlift, we handed them off to a crew for transport uphill, then rode up through bright sunshine, arriving at last at a mid-station some 1,500 feet above the valley floor, where a sizeable chalet lay in a snowy swale surrounded by alpine meadows. Though the peak lay another thousand feet above, it was set back sufficiently to be invisible from the base, making it impracticable for the purposes of the competition.

Nearby, a large assembly area lay next to a well-built take-off platform with an ample inrun, and after collecting our gliders we carried them onto the slope and started assembling them. In the vicinity of the chalet, a mass of skiers and spectators milled about, eating lunch and sitting in the sun as a steady succession of brightly-colored sails sprouted on the slope nearby and, one after another, took to the air.

After setting up the new glider, I awaited my turn at the launch platform and was soon airborne, the slope dropping away with dramatic suddenness and the view expanding until I found myself far above a swift river flowing between densely-wooded hills. Farther out, in the center of a broad valley, the village of Kossen lay snug in its mountainous surroundings—a fairy-tale setting, it seemed, where red-cheeked shop-keepers spent their days cobbling shoes while ample-bosomed hausfraus tended the fires of their gingerbread cottages. As I turned back toward the U-horn, the ski area swung into view, its broad snowfields dotted here and there with isolated stands of conifers.

It was easy to see how skiing had originated in such places, where a series of chalets served alternately as high-altitude farmhouses, shepherds crofts and skiers' havens. Stateside ski resorts, especially the eastern variety, seemed narrow-minded by comparison, with closely-confined trails hewn out of the forest in single-minded devotion to skiing, while every bit of open space at their base was devoted to commerce of one sort or another. Here, by contrast, the ski area wasn't a world unto itself, but existed rather as an extension of the nearby village, the slopes themselves ending in a series of broad fields belonging to a well-kept, working farm. For the purposes of the competition, a large portion of one such field was cordoned off and a series of concentric rings painted in chalk upon the ground, the object being to stay aloft as long as possible and land as close as possible to the center of the painted target. Lining up for landing, I drifted across the field and touched down within several yards of the bull's eye, feeling well satisfied with the new site.

If the setting was all that could be wished for, however, the same could not be said for my newly adopted glider, which had handled rather awkwardly throughout the flight. Due to its higher aspect ratio and flatter sail, the control inputs I was used to making in my regular glider didn't have quite the same effect. Instead of rolling easily into a turn, the inboard wing would dip without invoking an accompanying yaw, resulting in an initial side-slip, such that I found myself attempting to bring the nose around by means of body English, a sketchy proposition at best. The pitch response, on the other hand, was, if anything, too sensitive, requiring a delicate touch on the part of the pilot. Indeed, the wing seemed to have a will of its own, and flying it was like riding a headstrong colt compared to the well-behaved and stable mare of my old ship. While I had flown the new design several times before agreeing to the switch, changing equipment immediately prior to a competition suddenly seemed ill-considered. At the very least, it was going to take some getting used to, and I was anxious to get as much practice as possible.

In many ways, the warm-up days would prove more interesting than the event itself, giving the assembled flyers a chance to show their stuff unrestrained by the rules of the competition. Like the designs of the various gliders they flew, the pilots from each of the competing countries revealed their own collective style, showcasing techniques roughly analogous to the cultural disparities of their places of origin. Not surprisingly, perhaps, the tightest clique among the various national groups were the French flyers, who scarcely deigned to recognize the existence of their fellow competitors. This would have been easier to tolerate if they had not been such able pilots, carving steep, climbing turns that sent them pivoting around their wingtips in aerial pirouettes. More gregarious, but no less accomplished were the Austrians, whose trademark maneuver left even the California boys gasping with admiration. Rigging bicycle-issue foot straps to the middle of their control bars, once aloft they climbed into the uprights of their control bars, set their feet in the straps, and proceeded to warp backward and forward, alternately diving and climbing sharply skyward to carve a series of rhythmic parabolas across the sky.

For their part, the Californians tended to avoid such displays of aerial acrobatics, focusing instead on the critical issue of time aloft, for they well knew that all the trick flying in the world couldn't improve a wing's basic flight characteristics. The contest would inevitably be decided by subtleties of wing design, and while others were demonstrating their death-defying prowess for the crowds, members of the west-coast cohort spent much of their time fine-tuning their airframes, adjusting a wingtip here, adding a tube-faring there, tweaking the last little bit of performance from their equipment.

After a day of aerial maneuvering at the mountain, we spent the evenings trying out no-less-intricate moves in the local bars, where I struck up a friendship with a shy, doe-eyed fraulein who spoke English and was not entirely ashamed to be seen with the American crowd. We spent several evenings together, talking and drinking, and I ended up giving her my pilot's pin—a trinket we all received upon arrival—because she asked me for it, and I was a nice American gentleman.

In other respects, however, the attitude of the local population toward Americans was not nearly so welcoming, as Paul and I discovered one Sunday morning while walking into the village from our pension. Approaching us on the sidewalk was an older couple dressed in their Sunday finery, to whom we smiled and said good morning only to have our greeting turned down flat. Yielding not an inch of the sidewalk, they scarcely looked at us, and the brief glance they gave was more than chilly. They loathed us, and in hindsight, the response was hardly surprising. Dressed in well-worn, faded jeans and similarly tattered jackets, our eyes hidden behind aviator sunglasses, we no doubt came across as a pair of drug-crazed delinquents, and our attempt at familiarity had only made matters worse.

"Was it something we said?" I wondered aloud after they passed.

"Not unless 'Good morning' means 'Screw you' in German."

"You try to be friendly and where does it get you?"

"The hell with 'em! They probably had a bad piece of mutton for breakfast."

We started riffing on the local diet, and soon laughed the incident off, but it occurred to me, as if for the first time, that Americans might not be as universally admired as I had imagined.

After two days of practice flights and as many lay days in between, the first round of the competition got under way, in which contestants were to make two recorded flights, accumulating a combined score based on time aloft and spot-landing. With some 300 competitors to score, the event began early, and by mid-morning a steady succession of gliders began drifting out over the valley and making their way down to the landing area, where a large crowd of spectators had gathered on the outskirts of the field, listening to a public address system that announced the name of the pilot and the results of each flight as soon as it was completed.

It was nearly noon by the time I arrived at the launch platform and raced off into a freshening breeze. Though the glider was still not to my liking, I caught some lift on take-off and drifted west along the face of the lower mountain for a while, then headed out over the valley in hopes of finding a pocket of rising air above a number of plowed fields. Obliged to avoid all aggressive maneuvers in order to maintain altitude, there was remarkably little to do, and eventually lining up on final approach, I floated in for a landing some eight feet outside the bullseye. Not a bad result.

My second flight later that afternoon was not nearly as promising, however. Once airborne, I followed the pilot in front of me straight out over the valley, and somewhere far above the river was startled by an unexpected patch of turbulence that tipped the glider laterally at a sharp angle, forcing me to make a radical correction to counteract the resulting side-slip. Thinking to have entered the downdraft surrounding a thermal, I turned back toward the vicinity of the bump, hoping to find my way into a rising column of air, but to no avail, and the resulting maneuvers ended up costing me additional altitude. Soon, with the ground growing steadily closer, it was time to set up for landing, and by now the distance between me and the pilot in front had shrunk to perhaps thirty yards, close enough that his landing threatened to leave a wake of unsettled air for mine. Lining up at right angles to his approach, I tried to avoid his "junk," but as I flared for landing, I felt the air go mushy beneath the wing and touched down well short of the mark.

As feared, the second flight's results put me out of the final round of fifty, and when Paul had no better luck, the two of us, along with the great majority of our fellow competitors, spent the evening consoling ourselves in the bars. On the plus side, with the competition behind us, we had another four days to kill before returning home, and were now free to make the most of the time. Earlier in the week, with conditions unflyable, I had accepted an invitation to join some fellow pilots on a drive to Innsbruck, where we spent a couple of hours poking around the site of the recent Olympics. Now I was determined to go farther afield, and while Paul and a few of the other New Englanders made plans to go skiing at nearby Kitzbuhel, I decided to make a day trip to Munich. Thus, the next morning, with 35 Deutschmarks in my pocket (about eighty bucks at the operant exchange rate), I took a bus to Kufstein and boarded a train for the city in what was to be a glider-bum's version of a Grand Tour.

## A Not-So-Grand Tour

Looking back on it in the years since, I've often imagined myself stumbling into the Bavarian capital with eyes wandering vacuously in their sockets, a trail of spittle trailing from the corner of my gaping mouth. This was not strictly the case, but going it alone on a first visit to a European city tended to bring out the rube in me, a feeling that began the moment I stepped off the train into the immense interior of the Hauptbahnhof, a train station whose very proportions seemed intimidating somehow. Eventually arriving outside the station, I began wandering the streets, with little in the way of a plan and no particular interest in abiding by one. This was no American city, where glass and steel towers loomed at every turn. Instead, wide boulevards lay open to the sky, and the grid-work of city blocks was relieved by ample platzes with plenty of trees and public space.

Making a study of the subway system, I took a ride and reemerged on another side of town, where a magnificent baroque palace declared all that was modern to be a passing fad. Soon I was riding the trains like a ground squirrel in a vast new system of burrows, popping up in one new quarter of the city, taking in the sights, then scurrying off to find another. At one point, having resurfaced near a bridge over the swift-flowing Isar River, I happened upon a large complex with an imposing facade dominated by the legend 'Deutsches Museum,' and with a couple of hours to kill before the last train to Kufstein, I went inside.

Prior to this, I had never been a great fan of museums, which seemed to me too relentlessly educational to be of much interest. For some reason, however, the present experience made a believer of me. Maybe it was the fact that I was alone in a strange city with only my own thoughts for company, or maybe it was because I was content to let a series of impressions wash over me without trying to make strict sense of them. Then too, maybe it was simply the tremendous scope and variety of objects to be found in that place that made the difference, for this was a museum such as I had never seen before, in which the emphasis was on practical science and mechanical devices of all sorts. There were large architectural models showing bridges, dams and mines, as well as similar displays dealing with astronomy, biology, geology, medicine, physics, and every imaginable scientific discipline. Above all there were machines, hundreds of them:

*Near the Borderline*

tractors, paper presses, printing presses, hydro-turbines, lasers, clockworks, steam engines, combustion engines, jet engines, and, at one point a massive, intricately engineered cast-iron object that must have weighed several tons, yet whose purpose I could not determine despite careful study. Passing from room to room and floor to floor, I made my way through the building's labyrinthine interior, taking it all in. Here was the stuff of human invention, in such quantity and diversity that even the most confirmed misanthrope could not help but feel a grudging admiration for the industry and ingenuity of the species.

    I was mesmerized. And just when I thought to have exhausted my ability to wonder at all the many forms and varieties of such inventions, I came upon something that stopped me in my tracks, frozen with awe. I had been wandering through a large exhibit of early aircraft, working my way to the back of a high-ceilinged room crowded with all sorts of interesting planes and flying artifacts, when suddenly I looked up to find suspended above my head an object I had previously seen depicted only in crude sketches. Here, tucked away in a corner of the room and barely noticeable amid the many more recent designs, was the fragile collection of willow-wands and cotton sails of German aeronaut and aviation pioneer, Otto Lilienthal.

    They had saved it; God bless their retentive German souls! And here it was—the first flying machine worthy of the name—right before my eyes, nearly within reach! Hands clasping my head, I looked around for someone with whom to confirm what I knew to be true but could not quite believe, and, finding no one, I turned back to stare up at the wondrous device, studying its every feature. Designed around a circular yoke, the airframe was configured such that the pilot's upper body projected through the middle of the flying surface, leaving legs free for use as landing gear, with levers at each hand enabling a measure of control by means of wing warping. A full decade before the Wright Brothers first skimmed above the North Carolina dunes in their bulky, box-kite of a glider, Lilienthal had racked up hours of airtime in this elegant, bird-like craft, reaching altitudes over a thousand feet and performing a range of aerial maneuvers. We hang-glider pilots owed much to Lilienthal, whose design, like ours, was controlled in large part by weight-shift. A nearby display told of his enduring legend, including the circumstances of his death—the result of a tip-stall at an altitude of some fifty feet. Mortally injured in the ensuing crash, he survived long enough to utter the immortal words, "Sacrifices must be made."

Finding that amazing craft in such an unlooked-for way seemed fated somehow, and I stood gazing at it for some time, walking away only to return and stand beneath it again. So it was that, when I finally checked the time and raced back to the Hauptbahnhoff, it was only to discover that the last train to Kufstein had gone.

Now I had done it! Stuck in the city, I would have to find a place to stay for the night on a very slim budget, and with mounting anxiety I made the rounds of several hotels in the vicinity of the station. The limit of my purse was not my only problem, either, for despite my best efforts to make a good showing (trading blue jeans for a pair of corduroys, I had gone so far as to shave for the occasion), a succession of front-desk clerks looked me up and down and coolly shook their heads at the general state of my wardrobe and appearance. Following a third rejection, I pleaded with the clerk to recommend a place whose standards might be low enough to admit me, eventually prevailing upon him to confirm a vacancy at the place he suggested. Picking up the phone he made the reservation in German, casting a dubious glance in my direction only long enough to confirm my name, "—Eenglehart, eh?"

"Yah, Eenglehart!" I parroted in my best effort at a German accent, suddenly heartened to think that an ethnic heritage about which I knew precious little might serve me in good stead. It proved enough, at least, to get me a bed for the night, though the manager of the small, walk-up bed and breakfast to which I had been steered was not exactly thrilled to see me. Explaining in English my accidental circumstances, I attempted to convince him that I was not some witless vagabond, only an American, but he didn't seem to recognize a meaningful distinction between the two. With the severity of a reform-school proctor, he warned me that the front door would be locked promptly at eleven, after which I would not be admitted despite payment in advance. The accommodations proved entirely satisfactory, however, and I quickly availed myself of a brief nap before making another foray in search of a meal.

*Near the Borderline*

By this time night had fallen, and, returning to the Hauptbahnhof to get my bearings, I made my way to a small food kiosk, where I was soon in possession of a steaming hot bratwurst wrapped in wax paper, with a tub of mustard and a small beer to go with it, a combination which, after the day's adventures, afforded me one of the most satisfying meals I'd ever tasted. Next, with a couple of hours remaining before my curfew, I decided to do some more exploring, thinking to find the site of the notorious Beerhall Putsch where Adolf Hitler had embarked on his ill-fated political career. I had no idea precisely where it might be, however, and for some reason the travel brochures made no mention of a Hitler walking tour. Eventually starting down a likely looking thoroughfare, I thought to find my way to the scene of the infamous event by mere instinct.

In keeping with the beerhall district of my imagination, the street eventually grew noticeably darker, and so I kept going, peering into one honky-tonk nightspot after another as I passed. As I approached one particularly seedy-looking establishment, I was suddenly accosted by a scantily clad woman, who came out of the doorway of the place and leaned upon my arm in a well-practiced pantomime of good humor and conviviality. It seemed that, instead of the beer halls, I had stumbled into the red-light district. The realization came too late, however, for despite my protestations, the woman latched onto my arm with the tenacity of an anaconda and began dragging me toward the doorway, "inviting" me to join her for a drink. For a moment, I considered slugging her in the shoulder and lighting out, but I wasn't sure I could get the better of her, and the near proximity of a burly doorman further discouraged me. Thus, in we went, the doorman leering a grim welcome at me as we passed.

Having grown up in the hard-drinking environs of northern New York, I had seen my share of sleazy watering holes, but this one took the prize, making me long for the shabby, sawdust-on-the-floor roadhouses of home. Dark and low-ceilinged, the interior seemed to derive from the Boris Karloff School of Design, with utterly graceless furnishings and a variety of Musée-des-faux-arts paintings on the walls. Then too, the presence of what looked to be former Hitler Youth standing near the bar did nothing to relieve my disappointment with the decor. Getting out of there was likely to be

## A Not-So-Grand Tour

even more unpleasant than getting in. Nevertheless, I played along, following my captor to a cramped booth where a chintzy curtain afforded us a weirdly conspicuous sense of privacy. Sitting on a bench seat to one side of a small table, we were soon joined by a waitress, who poked her head through the curtain to take our drink orders: some kind of fancy cordial for my companion and a beer for me. When our libations arrived, the tab set me back more than three marks, which I considered steep even allowing for the added value of the ambiance.

Meanwhile, my new acquaintance chatted away in a strange parody of flirtation. Speaking fluent English, Marta—the name she gave me—was delighted to make my acquaintance and treated me to a good deal of physical contact to prove it. We talked and petted, drinking our drinks and making jolly for nearly twenty minutes, before the near approach of my curfew compelled me to end the charade. At this point, placing a hand on her ample thigh, I explained that, while I liked her and everything, I was only in town by accident and scarcely had enough money to get back to Kossen, let alone pay for the pleasure of her company. She acted crest-fallen for a moment, and then, abandoning her performance, confessed that she only did such work on odd weekends and because she needed the money. For all of her assertiveness on the street (and under the watchful eye of the doorman), it seemed she was not a very hard case after all, for which I was duly grateful.

The problem of effecting my departure remained, however, and the uncertain looks she began casting through the curtain in the direction of the bar were not encouraging on that score. No doubt the knowledge that she had literally dragged me into the place weighed on her conscience, and after thinking things over for a moment she told me to follow her and she would see me out of the place. Departing the booth, I trailed her to the bar, where she stopped to speak with one of the goons standing guard there, at which point, foregoing a formal leave-taking, I bolted toward the door, where, as luck would have it, the doorman was engaged in conversation with a new arrival, enabling me to slip across the threshold and make good my escape. Quickly deciding to get some exercise, I took to my heels in the direction of the train station, the sound of the doorman's shouted imprecations trailing me through the ill-lit street.

I could have stopped running whenever I wanted, but the urge never seemed to take hold somehow, and only after reaching the station did I slow to a brisk walk, eventually arriving at the door of the bed-and-breakfast some fifteen minutes before my deadline. Once safely inside, the thought occurred to me that, but for Marta's intervention and the fortunate shuffle at the door, I might well have spent the night in an alley somewhere, awaking with a lump on my head minus what little money remained to me. Under the circumstances, my modest room seemed a welcome haven indeed, and, falling onto the narrow bed, I slept the sleep of the innocent abroad.

The next morning, I made my way to a dining room downstairs for a breakfast of sausage and eggs, then started for the Hauptbahnhof to confirm the departure of the next train to Kufstein. It was a beautiful morning, with warm sunshine and the promise of spring in the air, and I was anxious to get back into the mountains and reconnect with the gliding scene; however, a quick check of the departure board revealed that my train was not scheduled to leave until 11:30, and it was not yet eight o'clock. With time to kill, I considered going back onto the streets for some more exploring, but after the previous night's experience the novelty of the idea had largely worn off. Now, uncertain what to do, I wandered aimlessly through the station, watching the morning commuters stream out of the trains, and it was while thus idly engaged that my eye chanced upon a familiar name on a sign-board above one of the platforms: Dachau. The name held dark associations, but whether any traces of its notoriety remained to be found there, I had no idea. Still, the place called out to me, and as the stop was only five minutes away, I decided to go and find out.

After a pleasant ride through the suburbs, with new buds beginning to show on the hedges and grass greening up along the streets, I found myself standing on an open-air platform, blinking in the bright sunlight. Heading inside the station house, I studied a wall-mounted map of the town but couldn't find what I was looking for and began to have second thoughts. Thus far, I was just another traveler, minding my own business and beholden to no one, but the prospect of asking for directions and revealing what it was I had come to see threatened to expose me somehow, filling me with a strange mixture of dread and embarrassment. A large part of my motive, after all, was morbid curiosity, and I was unsure how the locals might react. Furthermore, as I didn't know whether the object of my search still existed, I was unsure how to ask about it. Nevertheless, approaching the ticket window, I leaned in toward the clerk and spoke in an undertone: "Concentration camp?"

As I feared, the query had an ill effect, causing his face to fall ever so slightly, and without saying anything he pointed dismissively toward a taxi stand at the corner of the building. Upon learning my destination, the taxi driver motioned me to get in with similar impatience, and I rode through the town feeling a mounting sense of defensiveness. Surely others had come in search of the infamous place, and I was determined to carry out my own reluctant pilgrimage. The driver was not going to make it easy, however, for instead of taking me directly to the entrance as he might have done, he dropped me off at a bus stop a quarter mile away, where, after receiving his fare, he waved me in the general direction I was to go. Passing down a residential street lined with houses of fairly recent construction, I could see in the distance a large compound surrounded by an antiquated concrete and iron fence.

There it was, all right, the whole thing perfectly preserved as far as the grounds were concerned. Given the early hour, there were no other visitors to be seen, and, entering the headquarters/museum, I began making my way through a series of empty rooms in which large, black-and-white photographs covered the walls. Empty rooms with grainy enlargements on the walls and nothing more, creating an experience that attested to the museum's effort to convey simple, irrefutable facts. Though the captions included English translations, they proved of limited interest. One stood in the rooms and looked at the pictures. That was enough.

One of these images showed a group of high-ranking Nazi officials standing in front of the camp headquarters, arrayed on either side of a central figure whose dress and posture were clearly those of Hitler himself. A precise identification was impossible, however, for the image had been vandalized and the face completely scratched out. Indeed, whoever did the work of desecration had been in earnest, for not only had the photo paper been obliterated, but the plaster beneath it as well. Using some sort of crude implement, the perpetrator had dug down as far as the lathe of the wall, leaving a hole as much as half an inch deep where the Fuehrer's face had been. Of all of the photos I saw, it was the only one that had been vandalized and the only one I was the least bit glad of, for it seemed to explain something that had been bothering me ever since my abbreviated encounters with the clerk and the taxi driver. Whatever the facts might be, I wanted to believe that the vandal had been a local kid and that in scratching out that section of plaster with such obsessive thoroughness he had sought to remove some small portion of the infamy that had attached itself to his home town.

Another picture showed a room recognizable as the one in which I was standing, only filled with shoes. Hundreds of worn and tattered shoes of a simple, uniform design, lay in a pile reaching nearly to the ceiling. What there was about the picture that recommended it to memory, I'm not sure, unless it was the conspicuous absence of the many wearers of those shoes. Then too, there was something about the circumstance of standing in that room, now absent the shoes of those absent wearers, that seemed to resound with oppressive silence.

Finally, I recall the photo of a woman and two small children, presumably her own, whom she is leading by the hand. The three of them stand with their backs to the camera, their faces unseen as they make their way across the camp's squalid yard. There was no caption associated with it, nothing to explain the purpose of their journey or the hopeless set of the woman's shoulders and the abject submission of her two charges, but one couldn't help inferring the darkest of suppositions. In any case, upon leaving the main building, I soon found myself crossing what I imagined was the very same ground, making my way toward a squat, brick building on the far side of the compound. Along the way, row after row of large, rectangular plots marked a series of mass graves where thousands of bodies had been buried following the camp's liberation, and by the time I arrived in front of the door of the brick building I wasn't sure I could summon the will to enter.

Impelled by a dogged curiosity, I eventually went inside, where the shocking thing about the place was its ordinariness: a cramped, utilitarian interior in which even the appliances I had come to see—the cast-iron grates open on their hinges and the interior of the fireboxes perfectly visible—failed to excite horror so much as indignation. It wasn't the devices themselves that one recoiled at, but the industrial scale of their grisly purpose, and nowhere was the depravity of that purpose more evident than here. I looked around, seeing what there was to see, because this too was the stuff of human invention and had to be owned along with the rest.

Walking back across the compound, I reached the vicinity of the entrance at the same time a middle-aged English couple was arriving, and in the brief, furtive glances we gave each other in passing, I seemed to understand the reaction I had received from the clerk and the cabbie. It hadn't been deliberate rudeness, it seemed to me, so much as a general embarrassment on behalf of humanity. Maybe the science-fiction theorists were right, I thought, and the human race arose from some extra-terrestrial life form grafting itself onto an existing species. There had to be some explanation for what had happened in that place, and as I passed outside the gate, the sci-fi connection no longer seemed so bizarre.

I was to do a lot of walking that day, in the first instance hoofing it back to the train station in order to save the cab fare. Between my visit to the red-light district and the impromptu trip to Dachau, my available funds were nearly exhausted, and, after returning to Munich and catching the train to Kufstein, I arrived at the bus station to discover that my remaining funds were only sufficient to take me to a village some seven miles short of Kossen and no farther. Even so, I was glad to be back in the mountains on such a glorious spring day, and with sunshine and birdsong filling the air and towering escarpments on all sides, I started hiking along the side of the highway. At one point I stuck out my thumb and a car with three young men in it pulled over, coming to a stop some ten yards ahead of me. Breaking into a run, I trotted up to within a few feet of the rear fender only to watch the car speed away and the two passengers wave a snide goodbye through the rear window, clearly delighted to have put one over on a gullible American. Instinctively flying them the bird, I shouted more explicit instructions after them, and stood listening as my voice echoed off the surrounding cliffs. I may have been an outlander, but there was something restorative in the thought that for once I was not inclined to be deferential about it.

It was dusk before I made it back to the pension, and after a shower and a change of clothes I headed into town to catch up with the gliding crowd. As expected, Paul and several of the other New Englanders were in our favorite bar, and upon entering I received a lively welcome.

"Inglebird!" shouted my Sugarloaf crony from across the room, "Jesus, man, where you been? I was about to report you missing in action."

"To whom—the barmaid?"

"Well... sure, for starters. I figured we could get the locals to send out one of those St. Bernard dogs with a little keg strapped to its neck, only instead of brandy we'd fill it with reefer."

"Good thinking."

"So, what happened. —You get lost or something?"

It was nice to be back, and over several rounds of beer I told them about finding Lilienthal's glider and missing the train, and about my evening of golden memories with Marta. They responded with accounts of their own cross-cultural pratfalls as well as a thorough update on the championship. By this time, the competition had ended, with first place going to a Californian named Dave Cronk. Meanwhile, there was to be a final day of recreational flying before the event officially ended, and with this to look forward to, we all drank freely.

The next morning, we had a leisurely breakfast before trooping out to the mountain for a farewell performance. By noon a crowd had gathered around the chalet at the top of the lift, and the glider assembly area took on the cumulative energy and excitement of a tailgate party, with skiers and flyers mingling in a kind of alpine fraternity. As each pilot made his way onto the launch platform, a chorus of catcalls arose from the assembled onlookers, and the pilots did their best to play to the crowd, taking off while sliding downhill on cafeteria trays, or, once airborne, spinning around in their harnesses to mug for the audience.

Later, having made a couple of flights, I was standing on the landing field amid a large crowd of spectators and fellow pilots, when a distant popping sound was followed by the rapid fluttering of sailcloth and a collective gasp from the crowd. Far above the landing area, a glider could be seen undergoing a series of radical gyrations before entering a precipitous spin. It seemed a wing spar had failed outboard of the cross-tube, and despite the pilot's efforts to correct for the sudden loss of lift, it was all he could do to keep the wing reasonably level as he spun out of the sky in an ever-tightening spiral. In the course of some 20 seconds, he completed a trajectory that sent him into a stretch of forest along a narrow ravine, where he disappeared beneath the treetops, followed by a resounding KA-WHUMP that carried across the intervening distance with ominous finality. In the parlance of the hang-gliding cognoscenti, it seemed he had "augered in," not merely hitting the ground but digging a hole.

Suddenly there was a good deal of shouting and commotion as rescue personnel were mobilized and a snowmobile raced off in the direction of the crash. Many in the crowd stood gazing about with stricken looks on their faces, talking in low and sympathetic voices. Meanwhile, the response of the assembled pilots was more stoical. Instinctively huddling together, we started the process of rationalization that would enable us to continue flying in the face of such unsettling evidence of the sport's inherent dangers. From the design of the glider, the pilot was identifiable as British, and with this information to go on, we began to distance ourselves from what had likely been a fatality.

"Structural failure," said someone, matter-of-factly. "—I never liked the looks of those English rigs."

As we stood around, awaiting word from the rescue party, a couple of pilots who had taken off prior to the crash came in for landings, and soon the sky that moments before had borne a steady stream of brightly colored sails grew empty. Someone said it was a shame the event had to end on such a sour note, and all seemed to be preparing for the worst, when suddenly the mood of the crowd perked up. Someone had been in communication with the rescuers by walky-talky and a rumor quickly spread that the pilot was okay. The crowd buzzed with a sudden curiosity to know more, and soon one of the event officials made an announcement via loud-speaker, explaining that the pilot had been found sitting in a small clearing, smoking a cigarette, with only a few scratches—the trees having broken his fall.

Amid sighs of relief, everyone let out a collective cheer, none more loudly or enthusiastically than those of us who had recently contrived to remain detached. Slapping each other on the back, we reveled in the fact that one of our number had cheated death to enjoy a casual smoke, delighted to be associated with someone of such apparent sangfroid and British pluck.

That night at the closing banquet there was a good deal of optimistic talk about the next year's event, and the following morning we started on the return trip.

Chapter 11

# Sugar Mountain Farewell

U pon our return from Austria, Paul and I caught up with Jake, and the three of us took up where we'd left off, seeking ever more creative ways to enhance our flying repertoire at the mountain. One such opportunity soon presented itself in the form of an annual torchlight parade, a night-time spectacle in which ski patrol personnel, instructors, and other mountain regulars, all carrying special torches, skied down from the mid-station, creating a long line of moving lights for the esthetic enjoyment of the mountain community. Eager to add an aerial component to the parade, we hatched a scheme whereby the torchbearers, having once descended the mountain, would form a large circle on the open slope, giving us a target in which to land. Meanwhile, the three of us would fly with strobe lights attached to our airframes. The plan won ready approval from the other participants, and everybody looked forward to creating an especially memorable event.

On the appointed night, I got out of work early and joined Paul and Jake in the lodge, where a crowd of spectators was milling around in anticipation of the ceremony. Carrying our gliders to the gondola, we passed through the assembled torchbearers as they waited outside the terminal, talking excitedly.

"Sure hope these torches don't somehow go out when you guys are flyin'," someone called out.

"How much will ya give us to keep 'em lit?" sniped another.

"HEY, EVERYBODY. DRINKS ARE ON THE KITE-FLYERS WHEN WE GET BACK!"

## Near the Borderline

"NO, THEY'RE NOT!" yelled Jake.

Soon the three of us were on our way uphill for what promised to be a virtual "sled ride" in the still night air. Upon arrival at the mid-station, we unloaded the gliders and carried them out across the pale white surface of the trails, while on the slope directly below us the torchbearers were getting ready to begin the parade. Soon they were wending their way downhill, making a series of giant-slalom turns to create a long, sinuous display of moving lights.

Meanwhile, we finished assembling our gliders and taping the strobe lights to the top of our control bars, and by the time the skiers had formed their circle, we were buckled in and ready to go. Leading the way, Paul rushed forward and went airborne, floating silently out into the darkness, his strobe flashing dimly within the pervasive gloom of the cloud-covered night sky. Next, Jake followed suit, the ghostly image of his intermittent light drifting out and away, to be all but invisible amid the surrounding darkness. Soon I was following in their wake, watching the luminous white trail drop from sight and the inky blackness swallow me up. No sooner had I cleared the trees and entered the dark expanse above, however, than I was rocked by repeated bumps of turbulence that came as a considerable surprise. Unable to detect any signs of wind from the usual indicators, we had simply assumed that the night air would be calm, yet now, above the protection of the trees and the mountain's irregular terrain, conditions proved otherwise.

Continuing to undergo a steady buffeting, I tucked the control bar, thinking to descend into calmer air, but the maneuver only threatened to send me into an invisible forest of trees below. Searching the sky ahead, I spotted the two other gliders by the dim flash of the strobe lights against their sails. Both were well to the right of the circle of torches, indicating that the wind was westerly and blowing them off course, a perception not otherwise discernible in the general darkness. I responded by steering well to the left of the circle in an effort to drift crab-wise toward it.

While a flight from mid-station normally allowed plenty of altitude to maneuver for a landing, the crosswind had the effect of reducing the glider's over-ground performance such that by the time I descended below the turbulence I was too low to make it as far as the waiting torch-bearers. Meanwhile, upslope to my right I could make out one glider on a trail to next to the gondola line and another a bit farther downhill. Blown off course, both Paul and Jake had landed well short and were walking their gliders the rest of the way down. The chance to correct for the wind had helped somewhat, enabling me to land on the open slope, but short of the circle. Though I'd missed the chance to make a dramatic arrival in the center of the formation, I was glad enough simply to be back on the ground again. Meanwhile, the torchbearers parted upon my approach, and I walked somewhat sheepishly into their midst.

Before long, Jake made his way down to the vicinity of the lodge, followed shortly by Paul, who had banged up his glider upon landing, both of them still shaken at having been forced down in the dark and narrow confines of the trails. We compared notes, quickly coming to a consensus on the inadvisability of night flying, then returned the gliders to the storage room and repaired to the pub. For a second time, I was obliged to relearn a fundamental lesson—always determine true wind speed and direction before every flight—but at least this time I wasn't the only jackass in the zoo.

Not long thereafter I gave Sara a call for the first time in more than a month. Though unsure what to expect, I thought to fill her in on the championships and see how she was getting on. She responded with a nervous sort of energy, and I suppose I partly suspected, or might have guessed, what was behind it. Even so, her news came as a bit of a shock.

"Well... as a matter of fact I'm getting married."

"Really? –That's... great." It was the same thing I said upon first learning that she was a mom, since which time it seemed she had lost none of her ability to surprise me. "I mean it, congratulations."

"Thanks. It was kind of sudden and everything. I wanted to tell you sooner..."

"You don't have to explain."

"Well, I wanted to, anyway."

We both expressed a note of sadness at the way things had ended, but wished each other well and eventually rang off. I felt a pang of loss mixed with no small degree of guilt, but was happy for her just the same and relieved to think that my long-standing dilemma had finally been resolved. I hadn't been nearly as forthright about the situation as I might have been, but in the end my failure to declare myself had been a declaration of its own, and Sara had acted accordingly. It seemed things had worked out for the best.

Now, with the arrival of April, all signs foretold the end of the ski season. Throughout the valley the snowbanks were receding beneath the bright gaze of spring, while in the streambed fresh torrents surged through the boulder-strewn channels of the Carrabassett. On the mountain itself the relentless effects of sun and skis sent rivulets trickling across the open slope, while on the upper elevations the secret warmth of the rays had melted the hardpack, turning it into the loosely cohesive slurry of ice pellets known as corn snow. Even on the summit, where numbers of sun worshippers could be seen in pursuit of a high-altitude tan, winter was waning fast.

Meanwhile, in the cabin beside the highway a new sense of urgency filled the air, for soon the crowds of skiers would be gone, abandoning the mountain for the seacoast or some other summer place, and with them would go the basis for our existence. We denied this, of course, indignant at the notion that our activities should end just because the snow was gone. Who needed skiers, anyway? With a growing number of flyers to take their place, we could scarcely see why the ski area should not carry on operations right through the summer. We were scarcely prepared for it, therefore, when the area manager asked the three of us to stop by his office one morning to deliver some bad news.

"I figured you fellas would want to hear this in person," he began. "It seems our insurance carrier has written a new clause in the renewal policy, and well... it looks as if we're going to have to pull the plug on flying during skiing operations."

"WHAT?" we said in perfect unison.

"I've got somebody looking into it for me, but I'm afraid that's the way things are. We're talking about next season, you understand."

"Wait a minute," said Paul, reeling from the blow. "You're saying there won't be any more flying here next season?"

"That's the gist of it."

"—And all this time we've never had an accident or anything?"

"I know, and there's been lots of good publicity. Listen, if it were up to me, you guys could keep right on doing what you're doing, but I've got no control over the insurance companies and we can't operate without them."

"So some insurance guy just decided it was too dangerous?" Jake wondered grudgingly.

"It's not quite as arbitrary as all that. There are legal definitions of liability involved, and the insurance companies are bound to protect themselves. You can get any kind of insurance you want, of course, so long as you're willing to pay for it, and the potential costs make it prohibitive."

We looked at each other. –Somebody had simply decided.

Moments later, we staggered out of the office in a daze. At a stroke, the ski areas that might have served as a ready-made network of flying venues had seemingly been placed off limits. It was not the end of hang-gliding, but the end of a connection that promised to showcase the new sport and help it flourish.

At first, refusing to accept such a dismal prospect, we thought of building our own flying site. Directly across the valley was a west-facing ridge with an old logging trail to the top and an abandoned gravel pit at its base. It would be a relatively simple matter to clear a take-off site and landing field. We had already considered using the place as a back-up whenever the winds on the mountain were contrary, but the elevation was considerably lower than even the mid-station on the mountain, and hardly worth the effort of an unassisted trudge uphill.

It was no use. The idea of settling for such a diminished flying experience in the very shadow of the mountain we had come to see as our birthright was too humiliating to contemplate. We'd been disinherited, and with snowmelt coursing down the open slope and the afternoon sun actually growing oppressive, it was time to make new plans. When Paul and Jake drifted downstate, the world of the mountain, a world that weeks before had been full of activity, suddenly became unendurably lonely. At this point, rendered listless by the trend of recent developments, I had no idea where I might go or why, and it was a kind of migratory instinct that led me, one sunny spring morning, back through the familiar environs of Route 2 to the River.

*Near the Borderline*

Chapter 12

# The Story Behind the Stories

If force of habit led me back to the River upon my departure from Sugarloaf, it was a habit I was determined to break, for the idea of returning to anything resembling my old lifeguard job at this stage in life had become unthinkable; as heroically as I had struggled to resist its onset, the time had come to suffer the slings and arrows of long-term employment. Ever since the previous summer, when the prospect of living with Sara provided the incentive for my first, ill-fated foray into the non-seasonal working world, journalism had seemed a likely sort of job, and I returned to the idea now with renewed determination. So it was that, within a week of my return, I drove into town and applied for a job in the offices of the Watertown Daily Times.

Having by now grown more realistic about my prospects, I was prepared to start small and work my way up, which was just as well, for the only opening—that of Chief Go-fer in the mailroom—was about as small a job as they offered. Even so, there was nothing particularly onerous about the work, and I was reasonably content to be started at last on what I took to be a career path. The people I worked with were mostly older, long-time employees of the paper, and my immediate boss, a woman in her late fifties, was as gracious a supervisor as I could have wished for.

Arriving every morning at eight, I picked up and sorted the daily pile of mail, trotted it around to the various offices, and spent what was left of the morning hanging around downstairs, making myself useful. No one ever asked me to go for coffee, but I don't know how I could have refused if they had. During the better part of the afternoon, I delivered advertising proofs to various businesses about town, after which, returning to the office, I headed upstairs to spend time in a small room where some half-dozen teletype machines churned out fresh copy from the wire services. Standing amid the ceaseless clatter of the whirling print-heads, I pored over the ever-expanding reams of text for the right kind of stories and read to my heart's content.

For all the newsroom ambiance of the place, I wasn't much interested in the major events of the day, gravitating instead to the quirky human-interest stuff, where the writing tended to be more idiosyncratic and engaging. I was there purely for the entertainment value, and yet the time was not ill-spent, for I was not without ambitions of my own along those lines, and within a month of my arrival I worked up an article and sent it upstairs for consideration by the editor and publisher, Mr. Johnson. The piece took as its subject the antique boating craze at the River, soon to be highlighted in an annual show in nearby Clayton, a weekend-long event featuring all sorts of immaculately restored craft. From what I remember of it, however, my article made no mention of this important connection, but instead ruminated idly about the enduring appeal of old boats whose outmoded designs recalled earlier times. Despite the story's gauzy focus, Mr. Johnson—himself an antique boat enthusiast (a fact that hadn't escaped me in coming up with the idea)—was kind enough to publish it on the op-ed page.

My next piece took as its subject the sport of hang-gliding (of all things). Even less topical than my first effort, the article traced the development of the new sport and speculated about its future, presupposing a burning interest in such matters on the part of a readership rabid to try it for themselves. Lacking any perceivable organizing principle that might have placed it elsewhere, it too found its way into the op-ed columns, where readers no doubt puzzled over its relevance to local affairs. Even so, the story didn't go entirely unnoticed, and several weeks later a producer at the local TV station invited me to come in for an interview. I readily agreed, of course, showing up at the studio at the appointed hour with my glider on hand for a prop.

*The Story Behind the Stories*

After setting up the airframe on a soundstage, I stood in front of it alongside the station's sports reporter, who introduced me and wanted to know if the glider was typical of others at the world championships, prompting me to describe something of the basic Rogallo design and those variations on it that had been allowed under the rules.

"This was my regular ship," I explained. "The one I flew in the competition had a slightly better glide ratio but wasn't nearly as stable."

"I gather there's a trick to steering the things, right?"

"It's all done by shifting one's weight relative to the glider's center of gravity, but some designs are easier to handle than others. This one is a better all-around flying machine than the one I flew in the competition."

"You call it a machine, but it doesn't have any moving parts, does it?"

"It's a machine in the same way an inclined plane is a simple machine. It performs a specific function in a predictable way. In this case the function is controlled flight."

He went on to ask about the results of the championships, and about my plans, if any, to continue my hang-gliding career. This brought up the sad story of the end of flying at Sugarloaf, which no doubt came across as an indictment of the public's undue interest in personal safety, for so I had come to think of it. At that point a mere two months had passed since I'd last flown, yet I already felt strangely nostalgic about the whole thing, as if it had happened long ago in a world far away. While I had yet to give up my favorite pastime, the sudden involvement of the insurance companies seemed to have decided the issue for me.

The interview aired about a week later, and seemed to come off well enough, though without any video of actual flying it didn't make for riveting television. Still, the exposure provided something of a boost, and by the middle of the summer, at the behest of my mentor, Mr. Johnson, I started spending more time in the editorial offices upstairs, transcribing stories by phone from various stringers or editing material submitted locally. For the time being, my mornings continued to be spent sorting mail, which had become more tolerable in the context of my additional duties. Moving freely between the business offices and the newsroom, I imagined myself a free agent of sorts, with my own (largely delusional) sense of importance to the operation.

This comfortable frame of mind was suddenly dispelled, however, one otherwise pleasant summer morning in the midst of my duties at the mail desk. Partly out of consideration for my expanding role about the place, my supervisor had taken to helping me go through the usual mound of envelopes, and the two of us were thus engaged when suddenly she paused.

"What have we here? —A letter for you. Fan mail, no doubt."

"Let's see," I scoffed, dubious to the point of scorn at the suggestion that anyone might have responded to my scribblings.

My skepticism proved well founded, for a quick check of the return address revealed that it was not from one of my readers, but a personal missive from Sara. This came as a considerable shock. Some four months had elapsed since we last spoke, and I was at a loss to know how she had learned of my present circumstances, let alone what she might have to say. Indeed, such was my curiosity that rather than put it aside for a private reading, I tore open the envelope and began scanning its contents in front of my co-worker.

"Well?" she asked, seeking confirmation.

"It's from a friend," I explained, not bothering to look up, and, as I continued reading, something of its import no doubt registered in my expression.

"—Not bad news, I hope."

"No, not really," I said, abruptly folding the letter and stuffing it into my pocket.

But it was. It seemed Sara's marriage was not working out. She gave no particulars, but something had clearly gone wrong. She was afraid she'd made a mistake and needed time to think things over. Her tone was not pleading but disillusioned, and she wondered if she and Tasha might drive out for a visit.

Upon finishing the letter in private, my first thought was to phone her at the hospital and find out if she was okay. I was worried about her circumstances, and secretly glad of the chance to come through for her somehow. Even so, I decided to put off the call until the end of the workday, when we would both have more time to talk. Among other things, I wasn't prepared to make such a momentous decision without a chance to mull things over. Thus, I waited to respond until that evening, when I would be able to call her from my apartment.

By this time, I had moved into a place in Black River, a sleepy, crossroads village some few miles outside town, where I rented an apartment in an old limestone farmhouse: a kitchen/dining area with adjoining bedroom and bath. I took the place in hopes of escaping the summer heat and because the landlady, an elderly woman who lived in the main portion of the house, was delighted at the prospect of a presentable young man such as myself occupying the downstairs apartment. (For the sake of the job, I'd gotten a haircut and otherwise cleaned up my act).

Having stopped along the way to buy a six-pack of beer, on the evening in question I arrived in my meager quarters, stripped off my tie, loosened my collar, opened one of the beers and sat drinking it at a small kitchen table in front of the phone. Much of the day had been spent thinking about what I would say, but when the time came to make the call, I found myself at a loss. Among other things, I was worried about opening the door to a whole new level of responsibility with respect to Sara. After all, I'd been in a similar position before, twice, and twice had let her down. And so I waited, finishing one beer, then another, and eventually watching the sun set and the light go out of the sky without summoning the will to pick up the receiver. With the arrival of full darkness, I decided the opportunity had passed and thought to call the next day during my lunch break. There was still the chance for me to do right by her; I just needed some extra time to prepare for it.

The next day arrived, however, and I was soon caught up in the same round of debilitating speculation. I was going to call. I was sure of it. I just had to find the right moment. After all, it was a big decision, and I could see that if I were to put myself in the picture again, now that she was married, there were going to be weighty consequences for both of us, things we couldn't easily go back on. For her, the decision would likely be irrevocable. Leaving to stay with her family for a trial separation was one thing, driving off to see an old boyfriend was another; no husband was going to reconcile after that—not one worth taking back, anyway. And for me the prospect seemed scarcely less fateful. Having once agreed to interfere, my sense of obligation to her would only become more binding. It would be the same, familiar dilemma, only magnified several times over. Still, knowing her, I knew how difficult it must have been to make such a request, and part of me wanted more than ever to rise to the occasion, glad of the role she had cast me in. I leaned one way, then the other, made up my mind to call, then put it off until later. Failing to act during my lunch break, I once again waited until the end of the workday and went back to the apartment to reenact the scene of the previous evening, this time downing the rest of the six-pack for inspiration.

It didn't work. Every time I reached for the phone the uncertainty of who might answer and what might follow froze my will. Days passed, then, incredibly, a full week, and still I made no response. At one point, recognizing the difficulty of dealing with such an important matter over the phone, I decided to write her a letter and send it care of the hospital. But here too, the task of conveying my concern for her situation while expressing reservations about the prospect of her traveling so far under such unsettled circumstances, proved too difficult. I simply couldn't find the words.

So I did nothing. What it might mean for her, I had no idea. I could only hope that she would find a way through her difficulties and somehow come to understand my silence even as I tried to understand it myself. Indeed, whatever she might think of me could hardly be worse than what I thought of myself, for now the dilemma that had dogged me for the past year and longer had impaled me on its horns for good and all, and the worst of it was I was never able to arrive at a decision of any kind, even the decision to do nothing. Instead, I was left to play out the options over and over in my head, until I slowly grew numb to the torture.

In the mornings I got up and drove to work, did the job thing, then drove back to my dismal little rooms, had dinner and went to bed. On weekends, I went to the River and tried to sort things out amid happier surroundings. Nothing changed, however, and with the return of the work week, I headed back to town to resume my paltry progress toward nowhere in particular, the job now rendered all the more burdensome by the environs and circumstances in which I had, in effect, left Sara hanging. Every morning, while going through the mail, I was forced to revisit the moment of receiving her letter and replay the whole thing again in my mind.

The situation did nothing for my general demeanor, not to mention my job performance. Whereas I had formerly fulfilled my duties with a cheerful aloofness (the Managing Editor, a cynical, cigar-chomping veteran of the business, had taken to calling me "Smiley"), I now staggered about the place, preoccupied to the point of distraction. Even promotion to the newsroom in the role of staff writer scarcely snapped me out of it, and when the time came for me to clear-out my desk for transfer upstairs, the kindly older woman who had been my boss in the business office took me aside for a word of farewell, holding me by the arm and looking me straight in the eye.

"I don't want to seem a snoop, and I don't know what was in that letter," she said, "but whatever it was, I hope you work it out."

I stared at her, then through her, and nodded slowly in response. It was as close to acknowledging my troubles as I was prepared to go.

In time, however, the change of duties did me some good, if only by disrupting my former routine and giving me something else to think about. I was not assigned a regular beat, with established news cycles and sources, but rather was fed a series of likely stories that happened across the desk of the City Editor. This suited me fine, and with Mr. Johnson in the role of "Chief," I modeled myself along the earnest and ingratiating lines of Jimmy Olson of the Daily Planet, lowly understudy to my high-flying Superman persona.

On the trail of one of my first news stories I remember chasing down a set of stone lions that had gone missing from in front of the public library, a search that took me into the surrounding countryside and ended in an interview with an older man who looked after a place where the lions had last been seen. Something about my conversation with him got me sidetracked, and I ended up writing more about him than about the lions, indeed a good deal more, I suspect, than he cared to see printed in a newspaper. Whether my investigation actually turned up the missing statues I don't recall, but I soon came to recognize that my deeper interest lay not in uncovering facts so much as discovering the people to be found along the way. I was familiar with the standard journalistic dictum that Dog Bites Man is not news, whereas Man Bites Dog is, yet I was inclined not so much toward the unusual as toward the homely and mundane. Had it come to my attention that a man had been bitten by a dog, I would have wanted to talk to him anyway, find out if his wounds were serious and how he was getting along, get him to tell me something about himself and his story.

In any case, my pieces began appearing with some regularity, and I soon began socializing with several of the younger members of the newsroom staff, making the rounds of the local bars. During one such outing I met a woman named Sandy, who taught school in one of the outlying towns and happened to be a roommate of one of the assistant editors. We started going out, to movies, dinner, the usual stuff, and I ended up spending time in her apartment, though the proximity to my coworker made things a bit awkward. Every now and again she consented to spend the night at my place in the stone house, but the sleeping quarters didn't provide the height of comfort and convenience, and then there were my landlady's sensibilities to worry about.

One week followed another, and with the arrival of winter I started to grow restless. Flying or no flying, I still felt connected to the skiing scene at Sugarloaf, and sometime before Christmas I called the number of our old rental by the highway and was glad to hear Jake answer the phone. It seemed Paul had recently moved in with a girlfriend at a place on the mountain, making Jake and his "old lady" the sole occupants of the place, and in the course of a brief conversation he offered me a standing invitation to make use of my old room if I ever happened out that way. Having at this point worked at the paper a total of eight months, I hadn't accrued any vacation time, but through the indulgence of Mr. Johnson, I managed to wheedle a week's leave anyway, and shortly after the holidays I started east once again on another winter journey along Route 2.

Two years earlier I made the trip through a raging blizzard, arriving at the mountain on a pristine morning to make my first flight from mid-station. This time around, the trip was not nearly as dramatic or eventful. Under uniformly overcast skies, the once-evocative scenes of that earlier trip were rendered irredeemably plain in the flat light and still air. Even the sign welcoming travelers to Vacationland had lost its happy associations for me.

## The Story Behind the Stories

Darkness had fallen by the time I arrived in the valley and made my way up past the ski area, where the mountain's ghostly silhouette loomed against a starless sky. Pulling into the familiar driveway at last, I went inside to be greeted by Jake and his now-wife, and soon the three of us were sitting in front of the wood stove, smoking pot and recounting old times. Before long, it seemed as if I'd never left, although, as Jake explained, everything was different now. Following my departure in the spring, in a gesture of conciliation toward the fledgling gliding community, the ski area had offered to put on another summer fly-in, and there had been hopes that a restricted summer gliding season might present a way around the insurance problem.

The ensuing event had begun on a promising note, as some 15 participants showed up on the preceding Friday afternoon, many of them camping out overnight in the vicinity. While the next day revealed a heavy overcast and unfavorable winds, by afternoon the sky had cleared and Jake and Paul led several of the visiting pilots up to the summit for a series of test flights.

"It was gusting pretty hard out of the north—flyable, but just barely," Jake explained. "Paul got set up first, and I helped him launch, but he was getting tossed around as soon as he was away. I waited until he flew clear of the summit, then went back to setting up my glider, when the next thing I knew there was a lot of shouting and commotion and I looked up to see this guy do a wing-over on take-off and disappear onto the scree-field below. It happened so fast. The rest of us scrambled down and got him unhooked, but you could tell he was hurt. He kept complaining about a rock or something underneath him... kept asking me to get the rock out, so I slid my hand along, searching for it, but there was nothing there. That's when I figured he'd broken his back.

"Anyway, we were there with him until the rescue people showed up with a backboard, which took like forever, and a couple of us helped out with the carry, lugging him across the scree and boulders. You know what it's like up there. We got him down in one piece but were completely done in by the time it was over. Not that it mattered much. Nobody was going to do any more flying anyway."

"And the pilot?"

"They took him down on the flat-car and sent him to Portland by helicopter. The last I heard he'd regained the use of his upper body, but it doesn't look like he's gonna get out of a wheelchair any time soon."

"That was the end of it, then?" I asked.

"At the mountain—yeah, that was it. We've been doing some flying over in New Hampshire, but not here."

I let it sink in. At one time or another we'd all come close enough to disaster to know better, but I'd always preferred to believe that the mountain was somehow blessed, and now the spell was broken. I thought back to my first flight and the progress since then, and it seemed nothing was left of those days.

The next afternoon I caught up with Paul at the mountain and we did some skiing, at one point taking the gondola up to the summit and clambering out across the snowfields to the old take-off site. Though clearly disappointed about the way things had turned out, he was still looking for new places to fly and remained as irrepressible as ever. Having spent a good part of the summer and fall working construction, he was thinking of taking a regular job as an architectural draftsman, for which he'd had some training, but for the time being he was working on "a few deals." Later, we sat drinking beer at the pub in the company of his new girlfriend, a raven-haired ski instructor in whom he was well pleased. I was happy for him, and we agreed to stay in touch, but the future didn't seem to offer much in the way of opportunities to do so.

I stayed another day, skiing and hanging around at the pub. Somewhere in the back of my mind the thought of driving to Waterville and looking for Sara flickered briefly, but I couldn't trust myself to deal correctly with what I might find. Later that evening, I took my hosts to dinner at the Red Stallion and we sat talking about the future. They were planning to move to North Carolina in the spring, thinking to join a growing hang-gliding community at Grandfather Mountain. It seemed we had all come back to Sugarloaf for old time's sake, nothing more.

The next morning, I started back, driving down the valley past the familiar profiles of the surrounding peaks. By this time, however, I'd seen enough of Route 2, and as I made my way west a new logic entered my thinking. Ever since going off to college, I'd come to associate a sense of adventure with those eastern mountains, but all that time I'd been bucking the larger trend of history, for freedom and adventure, as every schoolboy knows, lie in the opposite direction. I started thinking of the possibility of chucking the job, buying a new glider, and touring the West in search of new flying sites everywhere from the Rockies to California. It was just a thought at this point, but for some reason idle road reveries had a way of turning into life-altering decisions for me.

In the meantime, I went back to writing my homely stories and living in my homely apartment. The job was not without its moments; that winter I 'scooped' a story about a dare-devil car jumper named Ken Carter, who billed himself as the "Mad Canadian" and planned to leap across the St. Lawrence from mainland to mainland in a jet-powered Pontiac. As the river is nowhere less than a mile wide, I found the idea frankly insane, but was assured that the event was being funded by one of the major television networks in consideration of exclusive rights. Work was underway for the construction of two gigantic earthen ramps for take-off and landing at a point several miles upriver from Montreal.

Wisely allowing for the considerable airtime such a leap would involve, Ken had thought to outfit the underside of his car with special wings that would serve to stabilize his flight, and in the (likely) event that something went wrong he would be wearing a full-body crash suit. I wrote it all up with a sense of personal interest tempered by no small degree of skepticism, going so far as to compare the planned jump to the daring feats of my favorite Japanimation cartoon character, Speed Racer, whose exploits in the fabulous Mach Five—likewise equipped with stubby, retractable wings—had provided me with many an hour of after-school entertainment. Even as a schoolboy, however, I had doubts about the Mach Five's basic airworthiness and could scarcely imagine how anyone beyond the age of twelve might think such a contraption would actually fly.

In any case, my first piece was picked up by the wire services, after which I remained in touch with Ken on a regular basis. While I had to admire the scope of his ambition, I dreaded the prospect of his rocketing back to earth in a fiery ball of wreckage. As it happened, recurring delays led to the cancelation of the TV deal, and five years would pass before the attempt was made by a stand-in named Kenny Powers, who, regrettably, was critically injured when his car disintegrated shortly after take-off and crashed well short of the landing ramp.

As I recall, most of my stories had to do with the River in one way or another. That spring, a major oil-spill took place in the shipping channel immediately upstream from Alexandria Bay, and on the morning of the incident I drove to the scene with more than professional interest. The spill occurred directly across from the village's main dock, at a point near the local Coast Guard station, where an upbound tanker hit a shoal, sending a heavy slick of glutinous bunker oil along some of the river's most scenic shorelines.

Arriving in the Coast Guard station within a few hours of the event, I wandered through the mayhem of station personnel, local officials, shipping company representatives, fellow reporters and curiosity seekers, all of whom had assembled to assess the situation. There was a good deal of interest in determining who was responsible and what kind of money would be available for remediation—strictly bean-counter stuff of interest to the shipping company and its insurers. Meanwhile, the real story, as I saw it, lay in the hiring and organizing of a small army of local day-laborers tasked with siphoning off, mopping up, and scrubbing away the results of the spill. While such efforts had little perceivable effect, they nonetheless served the purpose of providing lots of local jobs to compensate for the expected loss of tourist dollars. In the end, despite a good deal of public hand-wringing over the long-term consequences for the environment, the river's current readily carried the surface oil downstream to dissipate along the shore and into the atmosphere, leaving the rest to congeal and eventually be broken down by microbes.

As the initial interest in the story faded, giving way to various new crises du jour, my enthusiasm for the business of journalism likewise tended to dissipate under the tedium of the daily grind. Even so, with another summer in the offing I was content to keep at it. I was still seeing Sandy, and on odd weekends there was the chance to do some tow-kiting with my friend Sam, who had also succumbed to the meager inducements of a "regular" job in town. Our kiting outings were now few and far between, nothing like the day-long odysseys of yore, and when the Town of Clayton invited us to put on a flying exhibition during an upcoming weekend celebration, we readily agreed, eager to reprise our fabled (in our minds, at least) exploits of summers past. The show went off as planned, with an evening flight before crowds of spectators on the main docks in advance of a fireworks display, and for once we received a token amount of cash for our efforts.

As the summer wore on, however, I grew increasingly weary of the newspaper job. Soon, Sandy would be leaving to pursue an advanced degree at the state university in Albany, and while we talked about continuing to see each other, it wasn't clear how this would happen. Meanwhile, increasingly restless to pursue my pending western adventure, I ordered a new glider and traded my car in for a '68 Mustang (a make and model more in keeping with my westering impulse, so it seemed). Next, giving notice to my landlady and employer, I emptied my bank account of what savings I'd managed to accumulate, and prepared for departure. My mentor, Mr. Johnson, tried to dissuade me, citing indications of a slumping economy and wondering where I was bound and how I planned to make a living. As I didn't know the answers to these questions myself, I could only thank him for his solicitude and say good-bye. In all, I had spent a little over a year and a half at the paper—a respectable commitment, by my reckoning—and, having exhausted such occupational staying power as I possessed, I took my leave.

The next few days I spent at the River, installing a car-top rack for the new glider, collecting my gear, and gathering myself for the journey. Then, one crisp fall morning in which the first dark strands of geese could be seen trailing southward, I departed for the wide, open spaces.

*Near the Borderline*

# Chapter 13

# Westward Ho, the Rag-wings!

Leaving the island for the Canadian mainland, I followed the lake shore to Toronto and continued west, recrossing the border at Detroit and picking up Interstate 80. By the time night had fallen, l was somewhere in northern Illinois and, after stopping for dinner in a travel plaza, I found a quiet space in the parking lot and retired to the back seat. (Now unemployed and on a strict budget, my plan was to indulge in motels only every other day or so, a scheme which, however frugal, took little account of the value of a good night's sleep.) The next morning, scarcely refreshed but still energized by the adventure, I crossed the Mississippi and entered upon the plains, passing many miles of cornfields before fatigue caught up with me in North Platte, Nebraska, where, following a brilliant sunset and dinner at another truck-stop, I retired once again to my cramped quarters in the back seat.

Eight fitful hours later, I was up before dawn and driving hard for the mountains, watching the stars fade and the advancing day fill a wide and cloudless expanse of sky. Dropping south across the Colorado line, I caught my first glimpse of the Rockies from well out on the plains, the distant, snow-capped peaks barely perceptible at first, hovering above the horizon like a mirage in the bright morning light. Before long, the sprawl of Denver behind me, I followed I-70 up the eastern slope of the range, eagerly scanning the surrounding peaks for likely take-off sites. (After long months spent in the rolling pastureland of the north country, it would be weeks before I got over the urge to fly from every eminence in view.) An early snowfall in the passes made for an hour's delay, but by late afternoon I'd reached Grand Junction, where, turning south, I followed the western slope of the Continental Divide to Montrose and took a room in a run-down, fifties-era motel with a sign showing a poncho- and sombrero-clad figure slouching sleepily against a cactus. After a shower and a change of clothes, I had something to eat in a nearby cafe, wandered about the streets a bit, then returned to my room and the relative luxury of a broken-down bed.

At this point, though not sure where I might wind up, my immediate objective was the mining-turned-ski town of Telluride, home to a gang of hang-glider pilots recently featured in the pages of an outdoor-sports magazine. From its romanticized description, the town seemed just the place to stage my return to the sport, and the next day, continuing south from Montrose, I made my way into a narrow box-canyon and arrived at last in the center of Telluride's two-block business district. After three and a half days on the road, I'd reached my destination, but so what? Without a name to go by or any real knowledge of the people I'd read about, it occurred to me that I might have saved myself a lot of time and trouble by simply calling ahead. Then again, my larger mission was to see the West for myself, and I was content to dispense with formal invitations.

Happily, none were required. Heading for the nearest bar, I ordered some lunch and sat chatting with the bartender, who knew virtually everyone in town. Soon I was on the phone with one of the local pilots, introducing myself and hinting broadly at the possibility of getting a tour of the area's gliding sites. Later that evening, a low-key, pony-tailed fellow about my age showed up and the two of us sat drinking beer and comparing notes. It was nice of him to turn out like that, but I understood the purpose of the meeting to be more than merely social; he wanted to know something of my bona fides and whether I could be trusted not to get in over my head. In my wallet was a card from a gliding association claiming that I was an "expert" pilot, but such credentials didn't mean much. In a sport as ungoverned and ungovernable as hang-gliding, the truest sort of proficiency lay in a healthy respect for the vagaries of wind and weather, and above all a knowledge of one's limitations. He sounded me out and seemed to recognize a kindred spirit.

## Westward Ho, the Rag-wings!

The next two nights I spent on a sofa at his place, spending my waking hours roaming the town, making idle inquiries about job prospects. Perusing a copy of the local newspaper, a single page broadsheet, I noted the address on the masthead and paid a visit to a small, cluttered office, where the paper's editor was not unreceptive to the idea of my contributing to the enterprise in some as-yet unspecified way. With the start of the ski season at least a month off, however, it was too soon to talk in anything but generalities. Just as it had at Sugarloaf, everything would have to await the arrival of snow. Meanwhile, the town and canyon were the closest things to my former flying haunts as I could have hoped for, right down to the local gliding community, whose members were gracious enough to include me in plans for a weekend outing.

On the appointed afternoon, five of us—my host and I, two other pilots and a driver—loaded gliders and gear into the back of a four-wheeler and started uphill along a heavily switch-backed mountain road. Arriving at the base of a precipitous scree-field known as Mammoth Slide, we piled out and began carrying our stuff uphill to the take-off site, crossing a brief patch of sun-softened snow along the way. Though the climb was not particularly steep or difficult, at an altitude of over 11,000 feet, the exertion quickly told on us, and by the time we reached the top we were gulping the thin air at a rapid rate and glad of the chance to put down our burdens.

The view alone was worth the effort, for along the horizon successive peaks stretched away in every direction, while on the canyon floor some 3,000 feet below, the town seemed alarmingly small and distant. My admiration for the setting was not unmixed with a certain anxiety, however, for at this point I began to take stock of my recent flying experience, which had by no means been extensive. While I'd made a few brief flights in the new glider from a number of north country hills, the cumulative airtime was scarcely enough to familiarize myself with its handling characteristics, let alone get reacquainted with the finer points of gliding. After a year and a half spent away from the sport, it seemed I'd chosen a rather challenging site for a comeback. Nevertheless, I set about assembling the airframe and was soon ready to launch.

By this time, one of the local pilots had volunteered to serve as wind dummy, and once in position at the top of the scree field, he stood with glider at the ready, prepared to drive forward at the first sign of an oncoming breeze. As the air was remarkably still, however, there was a considerable wait, and when at last he stormed downhill and leapt into his harness, it was only to sink back onto the slope and skid violently to a stop on the rocky terrain. Despite the steepness of the slope, the thin air and lack of sufficient wind had failed to sustain him, and while he came away with only a few scratches, his glider was badly dinged up, summarily ending his flying plans for the day. He would ride back down in the truck.

Meanwhile, the rest of us stood around scratching the backs of our necks and pondering our options, regretting the fate of our companion yet more than a little grateful for the benefit of his example. Quickly settling on an alternate take-off, we carried our gliders down the slope to the edge of a ravine, where the ground fell away in a dramatic cliff. Though the new site guaranteed a clean launch, there was a catch, for instead of presenting a straight shot out into the canyon, it faced an equally formidable cliff on the other side of the ravine. This meant that immediately upon take-off one would be obliged to make a sharp left turn before breaking out into the open.

My host demonstrated how, charging off the top of the cliff, dropping precipitously into a glide and banking steeply away from the opposing rock wall to disappear around the shoulder of the ravine. This left two of us, and, deferring to the local pilot, I watched as he followed suit, driving forward and suddenly dropping out of sight, only to reappear moments later in a steep bank, whooping loudly as he went. Now, beset by lingering doubts (golf, after all, was a perfectly fine sport, and good exercise, too!), I awaited the necessary resolve to launch with the same apprehension I'd experienced on my first flight from Sugarloaf, a flight, as I recalled, that had taken a couple of botched take-offs to get right. The learning curve here, however, was as steep as the cliff; either you made it out of the ravine on the first go-round or in all likelihood you weren't going to require further instruction of any kind, having learned all you were ever going to know.

Summoning something of my former confidence, I bolted for the edge, leapt into the harness and waited a seemingly interminable two seconds for the wing to slip into a glide, at which point I warped left in a compressive turn that carried me out of the ravine and into an immensity of sky. Now thousands of feet above the floor of the canyon, I scanned the middle distance for those who had preceded me, one of whom was hunting thermals out in the open, while the other was exploring the vicinity of a pair of massive granite spires rising out of the base of the ravine. Meanwhile, at every point of the compass lay an unbroken series of rugged peaks beneath a bright blue sky, and suddenly whatever doubts I'd entertained about the sport or the purpose of my westering journey were rendered moot in the joyful rediscovery of my once and future pastime. I was back.

Flying straight out, I gazed down at the valley floor beneath my feet—so far below that individual people were scarcely discernible—and worked the upwelling currents in a long, leisurely aerial tour of the canyon. Eventually following the lead of the others, I flew west of the town and set up for landing in a pasture on its outskirts. Touching down not far from a group of grazing cattle, we carried our gliders to a nearby fence, beyond which the truck awaited.

"What d'ya think?" asked my host as we gathered to compare notes.

"Words cannot describe," I said, shaking my head in unfeigned awe.

"—Welcome to Telluride," he responded, grinning knowingly.

As restorative as that flight proved, however, I would not stay long enough for another. Later that evening, all toked up and pounding beers back at the bar, my newfound friends and I sat sharing stories and discussing the outlook for the coming ski season, when flying at the mountain would cease. The long arm of the insurance companies extended even here, it seemed, and as soon as the ski area opened for business the slopes would be off limits for gliders and the tote road itself buried in snow. If I wanted to fly through the winter, they explained, I should go to Utah, where there was reliable ridge soaring to be had just south of Salt Lake City at a place called Point of the Mountain.

Thus, a mere three days after I had arrived, I bid thanks and farewell to the Telluride Air Force, and got back on the road, departing the canyon and heading south, then west at Durango, leaving the mountains behind to start across long miles of high desert, where here and there a collection of wind-blown shacks masqueraded as a town. It was another fine fall day, and with the windows rolled down and the warm desert air whipping through the car, I settled in for the ride, ready for anything. With my first stop behind me, I continued my tour with a growing sense of self-assurance. Along the horizon stood the other-worldly setting of Monument Valley, the scene of countless western movies and now an appropriate backdrop to my own small legend, for I was an American adventurer and this my natural home.

The first town I came upon in Utah was Moab, where vague associations with the Old Testament kingdom of that name tumbled me to the fact that I was entering the domain of the Church of Jesus Christ of Latter-Day Saints, otherwise known as the Mormons. In any case, Moab seemed a well-appointed and orderly sort of place, and as a newcomer to the state I was duly prepared to accept the customs of the resident population, even if it meant drinking the state mandated near-beer my friends at Telluride had warned me about.

Proceeding north, I picked up the interstate at Provo and continued down the valley of the Jordan River (enough already with the Biblical allusions!) to the state capital, Salt Lake City. With plans to spend the winter in the area, I thought to begin my stay with a more or less concerted effort to find work, for which purpose I ended up taking a room in a small motel within walking distance of the downtown area. After a preliminary exploration of the immediate surroundings, I retired for a good night's sleep preparatory to an assault upon the concrete canyons of the metropolis, the lyrics of a classic Frank Sinatra tune running through my head: "If I can make it there, I'll make it anywhere. –So, here's to you, Salt Lake, Salt Lake!"

Alas, it turned out I couldn't make it there. In the morning, I visited the Magic-Kingdom-like Mormon Temple, and later snooped around the offices of the Salt Lake Tribune, buying a paper and studying it with a cool, professional eye. It soon became apparent, however, that I was not a likely candidate for a job in the city, in large part due to the dominant role the church played in local affairs, a role that tended to discourage all non-Mormons from rising to positions of importance or permanence in the community. There was always the option of becoming a Jack Mormon, the name given to converts of convenience, but having already reconciled myself to an inferior grade of beer, I considered any further concession to the prevailing traditions entirely unreasonable. Beyond this, as I had no intention of staying beyond the winter, any attempt to get a job with a future was bound to result in a good deal of wasted effort. Even so, I spent the rest of the day exploring the city before returning to my meager room to catch up with laundry and other chores. I still had a tune in my head, but from Sinatra's tribute to the big city I switched to Roger Miller's country classic: "I'm a man of means by no means—King of the Road."

  The next day I turned to my favorite pastime for consolation, retracing my route along the interstate to the local hang-gliding site the Telluride crew had recommended to me: Point of the Mountain—a prodigious end-moraine jutting into the valley halfway between Salt Lake and Provo. The previous evening on my way north, I had failed to recognize it in the faint light of dusk, but by daylight it was unmistakable—a steep and treeless ridge rising some 800 feet above the desert floor and running roughly east-west for nearly two miles. Getting off the interstate, I found my way to a dirt access road and followed it onto a brief shoulder of tableland at the base of the ridge.

  Otherwise known as Widowmaker Mountain, the landform was also the site of a special motorcycle event in which grotesquely-modified dirt-bikes sporting huge rear tires with paddle-like treads tore straight uphill, spewing rooster-tails of gravelly soil behind them and traveling as far up the slope as the steely nerves of their riders would take them. It was as a hang-gliding venue that the ridge's true potential was realized, however, for by a peculiar phenomenon of local meteorology it was soarable on nearly a daily basis, and indeed at almost any time of day. In the mornings, southerly breezes blowing up the valley created a steady band of rising air above the southern side of the formation, while in the afternoon—when the wind routinely blew in the opposite direction—the same conditions prevailed on its northern face.

  I learned all this from a local flyer and CB-radio buff who used words like "bodacious" to describe the wonders of the ridge. Like me, a transient, he was living out of a van and I remember him chiefly for his incongruous fashion sense, which bespoke a style perhaps best defined as hippy/disco. He was right about the ridge, though; it was indeed bodacious. With no road to the top (or none that would accommodate our vehicles) we were obliged to lug our gliders up to a take-off site on an outcropping some two hundred feet above the landing area, but from there we had only to step off into steadily rising air to be carried well above the crest of the ridge. Over the course of the next several weeks I spent hours there, catching up on the airtime I'd missed since leaving Sugarloaf, sometimes staying aloft long enough to watch dusk settle over the valley and car headlights wink on along the interstate far below.

As much as I reveled in such flying, however, I remember those days as a rather sketchy and troubled time. Having yet to find work and a place to stay, I was hewing to my original scheme, spending most nights in the car at or near the flying site, where my cramped back seat was rendered even more uncomfortable by the weird yowling of coyotes in the near vicinity. Then too, the fact that the Utah State Prison lay just the other side of the interstate did nothing to ease my mind, especially as the maximum-security facility was the subject of considerable media attention just then in connection with a notorious inmate named Gary Gilmore. Convicted of murdering two people while out on parole for a previous crime, Gilmore had thrown the legal system—and the country itself—on its ear by refusing to appeal his case, thereby igniting a firestorm of public debate over the death penalty. With only a few weeks to go before the scheduled execution, the Gilmore story was receiving intensive coverage, including considerable speculation about the possibility of an eleventh-hour breakout attempt.

Homeless and with a community of convicts as my nearest neighbors, I had to admit that I was living pretty close to the bone. Moreover, as I found myself often flying solo, without even a witness in the event something went wrong, I was getting pretty lonely. It seemed even my newfound friend, Mr. Bo Dacious (I never did get his name), had more of a life than I did.

> I knew a man, Bo Dacious, and he'd fly for you
> In a rag-wing kite,
> And every hill or mountainside he traveled to
> Was a take-off site...

*Westward Ho, the Rag-wings!*

    Even so, I was not without prospects. Nearby, in a narrow canyon of the Wasatch Range, the ski resort at Snowbird was gearing up for the season, and a visit to the Cliff Lodge, a large, upscale hotel on the mountain, landed me a job manning the front desk. With work scheduled to begin in another two weeks, I stayed on in the vicinity of the flying site, and one day while I was reclining against the windshield of the Mustang, taking in the feeble warmth of the November sun, a passing motorist pulled over and engaged me in conversation through his open window. A sturdy character with an easy-going western manner, he managed over the course of a five-minute chat to elicit something of my circumstances and background, taking particular interest in my newspaper experience and wondering if I had done any layout work. I hadn't, but this didn't seem to faze him, and before continuing on his way he dug into his wallet and produced a business card.

    "Listen, if you plan on staying around and are looking for work, give me a call."

    "Thanks, I just might."

    Indeed, I was in no position to take such an offer lightly, yet with the Snowbird job in the offing I had no intention of following through on it, and shortly thereafter, in anticipation of a regular income, I arranged to rent a small, unfurnished place in a suburb of Salt Lake. Roughly equidistant from the ski area and the flying site, the new place was spartan at best, but served the purpose of giving me a toehold in the community.

    Once the Snowbird job started, however, a better arrangement soon presented itself. While manning the hotel desk on my second day of work, I looked up to see three old college friends stroll through the lobby of the place, and we all did double-takes at the moment of recognition. It so happened they were working in a restaurant downstairs, and after the shock of the encounter wore off, we arranged to get together and catch up. A few days later, I paid a visit to the house they were renting at the base of Little Cottonwood Canyon, and when they invited me to join them, I readily agreed. Though I'd been obliged to put down a small deposit for the unfurnished place out in the valley, I hadn't signed a lease, and there was no question where I would rather be; having spent the better part of a month on my own, mostly on the move, I was glad of the chance to avail myself of the companionship of old acquaintances.

Things seemed to be looking up. In a relatively short time, I'd found old friends, a good place to stay, a job, and plenty of recreational options (when not flying my glider, I could take advantage of a free ski pass at Snowbird). And if this weren't evidence enough of my improving fortunes, shortly thereafter I signed up for the ski area's annual Thanksgiving tennis tournament, got paired with a ringer (the game was doubles) and won the thing. The next day my partner and I donated our winnings—two large, oven-ready turkeys—to the hosts of a massive staff party, at which the two of us stuffed our faces and drank our fill amid the grateful plaudits of our co-workers.

The only thing we all required at this point was snow, and there could be little doubt that it was on the way. The place was famous for snow, regularly getting more than 600 inches in a season. "The greatest snow on earth," the promo read. And yet, December rolled around and there was no snow. Everyone said it was fluky, but the season was still young. –Not to worry, soon there would be plenty of snow and the boom-times would begin.

When Christmas arrived with no appreciable snow, however, everyone truly started to worry. Vacation bookings were cancelled, the local patrons stayed away in droves, and those of us in the business of serving them were all thrown out of work pending the return of seasonal conditions. This proved a major inconvenience. We'd all been counting on a regular paycheck and now would have to scare up other sources of income. I looked around for a couple of days, and when nothing turned up, I recalled the stranger I'd met by the side of the road. The better part of a month had passed since then, but he still might have a job for me. Hunting around in my wallet, I found his card and placed the call.

When he answered, I identified myself as "the guy with the glider by the side of the road," and, readily recalling the encounter, he invited me to pay him a visit to learn more about the job he had in mind. Soon I was following directions to a modern, ranch-style house near the flying site, where he ushered me into a small office and started explaining his project. A former instructor of reading comprehension courses, he was engaged in publishing a special version of the New Testament designed to facilitate memorization. The idea was to cut the text of a large-print edition into individual thoughts—sometimes a single sentence, sometimes a whole paragraph—which could then be waxed and placed on graphed sheets along with related images that would serve as memory devices. Once the appropriate images had been selected and affixed adjacent to their respective thoughts, the individual sheets would be camera-ready, fully prepared for the final stage of offset printing.

When the job description failed to scare me off, we adjourned to a sizeable outbuilding next door, where a long table stood loaded with all the necessary materials: the large-print text to one side, an X-acto knife and metal ruler for cutting it into individual thoughts, a small machine for heating and applying wax to the verso, and stacks of layout sheets upon which the various elements were to be affixed. He plugged in the waxing machine, gave me a brief demonstration, and everything was clear.

Next came the matter of remuneration. Though I was to be paid by the piece (or completed sheet), rather than the hour, the rate seemed sufficient to be worth my while, and in any case, it was as good an offer as I was apt to find in a job market suddenly glutted with laid-off ski bums. As an added incentive, he invited me to take afternoon meals with his family as part of my compensation, an amenity not without its appeal in the context of my catch-as-catch-can existence. Though still somewhat bemused by the possibility—now an apparent fact—that a chance encounter by the roadside might lead to a viable job, I agreed to the terms and spent the remainder of the afternoon getting started.

It turned out to be interesting and oddly satisfying work. For the most part the individual thoughts were clearly noted within the symbology of the text, but not infrequently I was obliged to make determinations as to the relationship between words and images, decisions which required me to engage the material fairly closely. While the Gospels were not entirely new to me, I wasn't exactly intimate with their every detail, and the work gave me a new appreciation for them, if only as a series of ripping good yarns. Left to myself for much of the day, I worked at a steady pace, and in time the completed layout sheets began piling up beside me.

*Near the Borderline*

    The meals for which I'd contracted were not nearly as satisfying, however, consisting of proper, sit-down affairs that included his wife and a young man about my age whose relationship to my hosts I never quite understood. Overall, despite their best efforts at hospitality, I felt more than a little out of place, especially as the table talk routinely turned to matters of theology. While there were no overt attempts to proselytize me on these occasions, given the nature of the work I was doing, the subject could hardly be avoided, and I couldn't help seeing myself as a heathen in the company of true believers. In college, I had come to admire the lofty perspectives of no less devout a religionist than John Milton (an acquired taste, to be sure), and tended to approach the Scriptures from a literary point of view, enabling me to remain cheerfully aloof when dealing with the thorny matter of belief. My host, on the other hand, was inclined to a more dogmatic approach, and persisted in trying to pin me down on a number of basic tenets of faith, resulting in a conversational cat and mouse in which I found myself countering his every attempt with a suitably obscure reference to Milton's abstract cosmology.

    Even more unsettling than the conversation at these meals was the chow itself, which presented a clear and present challenge to my digestive tract. A woman in her late twenties, my employer's wife was considerably younger than he, and apparently still in training. The problem, however, lay not so much with her cooking skills as with the ingredients of the various dishes she served. According to Mormon tradition, upon their marriage the couple had stockpiled a year's worth of food, and rather than allow it to ossify beyond all recognition, she had taken to incorporating it into the family's daily fare. In any case, those meals caused me considerable distress, and I came to regret that part of the arrangement.

    Meanwhile, my housemates had taken jobs as waiters and bartenders at a local dive, and, determined to stick out the vicissitudes of the season, we carried on, awaiting the return of snow and the restoration of our jobs at Snowbird. As one snowless week followed another, however, our hopes grew more and more forlorn, and when, toward the end of January, national weather reports showed snow on Miami Beach, Florida, but none to speak of in the Wasatch Range, I lost all patience. It seemed entirely possible that, due to a freak in the jet stream, the entire winter might pass without appreciable accumulations, and with little time for flying and no skiing to be had at all, I decided to continue my westward journey, thinking to find work in California with the glider manufacturer for whom I was still a dealer. By this time, I had worked my way through Matthew, Mark and Luke, and, leaving the Book of John to another (good luck imaging forth that author's abstract idiom!), I thanked my employer for his kindness and got back on the road.

As it happened, the day after my departure a major winter storm buried the central Rockies under several feet of snow, but by the time the news reached me I was well on my way south by west and thinking only of sunshine and beaches and the blue Pacific. After an uneventful night in Las Vegas (my lifestyle involving risk enough of its own, I had no interest in the gaming tables, and the place frankly bored the hell out of me), I set off on a final day of driving, crossing the state line on a brilliant mid-winter afternoon even as the strains of the recent hit, "Hotel California," came pulsing through the car radio. Although going as far as the coast had not been central to my plans upon departing the River some months earlier, the idea had by now assumed a logic of its own, and, turning up the volume, I sped across the last stretch of desert to complete a journey that in many ways had come to seem predestined. I had set out, after all, to follow wherever the pursuit of gliding might lead me, and, consciously or unconsciously, California had always been on my mind. California, where hang-gliding had first taken hold, and where I was more than willing to become a "prisoner of my own device."

Following the freeway signs to Van Nuys, I arrived at the glider factory around quitting time. It turned out the owner was on his way back from a business trip, but a secretary in the office explained that I might catch up with him later that evening at a local nightclub owned by his wife. After a brief tour of the factory, I made my way to said nightclub, where the proprietress—a former show person, as I gathered—confirmed that her husband was expected shortly. Meanwhile, she bade me welcome and might have been pleasant company but for a nasty dispute she was having with her daughter, an attractive young woman about my age who worked behind the bar. Pressing me into service as a go-between, the mother insisted on asking my opinion about various aspects of her daughter's personal life, which put me in something of a bind. I couldn't very well side with either one of them without offending the other, and the fact that I had yet to find a place to stay the night didn't leave me with a lot of patience for the quarrel.

At last, my would-be employer arrived, and after giving him a chance to meet with his warring family, I presented myself and asked for a job. As it happened, he recognized me from the championships in Austria and quickly recalled that I'd been flying another make of glider (I was hoping he might have forgotten). The issue was my loyalty to his product, and I had to admit to having been wooed away from the true faith. Though I made a point of explaining that I'd come to regret the move, the lapse had been a serious breach of trust and he wasn't sure he should take me back. After struggling with his conscience, he decided he would, but only if I agreed to rent an apartment for which he held the lease. Pretending to have likelier options, I held out for a tour of the place before accepting, and was soon accompanying him on a short trip across town to have a look.

The apartment complex in question overlooked a palm-lined thoroughfare, with two floors of units above a basement garage. Making our way upstairs, we arrived at a modern, furnished suite with wall-to-wall carpeting, ample bedroom, kitchen and sitting room. Compared to my previous accommodations, the place was palatial, and when the rent worked out to a mere week's pay at the factory, the deal was sealed. I moved in at once, establishing a local address far sooner than I had any right to expect. On closer inspection the next day, I was less impressed with the place, which, as it turned out, I would be sharing with a sizable population of cockroaches. A daylight tour of the larger complex likewise revealed a pervasive shabbiness. From the dazzling sunlight of the street, a vestibule opened onto a dark courtyard, where a tired-looking assortment of large-leafed plants encumbered a fetid pool area. Apart from a few hours at midday, the pool remained in the shadows of the surrounding floors of apartments, a dank and claustrophobic space where I never once saw anyone swim or make use of the lounge chairs.

Nevertheless, when it came to the larger objective of my western tour, I was soon "living the dream," building gliders during the week and exploring all manner of new flying sites on the weekends as part of Delta Wing's factory team. Within six weeks of my arrival, I'd flown from sites as far south as La Jolla, where oceanside cliff-soaring afforded close-up, aerial views of the mansions at Torrey Pines, and as far north as Big Sur, where long, leisurely flights from the top of 6,000-foot Mount Pruitt revealed the ghostly forms of gray whales making their yearly migration along the coast far below. And just when the novelty of such adventures was beginning to fade, I received fresh incentive to go still farther afield.

One day while at work in the factory, I got a message to report to the front office for a phone call, a bewildering prospect in itself, for apart from the gang I worked with, I couldn't think of a single soul who knew where I was, let alone how to reach me. My surprise was only the more complete when it turned out to be my old Sugarloaf crony, Paul. Still a dealer for the company's products (like me, he had returned to the fold following the championships in Austria), he learned of my presence at the factory while checking on the delivery date for a new order, and was as amazed to discover my whereabouts as I was to be discovered. The last I'd heard from him was during my brief visit to the mountain the previous winter, since which time it seemed he had done rather well. Now flush with cash and eager to resurrect his gliding career, he was instantly envious of my situation, and in the course of our phone conversation he decided to treat himself to a west-coast tour of his own. Several days later, he called to confirm that he'd booked a flight to Los Angeles for himself and three gliding buddies from southern Maine. Their plan was to rent a motorhome for a two-week survey of gliding sites throughout the state, and I was cordially invited to serve as tour guide.

In preparation for their visit, I made arrangements with the boss to take a week off from the factory, to which he agreed on condition that the bunch of us take part in an upcoming promotional fly-in to be held near San Francisco. So it was that on the day of Paul's arrival I borrowed a company truck and drove to LAX, where I found the four Mainers in excellent spirits after multiple trips to the onboard facilities for snorts of marching powder—the source, it seemed, of Paul's recent largesse, which included ample cash reserves. After loading the two dismantled gliders they brought with them (Paul's new ship was awaiting him at the factory), I drove them back to the Valley, where they spent the night in a motel.

The next morning, they arrived at the factory in a rented, late-model motorhome, and after loading the boxy vehicle with gliders and gear, the five of us clambered aboard for what promised to be a memorable road trip. Thinking to start off with a flight from the coastal range, I plotted a course northward to Santa Barbara, where we made our way to a peak in the Santa Ynez Mountains overlooking the city. Though I hadn't flown there before, it seemed a likely enough spot to begin our aerial exploits, the only problem being that the landing area was not directly visible from the take-off site. Nevertheless, I figured it would be easy enough to spot from the air, and on this sketchy basis we prepared to take off, telling our designated driver to do his best to find us.

Launching at an altitude of some 2,000 feet, we floated high above the city, but when the landing site proved unrecognizable from the air, we ended up trailing each other in search of it like a flock of bewildered geese. Eventually dropping out of the sky in the middle of a housing development somewhere in the foothills, we were out of touch with our ground man and far from any clear landmarks. By previous agreement, we had planned to coordinate, if necessary, through the local police department (a risky choice under the circumstances), and after calling in our position from a nearby house, we loitered about until, miraculously, the motorhome came lumbering into view. Despite a woeful lack of planning, it had been a spectacular flight, and the recovery effort added a certain picaresque quality to the day's adventures.

Next, we continued north along the coast to Santa Maria, where we spent a rainy night in the motorhome. When the next day dawned cloudless and balmy, we drove out to nearby Guadalupe Dunes, a series of low sand hills overlooking the wide Pacific. By noon, the site's reliable onshore winds were blowing, and though the dunes themselves rose little more than a hundred feet above the beach, their contours were such that the lift they produced carried us far higher. It was the first time the Maine boys had done any extended ridge soaring, and they liked it so well we decided to stay another day, parking that night at the edge of the sand and cooking steaks over a campfire on the beach. The next morning, we roamed around the site, waiting for the wind to build, then spent another brilliant afternoon in a continual series of impromptu flights.

Climbing to the top of the lift, we gazed far out to sea, calling out to each other, wheeling and diving like gulls. Finally, sunburned and exhausted, we packed up and got back on the road. With the lion's share of their trip still ahead of them, the newcomers were already amazed by the amount of airtime they'd logged.

Continuing up the coast, we stopped at a campsite in Big Sur in hopes of catching a ride to the top of Mt. Pruitt the next day. As it turned out, conditions were marginal, however, as were our prospects for finding a means uphill on roads the motorhome couldn't possibly manage. Three weeks earlier I'd made a memorable flight there, taking off in clear skies only to see building clouds close out the landing area. At the prospect of getting lost in the clouds and ending up far off course, I opted to land on a grassy ridge about half-way up the mountain and was soon joined by two other pilots, who dropped out of the sky nearby. After hunting up a likely take-off site, we waited for conditions to change, and, when at last an opening in the clouds gave us a clear view of the landing area, we charged back into the air to complete the flight.

Now stymied in our attempts to find a way uphill, we got back in the motorhome and continued north, eventually arriving on the outskirts of San Francisco, where the scheduled weekend fly-in was about to begin at Fort Funston, an old missile base overlooking the Pacific near Daly City. Once a strategic outpost in the Cold War, the base had been rendered obsolete by new technology, whereupon the existing missiles were removed and the site opened to the public for day use. Rising above a sandy beach, its bluffs presented a steep, uniform barrier to the prevailing wind, creating one of the best coastal soaring sites in a state famous for them. We spent the night in a small state park nearby, and the next morning arrived bright and early in the base's ample parking lot, soon to be joined by a large gathering of pilots from as far away as New Mexico.

About mid-morning the wind set in, giving rise to a flurry of activity, and soon dozens of gliders were wheeling back and forth above the cliff in a constant stream of brightly-colored sails. Getting in line for take-off, we quickly adapted to the site's carefully monitored traffic pattern as well as the 20-minute time limit allotted to individual flights. By noon, crowds of spectators had flooded onto the top of the cliff to gaze at the spectacle of airborne traffic passing directly overhead. Taking to the air in a continual series of flights, we danced our gliders back and forth above the cliffs, swooping low for the benefit of the spectators, feigning sleep as we rested comfortably in our prone harnesses, and generally playing every moment for all it was worth. Such flagrant exhibitionism was partly redeemed, perhaps, by our own self-absorption; "Look at us or don't look," we seemed to say, "but we can fly, really fly!" Everyone was looking.

Eventually, with the sun sinking low in the sky and winds diminishing, we packed up our gear and headed into the city in search of a likely eatery. Along the way, somebody produced a hash-pipe and before long we had slipped into a state of heavy-lidded befuddlement. Soon we were lost in an unfamiliar maze of city streets, peering out the windows of the motor home as throngs of pedestrians spilled from the sidewalks, slowing traffic to a crawl. By chance, we had driven into the heart of Chinatown during the New Year festivities and, surrendering at last to the crowds, we parked our cumbersome vehicle along a side street and were soon swept up in a sea of celebrants.

Given our collective state of mind, the occasion threatened sensory overload as a blur of innumerable faces, some wearing grotesque and gaudy masks, appeared and disappeared within an ever-moving mass of humanity. At some point in our wanderings, we made our way into the placid interior of a likely-looking restaurant and gratified our hash-induced appetites with a small feast before venturing back onto the streets to mingle with the crowds once more. How we managed to remember where we parked the truck, I don't know, nor do I recall the feat of navigation that landed us first in a bar on the waterfront, and later that night across the Golden Gate at an RV park in Sausalito.

For sheer activity, that day was going to be hard to top, but the next morning we prepared to give it a try. After lingering over breakfast at a harborside diner, we returned to the missile base and, with the arrival of an onshore breeze, took up where we'd left off the previous evening, soaring high above the cliffs and mingling with prospective customers in fulfillment of our promotional obligation to Delta Wing. As I was scheduled to be at work in the factory the next morning, however, when the flying was done, we packed up and started on the long trip back to Los Angeles, taking turns driving

*Westward Ho, the Rag-wings!*

through the night. Come daybreak, we were back in Van Nuys, and, after pointing the Mainers in the direction of La Jolla and the cliffs at Torrey Pines, I got off the bus. For the final week of their trip, they would be on their own, and were well-prepared to make good use of the time.

Several days later they returned, road-weary and flown out, yet not wanting to leave. When I drove them back to the airport, they were complaining of another New England mud season, openly envious of my situation, and effusive in their appreciation for the part I'd played in their tour. I had to admit that, where flying was concerned, I felt lucky to be able to visit all of the better-known sites throughout the state, but there was another California, too. For all of its laid-back reputation, the place was full of a pervasive restlessness, and every week when Friday rolled around, the rush of traffic getting away from the city was nothing less than life-threatening. Indeed, as my time there wore on, I found myself growing tired of the culture.

One day, having found a public tennis court not far from my apartment, I got involved in a pick-up game of doubles. We hadn't been at it long, however, before a serve into my court was called out by my partner and instantly disputed by the server, who grew increasingly heated about the call. Asked for my opinion, I confessed to having seen the ball land out as well, but was perfectly willing to play the point over. It didn't matter—the two of us were cheats and not to be trusted. There was talk between the server and my partner of resolving the issue with fists. I protested it was only a game. More insults ensued, whereupon my partner dropped his racket and moved to the net, to which the server responded with the reductio ad absurdum: "I'll get my equalizer—then we'll see. I'll get my equalizer!" At this point I walked away (talk of gunplay always puts me off my game), and for some time afterward I found myself looking warily over my shoulder, half-expecting to become the victim of some insane attempt at retribution. An isolated incident, the episode only highlighted the importance of choosing tennis partners (and venues) carefully, but I couldn't help extrapolating from it.

Another discouraging encounter took place during a visit to a local night club with a co-worker from the factory, a native Californian who spent his free time surfing and skateboarding. While his workdays were occupied building gliders, he considered anyone who flew them to be tetched in the head, an opinion he shared freely at the shop. In response, I dubbed him "Wingnut," and made fun of his passion for rolling around in empty swimming pools.

The nightclub in question was a nondescript, one-story bunker of a building surrounded by parking lots, where a rock quintet of local repute provided the featured entertainment. The place was jammed, and with high expectations for the show we stood at the bar drinking bottled beer and studying the scene. Soon, the band arrived on stage wearing skin-tight leather vests and pants. Of Native American extraction, the lead singer had the impressive build of the Navajo as well as what in locker-room parlance is known as 'the gift,' an attribute his movements and attire, as well as the songs he sang, tended to advertise as much as possible.

Meanwhile, sitting at a large table to one side of the dance floor were the band's nubile consorts, all dressed and coiffed according to the latest fashion and, despite their best efforts to affect sophisticated poses, all painfully young. No one ever asked them to dance. The response was a foregone conclusion. They were not there to dance, but rather to be ogled. Sitting with elaborate mixed drinks in front of them, they dutifully watched their paramours strut about on stage, leaning towards each other every now and again to discuss some nuance of a show they'd no doubt witnessed a hundred times before. But discuss is not the right word. Given the din of amplified noise within that low-ceilinged place, discussion was quite impossible. At best, one could only hope to shout brief comments into another's very earhole, and even then, there was every chance of being drowned out.

Among the band's signature offerings was an endearing number called Big Ten Inch, a song that might have been funny as a send-up of male braggadocio and sexual pretension. If its aim was satire, however, the performer did nothing to suggest as much. Treating the lyrics with all the sincerity due a love ballad, he proceeded to pay tribute to the frightful proportions of his manhood with such single-minded devotion that the role of a sex partner seemed perfectly irrelevant.

Noticing a likely young woman seated solo at a small table near the dance floor, I grabbed my beer and wandered across the room in the relative quiet between songs. By the time I arrived, however, the music was blaring again, and with no hope of actually speaking to her I simply presented myself and gestured toward the dance floor. She responded by staring at me long enough to put me in doubt, then relenting, whereupon I put my beer on the table and followed her onto the floor. Back in college, I had enjoyed such dancing for the opportunity it afforded to show off in a socially acceptable way—a kind of dancing, it seemed to me, to be engaged in with a playful swagger. Under the circumstances, however, such whimsical considerations seemed entirely out of place. Indeed, my partner of the moment wore an expression of such calculated indifference that I wound up feeling like the character in the fairy tale whose challenge is to make the despondent princess laugh or be summarily put to death.

Even so, I was prepared to give it a try, and when the song ended and the band announced an intermission, I asked if she would like some company and was accepted. We talked. Or rather, I talked while she responded with cool smiles and the kind of personal warmth one comes to expect from the counter help at a Seven Eleven. I asked questions, the usual ones, and she answered. She was twenty-one, lived in the Valley, and worked for a local talent agency. Upon further investigation (I was beginning to appreciate the difficulty prosecutors face in dealing with balky witnesses) it turned out her agency had booked the night's band, and for a moment, expecting to be asked for my musical opinion, I was prepared to say how much I enjoyed their—heh, heh—'sound.'

No such luck. She didn't ask me anything. I might have been the Boston Strangler for all she knew, yet the possibility seemed of little interest or concern. There was always the chance she was trying to get rid of me, of course, and I was perfectly open to the possibility. All I needed was a sign, some indication one way or the other. The idea of revealing anything like spontaneity seemed quite beyond the role she envisioned for herself, however, and I eventually ran out of legs trying to carry the conversation single-handedly. Indeed, it seemed I had fallen into an etiquette trap from which there was no graceful means of escape.

Compounding my predicament, the band eventually returned to the stage and started playing again, emitting a barrage of noise so grotesquely unmusical as to seem a deliberate assault on one's hearing. At this point, confronted with the prospect of another set of mind-numbing, genital-wagging performances, I resolved to leave no matter what. Getting up, I shrugged awkwardly and made my departure.

"What was she like?" asked Wingnut upon my return to the bar.

"Nice enough, I guess. Only thing missing was a personality."

"Pfft," he scoffed. "–Aren't you the picky one!"

Not all my social encounters were quite so discouraging, or at least not in the same way. One weekend at a gathering attended by a number of women familiar to the gliding circles in which I found myself (some of whom were themselves pilots), I met an extremely outgoing party-goer with lots of interesting things on her mind and not the slightest scruple about acting on them in the midst of a room full of people, to the extent that I was obliged to dissuade her from any further familiarities until a more opportune moment should arise. Despite my best efforts to nuance the situation, however, the next thing I knew she had stormed off in a huff, leaving me quite dejected and, what was worse, in a debilitating state of arousal.

My failure to adapt to the prevailing social norms was mostly my own fault, I suppose. In truth, I was never able to take west-coast ways very seriously, and no doubt I gave people the wrong impression. In any case, I couldn't seem to strike the right pose, and with the passage of time the extremes of the culture only seemed to grow more pronounced. Between being groped in public and having my life threatened on a tennis court, I couldn't help thinking there was something out of balance in the world I'd traveled so far to see.

Then too, the very changelessness of the climate came to annoy me, the persistent sunshine and balmy temperatures that had been such a welcome novelty in mid-winter having somehow grown oppressive over time. Toward the end of April, I found myself yearning for a change of seasons and knew I wasn't long for a move. Summer was on its way (not that you'd notice the difference in SoCal), and somehow the thought of its return to northern regions was more compelling than its actual presence in the south. I couldn't go without treating myself to a new glider, however, and, after overseeing its production at the factory, I sold my old one and prepared to move on.

Departing the Valley one bright morning in early May, I headed north to San Francisco with plans to spend the next day at Fort Funston, then continue up the coast to Oregon and Washington. Beyond that, I wasn't sure what I might do. Something would turn up. It always had. Arriving in the Bay Area at dusk, I decided to forego the small state park where the Mainers and I had stayed some five weeks earlier, thinking to spend the night at the missile base instead, the better to get an early start in the morning. Thus, after taking a leisurely meal at a diner in Daly City, I made my way out to the flying site and parked surreptitiously near a clump of bushes in the lot at the top of the bluffs. It was going on ten o'clock, and, worn out from a long day of driving, I retired to the back seat and went readily to sleep.

What I'd failed to consider was that the site was technically a restricted area. Granted, signs to that effect were posted at the entrance, but having once again returned to "road mode" I scarcely paid attention, discounting their warning as no longer valid and thinking to make myself somehow inconspicuous. This would prove a mistake, for shortly after midnight I was awakened by an assortment of colored lights racing across the darkness. Moments later a loudspeaker-amplified voice blared:

"ATTENTION IN THE CAR. OVERNIGHT PARKING IS NOT ALLOWED. YOU NEED TO VACATE THE PREMISES."

Bolting upright, I spent several moments mesmerized by the flashing lightshow before thrusting my feet into a pair of sneakers and preparing to face the law. Outside, the glare of a flashlight was added to the bewildering collection of beacons as an unseen figure looked me over from the seclusion of the surrounding darkness. Dressed in tee-shirt and blue jeans, the laces of my sneakers dragging, I stood with hands thrust awkwardly in my pockets and shoulders huddled against the chill of the night air.

"You'll have to move on," began a faceless voice, speaking in the practiced tones of the public servant. And as if the situation weren't embarrassing enough, the voice was clearly that of a female.

"—Public access is allowed from eight a.m. to eight p.m. only," she continued, choosing this moment to direct the flashlight out of my face and play it over the car and glider. Regaining my vision in the interval, I was able to glimpse the features of a young woman scarcely older than I, clad in the uniform of a security guard.

"Oh," I responded. "I figured since it's a regular flying site and everything. ..."

"Didn't you read the sign?"

"No," I lied, "it was dark when I got here. −I'd only be staying the one night."

"It's not allowed and besides it's not safe—a car was pushed over the bluffs a couple of weeks ago. There's a public beach three miles up the coast highway," she suggested. "You can park overnight there."

The lot she had in mind was a wide field of asphalt along Ocean Beach, and, even as I parked and shut off the engine, I had reservations about the place. Within the stillness that followed, I could hear a distant exchange of shouts, and at the far end of the lot a lone figure was moving furtively among a group of cars. Crawling into the back seat, I prepared once again to sleep, but by now it was no use; between the discomfort of my accommodations and the lurking of imaginary vandals intent on making off with the glider, I managed only a fitful state of half-sleep, and after an hour or two of anxious contortion I gave up and started in search of some more secluded spot.

Driving back along the coast highway, I passed the road leading to the missile base and followed the turnoff for the state park immediately below it, eventually arriving at an iron gate that barred entrance to the secluded camping area I had shunned earlier in the evening. I thought better of the decision now, of course, but there was nothing to be done about it. Pulling over onto the roadside in front of the gate, I collapsed into the back seat once more and eventually drifted off to sleep... only to wake up three hours later in the predawn twilight, huddled in a sleeping bag which, beyond a thin perimeter of tepidity, was as cold and clammy as could be. It turned out I had left one of the windows partially open, and during the night a thick fog had rolled in, thoroughly permeating the interior.

At this point the wind wouldn't set in for hours, and to pass the time I paid another visit to the diner in Daly City, lingering over breakfast before proceeded to the base, where the wind telltale along the edge of the bluffs hung lifeless. Setting up the glider anyway, I sat beneath the up-tilted wing, waiting for conditions to improve, but it was long wait, during which I was beset by growing doubts.

Over the past several months, each time I had returned to the road a persistent westward impulse had served to sustain me. Now, having crossed the continent and covered a good portion of the coast, my tour seemed to have run its natural course. And here I was, twenty-five years old, sleeping in the back of my car and being chased out of parking lots by otherwise likely young women. Twenty-five years: a quarter of a century. At twenty-five, Lindbergh had made his solo flight across the Atlantic, altering the world's perception of time and space, whereas, when not engaged in altering my own consciousness, I'd been pursuing a pastime of no earthly benefit to anyone. The comparison was not pleasing to contemplate, and for many moments I sat struggling to rationalize my existence. If only I could get airborne, I thought, things would be different; the future would look bright again when seen from high above the cliff.

In time, the fog began to lift, and though the sky remained overcast, a steady onshore breeze set in. It seemed I was going to get my wish, and with the wind continuing to freshen, I strapped in and took off, slowly gaining altitude with successive passes along the cliff. Before long I was well above take-off with the sky all to myself, yet no sooner had I begun to settle in for a long, leisurely flight than a thin drizzle began to fall, and as moisture accumulated on the wings, I began to lose altitude as steadily as I had gained it. I held on as long as I could, but it was a losing battle, and, surrendering to the inevitable, I turned out of the lift and came in for a landing.

Now, with glider and clothes as damp as my spirits, I sat once again beneath the airframe and waited as the rain continued and the winds began to strengthen. A half hour later, I folded the wings to avoid stressing the air-frame and retreated to the car, where I sat staring morosely out to sea. Somewhere in my mind a door was closing and I struggled to hold it back. Then, shortly before noon, with conditions getting still worse, I called it quits. Packing up the glider and lashing it to the car, I started driving without anything resembling a considered plan. It was as if the incoming gale had blown me off my moorings, and I was simply running before it. Only later, with a reluctant sense of finality, would I recognize that my eight-month tour had entered its final leg.

*Near the Borderline*

    My original plan had been to cross the Golden Gate and continue north, but the incoming gale changed all that, hurrying me on my way with a prodigious tailwind. Driving through the city, I crossed the Bay Bridge and continued east, watching the coast range rise up and fall away behind me. Somewhere in the middle of the inter-mountain desert I spent another fitful night in the car, and the next morning, awaking to the same high winds and dismal sense of failed ambition, I thought to get out of the path of the storm by heading north, up through Idaho, across the Divide, and into western Montana. But the winds of change found me out even there, sweeping me down the eastern slope of the Rockies and onto the northern plains. Forty-eight hours later, four days since I'd watched it blow in at San Francisco, the gale continued unabated, blasting the car with such force along a stretch of highway south of Chicago that I nearly ended up in a ditch. Another day's travel took me across Michigan and southern Ontario, back to the island.

    By this time, night had long since fallen, and I drove the final stretch in a road-weary trance, down the island road, past the golf course of the Thousand Islands Club, across the narrow wooden bridge that spanned an abandoned cross-island canal, and onto the gravel leading to the lesser of the two cottages that comprised the family's summer home. Finding the place much as I had left it eight months earlier, I went inside, fell upon the winterized bed, and was instantly asleep.

# Chapter 14

# Asylum in Academe

The morning after my return from California, I awoke to find the sun well up and shining brightly through the windows of what family members, with appropriate lack of pretense, had always referred to as the Little House: a one-story, flat-roofed, and singularly unadorned cabin a short distance from the main cottage. Ever since leaving the missile base five days earlier, I'd been struggling to understand why, at the first signs that spring was returning to the north country, I had abandoned my western tour and started back across the continent.

The answer, it seemed, could only be found in the mythic environs of the River, and for me the cabin was its epicenter. Built under somewhat mysterious familial circumstances some years after the completion of the main house, the place had always held the most pleasant associations for me. Out the front door, a patch of lawn sloped down to the water's edge, where a brief stretch of sandy beach was flanked on one side by a granite outcropping and on the other by a stand of cattails. On the opposite shore Hill Island, Ontario, enclosed one end of a closely confined bay known as the Lake of the Isles, while out the back door, a broad pasture was bordered by deep woodland on one side and river shore on the other. Originally part of a working farm, the pasture had once been populated by a small herd of dairy cows, and I remember getting my first lesson in animal husbandry at age seven when, after idly pelting individual members of the herd with the fruit of a nearby apple tree, I was summarily chased up into its branches by an angry bossy who wouldn't let me down for the next half-hour.

Later, the dairy operation was replaced by a riding stable, where I was a regular visitor as a pre-teen. The main barn was only a quarter mile from our place, and after taking me on a number of trail rides, the young woman in charge allowed me to ride on my own, a rare privilege for a fifth-grader. Roaming freely about the nearby woods and fields, I made a point of stopping by the main cottage, where I tied my mount to a tree in the yard and went inside for something to drink, just like a cowboy.

The novelty of such experiences was such that I soon became a nuisance around the farm, and, if only to be rid of me, my erstwhile instructor let me take one of the older, less active horses out for some exercise at no charge. Granted, I practically had to flog the animal to get it to move faster than a walk, but riding was riding, and nobody could accuse me of failing to take my new duties seriously. Indeed, one day while preparing for another outing, I was patting the ancient beast's flank through a corral fence, when it suddenly stiffened, tottered slightly, then fell over heavily on its side. Upon closer inspection, it was stone dead, and while I tried not to take it personally, I couldn't help thinking that it had given up the ghost at the prospect of another of my enthusiastic exercise routines.

Then too, there were all manner of water-borne adventures to embark on in a wide assortment of vessels. The first boat I was allowed to paddle on my own was a double-ended, canvas-covered, flat-bottomed, and manifestly unseaworthy craft that floated me on my first tentative forays in the immediate vicinity of our boathouse. Eventually growing big enough to handle oars, I graduated to a sturdy rowing skiff of indigenous design, in which I ventured across the river and along the nearby shores.

Among the several power boats that had, over time, come into the family's possession was an early metal-hulled craft with a one-cylinder, inboard power plant scarcely more advanced, it seemed, than a steam engine. Variously known as the Tin Boat, the Putt-Putt, and the One-Lung, the vessel proved so unreliable that it scarcely ever left the dock, and one day my father decided to put it out of his misery by towing it out to the Canadian channel and sinking it. Inviting myself along for the ride, I climbed aboard our 22-foot Chris

Craft and we were soon on our way, the condemned hulk plowing along behind us under tow, veering precariously from side to side as if attempting to escape its fate. When we arrived at a suitably deep spot, my father wrestled it alongside and climbed aboard while I watched from the safety of the towing vessel, a bit frightened at the prospect of the impending burial-at-sea.

After removing various intake hoses and drain plugs, my father got back into the Chris Craft and together we watched as water rushed into the hull. Despite a long history of incessant leaking that regularly saw it awash to its gunwales, however, the old hulk refused to go down. Instead, it rolled over like a dead fish and clung to the surface, posing a serious hazard to navigation. Armed with a crowbar, my father eventually succeeded in punching several holes through the hull, and to a prolonged hiss of escaping air The Tin Boat slowly disappeared into the murky darkness, sinking down and down, into the depths of memory.

At age eleven, I was allowed to operate on my own a thirteen-foot Lyman outboard with an eighteen-horse engine, earning the privilege by swimming across the river immediately in front of our point and passing a written test. Thus checked-out and certified, I exercised my new privilege with a vengeance, embarking on excursions that took me as many as five miles upriver and down, a radius within which lay every sort of riverscape imaginable, from busy shipping channels to shallow inlets; from wide, backwater bays to narrow passages through which the current rushed in standing waves. Taken together, such settings represented a world unto itself. When locals referred to the River, they didn't mean the whole of the St. Lawrence, only that part of it containing the Islands—another local alias. While these names were not generic in reference, neither did they indicate a distinct archipelago or body of water. Instead, they represented mutually agreed-upon abstractions in which geography, history and memory combined to signify a place as inherently mysterious as the stream of time itself.

Beyond its fame as a summer resort, however, the place was an employment desert, presenting an all-but-insurmountable barrier to year-round habitation and leaving me right back where I'd started the previous fall. With another five weeks to go before the official start of the season, the summer people had yet to arrive in force, leaving me with nothing much to do except contemplate the familiar subject of my uncertain future. So it was that, at the end of a two-week hiatus in which the specter of another stint as a lifeguard haunted my sleep, I packed up my things once again, lashed the glider to the car, and set out to find a year-round community in which to anchor myself.

For some reason I thought to begin this search in Vermont (the long ridges of the Green Mountains seemed so eminently soarable), and thus, skirting south of the Adirondacks, I drove east, crossing the state line near Glens Falls and arriving in the town of Rutland. Its name notwithstanding, the place had seemed auspicious enough, nestled as it was between rich farmland and a major ski resort at Killington. On the dreary, rain-soaked evening of my arrival, however, its charms were nowhere to be found, and that night—spent in a cheap, roadside motel—would be among the bleakest in my memory. After leading me across the country and back, the road seemed to have run out of fresh horizons.

The next morning brought cloudless skies and the first real warmth of the season, and, restored to hope, I set out once more, heading north with the semblance of a plan. At some point during my western tour, I had learned of a summer graduate school in English at a college along my route, and, with nothing but hearsay to go on, I resolved to find out more. Making my way to the school's main admissions office, I was directed to another stately limestone edifice, where I was soon in the presence of a genial professor-type who explained the program and went on to describe the school's secluded, mountain campus some twenty minutes away. When I continued to show an interest, he proceeded to the matter of admission requirements and costs, and encouraged me to apply for a place in the upcoming session.

It remained for me to send transcripts and personal evaluations, but chance alone seemed my chief recommendation, and, laden with a packet of brochures and introductory materials, I left the office feeling all but assured of a place. Driving through the center of town, I took a new, proprietary interest in things, and, parking on the main street, got out to walk around, eventually entering a small pub, where I sat at the bar, ordered a sandwich, and chatted up the bartender.

"Pretty quiet this time of year," I offered.

"Yeah, the lull only lasts a couple of weeks, though. When the foreign language schools start up, the place will be humming again."

"What do you know about the school of English up in the mountains?"

"Not much. It's a ways out of town, so we don't see much of that crowd in here. You planning to attend?"

"Thinking about it. Ever been up there?"

"Sure. It's just this side of the ski area."

"Really?" I said, perking up at the prospect of finding a new flying site. "What's that like?"

"Nice spot. Interesting terrain, a dozen or so trails."

"And it's just up the road from the school?"

"Yep. Just the other side of the ridge. Can't miss it."

After lunch I got started, traveling south several miles before turning east to follow the course of a lively stream up through dense, hardwood forest. Soon the woods gave way to a series of open fields, where a well-kept Victorian inn was surrounded by several dormitories, an assortment of cottages, and a large barn. Formerly the site of an equestrian resort, the place had the blissfully bucolic appearance of a Hudson River School landscape, and if this were not enough, the campus' broad meadows were dominated by a towering ridge that faced due west, into the prevailing breeze. Interesting terrain indeed.

Following a brief tour of the grounds, I returned to the highway and continued uphill over the crest of the ridge and down the other side. There, as promised, was the ski area, and, pulling into the empty parking lot, I got out to hike along the nearest route to the summit. It was a nice spot alright, but with no trails offering a western exposure and nothing in the way of a landing area, its potential for gliding purposes was negligible. Still, the ridge itself was promising, and with a bit of bushwhacking I was likely to uncover a take-off site overlooking the campus. Thus encouraged, I started back downhill transformed. After months of transience, it seemed I'd found a refuge of sorts, and the promise of a future. The road hadn't let me down after all.

Feeling much restored, I reverted to familiar habits, setting out on another quest for the ultimate flight. Retracing my route of earlier that morning, I returned to Rutland (not such a bad place, after all) and crossed back into New York State. Continuing south along the Hudson, then west into the Catskills, I arrived at last in Ellenville, home to a number of spa resorts and one of the best hang-gliding spots in the East. Arriving about mid-afternoon, I found my way to the site by scanning the sky, where a dozen or more gliders could be seen soaring above a prominent ridge. After checking out the take-off area, I returned to the village, where I took a room in a likely-looking motel and prepared to make a fresh start in the morning.

Earlier in the day, in the vicinity of Albany, the thought occurred to me to get in touch with my friend Sandy, who, the last I knew, was attending the state university. Now hoping to embark on my own grad-school career, I was eager to hear about her experience and see how she was doing. Though I hadn't been in touch since my departure the previous fall, I still had her number, and later that evening I called her from the motel room. In the course of a lively conversation, we quickly brought each other up to date and I was pleased to learn that she was free and willing to drive down and join me the next afternoon. My return to the road seemed to have turned a corner, and with ever-brightening prospects for the future, I looked forward to our reunion.

The next day brought unflyable conditions, however, and I spent much of the day killing time until Sandy's arrival. She showed up at the motel around dusk, and we renewed our acquaintance over dinner in a nearby restaurant. It was good to see her again, and between her grad-school experience and my western adventures we had no shortage of things to talk about. Over the course of the evening, we caught up with each other and then some, and the next morning over breakfast we made plans to spend the rest of the weekend together at her place in Albany.

Meanwhile, there was flying to be had, though for once it seemed something of an afterthought. Indeed, while I had hoped to get an early start, by the time we had finished breakfast and made our way up to the flying site, it was mid-morning and cumulus clouds had already begun to form above the ridge. Many pilots were already soaring high over the valley, while others were scrambling to set up and launch before the thermals in front of the ridge became too unstable to allow for a steady ascent into the smoother air above. Late for the sky and finding the turnout beneath the primary take-off already littered with cars in the process of unloading, I turned around and drove back down the highway several hundred yards to another overlook, where a lesser launch site appeared along the side of the road just outside a section of guard rails. Difficult enough for those launching from the upper platform, catching a thermal from this take-off was going to be a long shot, but given the crowded circumstances, was likely my best chance.

Racing to assemble the glider in anticipation of what I hoped would be some extended soaring, I gave Sandy directions on how to get to the landing field and asked for her help in maneuvering the airframe over the guard rails and onto a narrow ledge, where she steadied it against a series of downdrafts. When a fresh breeze began to cycle uphill, I jumped out into the rising air and began a steady ascent across the face of the ridge. Soon I was level with the upper launch site and anticipating a steady elevator ride to the top of the lift. Just when I thought to be home free, however, the bottom fell out and I started sinking. Turning for another pass in front of the steepest part of the ridge, I awaited another upwelling pocket of air, but the thermals had by now become overdeveloped, forcing me to drop out while I still had sufficient altitude to reach the landing field.

And that wasn't the worst of it. While on short final across a plowed field, I was summarily driven to earth by a violent downdraft. Coming to rest full-length in the dirt, I picked myself up and took stock. Though the crash had been cushioned by the freshly-turned soil, upon extracting myself from the harness I discovered that one of the glider's wing-tubes had been deformed by the impact. Now, rather than staying aloft for a leisurely flight as I had hoped, I would be unable to fly at all until such time as I could make the repair.

Meanwhile, having watched my abortive flight, Sandy drove down to the landing field, where I was dismantling the glider in a less than sunny mood. I explained what had happened, and was disappointed, to be sure, but not upset, not angry. How could I be angry? Okay, maybe I was a little angry, but not with her. I just happened to be angry, and she just happened to be there. The truth is, I was angry at the persistent aimlessness of my existence. I couldn't explain it, really, least of all to her, but somehow the incident made me realize how desperate I had become, knocking around from place to place, engaged in an idle pastime to the exclusion of more seemly or respectable pursuits. In some unaccountable way, she seemed to have come between me and my flying habit, and like any hopeless addict, I instinctively rushed to the defense of my diversion of choice, locking out all who threatened to reveal its power over me. In what way, precisely, she represented such a threat, I couldn't say; her presence, it seemed, was enough.

The whole thing was perfectly ridiculous. Having asked for her help me with a difficult launch, and having nearly made good on the attempt, I now found myself stuck in a churlish mood. There was nothing obvious about it, however, nothing you could call openly rude or disparaging. Instead, in a thousand subtle ways over the course of the ensuing afternoon and for the rest of the weekend—spent, awkwardly enough, in her apartment in Albany—I managed to sabotage our rediscovered friendship, making her feel every bit as miserable as I did. In truth, I suspect she understood well enough what I was about and was sufficiently bewildered by my self-destructive mood to let events run their course.

The next morning, I cheered up a bit, trying to put a good face on things, and we got around to saying goodbye. Once the session started in Vermont, I would only be an hour and a half away, but we refrained from talking about getting together again, both recognizing that it wasn't going to happen.

Some three weeks later, having duly applied and been accepted to the grad program, I arrived back at the school's bucolic campus. Receiving my room assignment, I moved in, getting my first look at what the introductory materials had indicated were no-frills dormitory accommodations: bare, wooden floors, uninsulated walls, a metal-framed single bed, spindly wooden desk and chair, and a reading light. According to school policy, there were to be no TVs, no stereos, and—apart from electric typewriters—no appliances of any kind.

Having spent much of the previous year living mostly out of my car, the austerity of the place was not of great concern to me. It was one thing to do without the comforts of modern life on one's own, however; what such privation might mean in a larger social setting wasn't clear. And when, in an opening lecture riddled with arcane literary allusions, the director celebrated the cloistered, monk-like atmosphere of the remote campus, giving heavy emphasis to the rigors of the course work and the glories of the school's rich intellectual life, I began to suspect that fate had played a cruel trick in steering me thither. For a moment, I contemplated a discreet exit, but in the end I stayed. It seemed the responsible thing to do, and I wasn't exactly flush with likely alternatives.

As it happened, the course work would prove less formidable than the various social adjustments I would make over the ensuing weeks. While the majority of my fellow students were teachers of English at various private schools, there were inevitably those of us whose reasons for pursuing an advanced degree in the subject were not immediately apparent, having to do, it seemed, with the idiosyncrasies of the literary soul. It seemed that, in addition to myself, the school had its fair share of eccentrics.

Take my roommate, for example: a rangy fellow whose two passions were opera and mountaineering. I first became aware of the former interest early one morning soon after the start of the session, when, upon hearing the sound of distant singing, I went to the window to see someone strolling across the broad, open fields of the campus giving voice to an obscure Italian lyric in a booming tenor that pervaded the misty morning air. Dismissing the far-off figure as, well... a bit of a showboat, I returned to my reading only to hear the singing grow louder and louder until, with something like horror, I recognized the voice and realized that its owner was making his way to my very room. Even so, I was prepared to befriend him, and when in the course of conversation, I learned of his enthusiasm for mountain-climbing, I thought to have found a substantial basis for comradeship. When I made bold to speak of my own mountain-related experiences, however, he responded with a patronizing sort of tolerance, implying that mine was a second-rate sort of sport, unworthy of a true alpinist. Thus ended all but the most cursory dialogue between us.

Shortly thereafter, I got to know my neighbor from across the hall, name of O'Malley, whose loud, thick-tongued singing awakened me from a deep sleep late one night about a week into the session. It seemed that certain of his ancestors had worked on the railroads, and with fierce Irish pride he had begun working his way through a litany of old railroad chanties, thunderously thumping his feet in time to his raucous vocalizations. This went on for some ten minutes, at which point, wearing only a pair of boxer shorts, I knocked briefly and made entry into his room, where I found O'Malley lying on his bed, propped upon his elbows in a posture of hideous drunkenness, while two women and another fellow, all well in their cups, sat listening along the opposite wall. With a look of bleary-eyed incredulity, I stood looking from singer to audience.

"I'm trying to sleep," I ventured at last.

"Then sleep!" bellowed O'Malley, as if the matter were no concern of his.

"I can't. You're keeping me up."

"Why, I wouldn't dream of coming between you and your slumbers, my good man. Go—and may flights of angels sing you to your rest."

"As long as you stop your caterwauling."

At this point, the conversation threatened to devolve into a series of maledictions, whereupon O'Malley invited me to take my complaint to the director of the school, the implication being that he had some sort of favored status with the latter and would inevitably be exonerated. For several moments I stood trying to imagine what sort of crazy accommodation he might be referring to, and, shaking my head in disgust, I left.

The singing did in fact stop, but not my bewilderment at his assumption of some sort of privileged status. What was with these people? Between Italian opera and Irish railroad chanties I was like to be driven mad, and again I wondered if I had made a grievous mistake in signing up for the program.

The next day, upon returning to the dormitory from an early class, I found O'Malley shuffling groggily down the hall in his bathrobe, having just rolled out of bed and on his way to the shower.

"What, up so early?" I gibed in my most stentorian and obnoxious voice. "Why, it's scarcely noon!"

To this he responded with a pained expression that seemed to pass with him for a *mea culpa*, and when I recalled for him his challenge of the night before, his face dissolved in a fit of horrible giggling. Clearly his claim to some special clout had been a ruse; even so, I never quite shook the feeling of being an outsider in a world of secret and unfathomable considerations.

In other respects, there was a certain timelessness about the place. With two courses to complete in six weeks, each involving at least half a dozen books, the days passed in a steady round of lectures, mealtimes, and reading, reading, reading, with oral and written responses required on an ad hoc basis. It was work, to be sure, but a more genteel and engaging sort of regimen would be difficult to imagine. After all, the subject of study was itself a form of entertainment, and it seemed a surprisingly short step into the pre-electronic past, when reading played a more prominent role in leisure-time pursuits. Then too, the weekly regimen was not completely without diversions. Movie showings in the barn every Friday and Saturday evening featured an eclectic selection of arthouse and foreign films and were always well-attended, representing the school's sole concession to modern diversions. Other than this, a small pub lay down the hill in the parlor of an inn, but that was about it. Other options lay a world away down in the valley.

Among the more memorable titles I read that summer was Melville's *Typee*, an account of his daring escape from the tyranny of a whaling ship in the South Seas and subsequent capture by a tribe of Polynesians. Great stuff it was, all about his discovery of strange, aboriginal customs (including a scandalous hint of cannibalism) and his intriguing dalliance with a dark-eyed native gal named Fayaway. He wrote it all up with due regard for the moral standards of the day, but it was pretty clear that he'd had a good time while the opportunity offered, smoking the islanders' version of pot and getting more than friendly with the nubile Fayaway. In the end, he breaks free of his captors and is rescued by a passing warship, but his brief stay in paradise leaves him less than enthusiastic about getting back to civilization, which helps explain the gloom and doom of his later books.

Another literary corker was Flaubert's *Sentimental Education*, in which a college graduate named Frédéric falls in love with an older woman and squanders his youth pining away for her. The trouble is, the woman is happily married and doesn't seem to know he's alive, despite the fact that he spends a lot of time moping around in her presence, fondling her shoes and things like that. The situation goes from bad to worse, and by the time he's prepared to confess his feelings, the object of his desire has grown long in the tooth and he loses interest. By which time, coincidentally, the reader has concluded that Fred is not the noble lover and artist he makes himself out to be, but a pretentious fop with an insufferably egocentric attitude. This, of course, is the whole point, and once you get onto it the book makes a lot more sense. In the end, despite all his sorry attributes as a hero, you have to admire the brutal honesty with which he is portrayed.

    I enjoyed these books. They were good reads, and interesting to write about, yet I had to wonder what earthly good the whole experience was doing me. From the uncertainties of the recent past, the school provided an asylum of sorts and the chance to rediscover something of the unfledged enthusiasms of my undergraduate days, but meanwhile, back in reality, my old predicament awaited me. The end of the session brought a return to the same unsettled circumstances I had faced at its outset, and having yet to find a suitable job or even a likely place to look for one, I was facing another stint on the road.

    So it was that, with updated resume in hand, I set out to reassert my claim upon the noble profession of journalism. A wiser, more disciplined candidate might have begun by researching the job market, isolating likely prospects, and arranging interviews. But accustomed as I was to seeing my future through the windshield of a car hurtling down the highway, such an approach seemed far too abstract and time-consuming. Instead, taking the business of a job search literally, I got into my car and went looking for a likely opening as if it were an item on a scavenger hunt. Still focused on Vermont, I sought out newspaper offices from one end of the state to the other, but the response in each case was polite appreciation for my interest followed by the announcement that no positions were available. My resume would of course be kept on file in the event of an opening, the chances of which were virtually nil.

    At this point, I was officially out of ideas, and, having given my rural route P.O. box number on the island as a permanent address, I headed north from Burlington along the familiar route leading to the to the River. Somewhere east of Ogdensburg, while brooding about my general aimlessness, I happened upon the scene of a minor traffic accident: a couple of cars were pulled over on the shoulder with a state trooper gesturing to the passing traffic to slow down. Indeed, the officer appeared to be especially insistent in my case, but having dutifully reduced my speed I kept going, unaware of any reason for him to stop me. A few miles later, however, I looked in the rearview to see a patrol car bearing down on me, its lights flashing, and with a deeply disgruntled, what-next attitude, I pulled onto the shoulder and came to a stop.

Normally, it was my habit to respond to such situations with a pleasant and tractable manner, a practice that had always served me well during encounters with the Law. On the present occasion, however, feeling badly used by fate and indignant into the bargain, I rolled down the window and waited peevishly with license and registration at the ready. Whatever my offense, I reasoned, he could scarcely make me feel any worse than I already did. In this I would be mistaken.

"Didn't you see me wave you over back there?" began the uniform, clearly angry at having been obliged to give chase.

"No," I responded flatly, "I thought you just wanted me to slow down."

"Did you know your vehicle inspection has expired?"

Directing my gaze to the windshield sticker, I noted that it was three months overdue, and, returning his gaze, replied curtly, "Nope, wasn't aware of it"

Three months. At any other time, I might easily have talked my way out of it. Instead, I simply stared at him.

"What are you hauling here?" he asked with more than idle curiosity.

"It's a hang-glider."

"Uh-huh. Mind showing me what's in the glove compartment?"

"Not at all." Tossing my collection of roadmaps onto the passenger seat, I quickly emptied the contents.

"Alright," he muttered, "wait here."

Making a quick inspection of the vehicle and its cargo, he went back to the patrol car to write me up while I waited with growing frustration. During the course of my recent cross-country tour, despite a number of encounters with local constabulary, I hadn't received a single ticket. Now, within an hour of home, I get nabbed for a delinquent sticker. Perfect.

"Okay, so you don't forget," he said upon his return, "I've got a ticket here to help you remember. You've got another ten days—either get it inspected or get it off the road."

With that, he returned to his car and drove off, leaving me to continue on my way with his final admonition echoing in my thoughts: get it off the road. Taking the expression both literally and obtusely, I wondered how it was possible to take a car off the road. Didn't the road lead everywhere a car might go? —It was time to rethink my options. For the past year, I had surrendered to the popular culture's fascination with the automobile, and, if nothing else, the experience had cured me of wanderlust for some time to come. Now, as I crested the span of the Thousand Islands Bridge to arrive back on the island, I began to contemplate the possibility of a carless existence.

# Chapter 15

# Going Off-Road

Taking up residence once again in the Little House upon my return from Vermont, I scared up a number of odd jobs and eventually found steady work on the island of old friends of the family—the same island, as it happened, from which I'd witnessed the passing of *Britannia* some ten years earlier. A regular visitor as a kid, I had fond memories of the place, not the least of its attractions being a large game room above the boathouse where we kids used to play shuffleboard and ping-pong while our parents sipped cocktails in the main house.

From the island's unique vantage point, we kids could watch as the massive freighters of the seaway negotiated one of the narrowest parts of the river, pivoting through a critical turn, and continuing on their way up or down the river. The spectacle became all the more engaging when the vessel happened to be of foreign origin, for as soon as the approaching ship's nationality was determined—in more obscure cases by reference to a large, bound copy of the shipping registry—we would race to find its appropriate ensign from a large collection in the boathouse, and send it up a nearby flagpole. Next, waiting for the ship to come abeam of the island, we delivered a series of ear-piercing blasts from an air horn, alerting it to our carefully choreographed display. The reward for all this activity would come in the form of a series of corresponding blasts from the ship, and, not infrequently, the cheers of crew members who appeared on deck, waving enthusiastically in return.

Indeed, at no time were such exchanges more enthusiastically given or received than on those rare occasions—the Cold War then at its height—when the ship happened to be Russian.

"It's a Russian! It's a Russian!" we kids would shout upon identifying it from a distance with the help of binoculars. Then, our arms flailing, we raced to prepare our tribute, convinced that the cause of world peace rested with us alone. Next, up the flagpole would go the lurid red banner with its strange insignia, the air horn would sound with special insistence, and moments later the passing ship would respond with such spontaneous cheering and salutation from the crew that we could scarcely imagine how they were perceived as our country's enemies. As it happened, in later years a Russian crewmember from one of these ships would attempt to defect by leaping into the river at a point very near the island, and I've often wondered if the incident was somehow inspired by one of our effusive receptions. If so, our youthful idealism would be betrayed, for the man was denied asylum and summarily returned to his homeland, a candidate, no doubt, for the gulag.

Now, with fall beginning to settle over the river and the summer population drifting away, I was back once more, revisiting the haunts of my younger days and glad to be engaged in the upkeep of a place dear to memory. Scarcely an acre in size, the island enjoyed the distinction of being man-made, the result of many barge-loads of fill and soil deposited on a series of prominent shoals. But for a stone wall running around its perimeter, the whole thing would readily have been swept away by the current, and, as it happened, the greater part of the job I undertook was to maintain this wall. With late-season water levels at their lowest, I towed a small raft to the head of the island, secured it in front of the damaged areas, and began laying in fresh mortar, adding new cobblestones, where needed, from a pile I had loaded onto the raft.

It was oddly satisfying and contemplative work, too. From my perch in front of the wall, I could look out across the river's main channel to the shores of the surrounding islands, where the hardwoods were slowly taking on their fall colors. Meanwhile, from the depths below, the swift currents of the channel sent spring-like surges welling up to the surface with all the ceaseless dynamism of memory itself. During such moments, I found myself thinking about my long yet inconstant attachment to the region, for it seemed I had been little more than one of the many tourists who gaped at the islands from the decks of passing excursion boats before returning to more hospitable climes as soon as the weather turned. Now, as the season advanced beyond the point at which I had always departed in the past, I began to experience a new attachment to the place, growing more proprietary about the islands even as they became more isolated.

Soon the many boats that had crowded the main channel in previous months would be laid up for the winter, and as I traveled back and forth to the work site it seemed the river was slowly becoming my private domain, if only by a kind of squatter's rights. By the time my work on Artificial Island was done, October had drawn to a close, and I found myself growing increasingly comfortable with an idea that at first had seemed unthinkable. Thus, by slow degrees I came to the decision to "winter over" in the Little House.

Considering the dwelling in question, the proposition could scarcely be taken lightly. Completely uninsulated, the cabin consisted of two-by-four framing with tongue-and-groove pine planks on the outside and beaverboard inside: a mere shell with a flat, single-layered roof and no basement, its foundation a simple concrete slab. For ventilation, ill-fitting, wood-framed windows opened horizontally (when the primitive tracks on which they slid were not jammed or obstructed) and on the wall facing the river, a large overhead door separated the main room from a screened-in porch. In warm weather this door had clear advantages, readily admitting the welcome breezes of summer, yet as a barrier against the chill of spring and fall—to say nothing of the winter winds that all too soon would begin sweeping down from the Canadian tundra—it was completely inadequate. For this as well as aesthetic reasons, the overhead door concept never quite caught on in domestic applications, and newcomers to the place were invariably heard to ask, "Was this once a garage?" Clearly, there was much work to be done if I hoped to survive in such a structure, let alone live in any degree of comfort.

My first concern was the roof; without insulation or the buffer of an attic space, any heat would readily dissipate through the thin planking and tarpaper, and apart from the inefficiency of such energy loss was the problem of snowmelt. So long as the interior of the cabin remained below freezing, the bulk of any snowfall would simply blow off in the wind, but heat escaping through the roof would inevitably melt any accumulation, creating a steady built-up of ice with the potential to bring the whole structure crashing down around my ears. To prevent this, I tore down the old beaverboard ceiling and installed bats of Styrofoam insulation between the joists, finishing all with sheetrock. With no dead-air space between the insulation and the roof boards, the solution was less than optimal, but it was better than nothing, and as an added precaution I fitted an upright six-by-six post between ceiling and floor at a central spot in the main room to provide additional support.

Next, I sealed the windows from the outside with clear plastic sheeting drawn tight to the frames, which was little help in the way of heat retention but at least kept the wind from blowing visibly against the curtains. The overhead door was another matter. As the track on which it was mounted lay on the outer wall, the best I could do was tack a sheet of heavy plastic along the inner threshold, the inadequacy of which became readily apparent whenever a strong north wind penetrated the many gaps in the door's extensive jamb, causing the plastic to balloon into the room. Responding to the ebb and flow of the air currents outside, my makeshift solution eventually took to bulging back and forth like a huge diaphragm, making the cabin seem alive with its own labored breathing.

Beyond such efforts at winterization, I was confronted with several equally pressing logistical considerations. The nearest paved road lay a quarter mile away on the other side of the island, and while state crews could be counted on to plow it on a regular basis, its relative remoteness from the cabin coupled with my recent disenchantment with the automobile convinced me to forego the use of my car altogether. For the time being, I scarcely needed it; my trips to and from the mainland for food and supplies were more easily accomplished by boat, but only by a roundabout route that would soon be rendered impassable by thick river ice.

Even in the dead of winter, however, the main shipping channel directly across the island from the cabin would remain mostly open, providing a crossing point to Alexandria Bay. When the time came, I planned to skid a canoe across the island and stash it in a secure place along the shore for just such a purpose. Meanwhile, possessed of a shotgun and fishing pole, I planned to augment my supply of animal protein from the river and surrounding woods. Fish were easy enough to catch, and in an effort to test my marksmanship I shot a squirrel and prepared it for dinner. The resulting meal was not exactly a gourmand's delight, however, and when the reek of parboiled rodent persisted about the cabin for several days, I decided to take fur-bearing game off the menu.

Then there was the question of how to occupy my time during the long periods of solitude. After a year of nearly continuous travel, the idea of staying in one place throughout a long, north country cold season presented an alarming sort of contrast, yet it was partly for this reason that I came to see the winter-long retreat as a challenge of epic proportions, which made me take the plan all the more tenaciously to heart. After all, I told myself, it was only a matter of twelve weeks, give or take. Twelve weeks—what sort of hardship could I not endure for a mere twelve weeks? So it was that, partly in response to a chance encounter with a state trooper, I prepared to take myself "off the road."

Meanwhile, a few unseasonably warm days remained, and one bright November afternoon I decided to go visiting via canoe. All day long the sun had been shining in a clear blue, windless sky, mimicking the balmy days of summer. (Water temperatures were another matter; already skim-ice was forming in the bays.) Crossing the narrow channel in front of the cabin, I arrived in front of the island of a long-time family friend who lived on the Canadian side. One of the few summer people still on the river, Janet was in her late fifties and would soon be leaving for her winter address in France. I found her puttering about her yard, enjoying the day's limited warmth, and when she invited me to join her on a short hike I readily agreed.

We followed a narrow path running along the spine of the island, eventually arriving on a rocky beach across the channel from the cabin. Here we stopped to bask in the receding rays of the afternoon sun, and were quietly contemplating our own thoughts when I heard an all-but-imperceptible call coming from somewhere upriver: a single syllable, muffled and indistinct, dying out even as it arose within the abiding stillness of air and water.

"Did you hear that?" I asked.

"No, what was it?"

"I'm not sure. Something. —A call."

For some time, we stood motionless, waiting, but all was silence, the air perfectly calm.

"Where did it come from?" she asked after a long, listening interval.

"I don't know… it sounded almost like a call for help."

"It might have been the geese," she suggested. "They've been flying over all day."

"Yes, I suppose."

At that time of year on the river, sounds were apt to travel great distances across the water, bouncing off islands and other obstacles until the source became hopelessly obscure and indistinct. Even so, a sense of some unknown urgency continued to nag at me.

"Maybe I should go check it out."

"If you really think so. I'm ready to head back anyway."

"Yeah, I'll make a swing along the shore over there, just in case, and stop by again on my way back across the channel."

"Yes, be sure to let me know."

Though I started back down the path with a purpose, it didn't occur to me to run, that someone might really be in trouble, and by the time I got back in the canoe the whole thing had begun to seem increasingly pointless. In the oblique rays of the afternoon sun, the river was a perfection of serenity, with no hint of trouble or alarm.

Paddling across a narrow inlet, I passed quietly down the shore of Hill Island, pausing between strokes to listen as the canoe slipped effortlessly over the mirror-like surface. There was only one cottage on that part of the island, and as I came within fifty feet of its boathouse, a shout suddenly issued from the interior, startling me.

"HAAALLLLL!" came a garbled cry from within one of the boat slips.

Despite the confirmation of my original suspicion, I was still somehow skeptical, and though now paddling with a will, I called back with a tentative and, in hindsight, maddeningly obtuse question: "—Are you calling for someone in particular?"

"Help, I've fallen in!" came the reply in a voice charged with frustration and growing weaker by the moment.

Rounding the corner of the nearest boat-slip, I peered inside to find a small Boston Whaler docked at the far end, and nothing more. For several seconds I was at a loss to know where the voice had come from. Then, as my eyes adjusted to the gloom of the dark interior, I made out a pair of hands and forearms clinging gamely to the Whaler's gunwale, and, upon closer inspection, a thin portion of a face barely breaking the surface of the water.

It was Jack.

Ever since I could remember, Jack had been the caretaker of the place across the river from ours, and though I didn't know him well, his longstanding reputation as a native riverman had always made him seem somehow familiar. A year-round islander from the Canadian side of the border, he knew that part of the river as well as anybody and wasn't shy about letting people know it. Though well on in years, he continued to look after the place, and now the frigid water had left his face drawn and colorless, making him look every day of his seventy-plus years. Hanging on for dear life, he'd been paralyzed by the cold.

"I'm coming! Hold on," I said, fully aware of the emergency at last.

Maneuvering the canoe into the slip, I clambered into the Whaler and, taking hold of the old man's wrists, began hoisting him upward. From the appearance of his drawn and sunken face, he seemed no more substantial than a scarecrow, yet the effort required to haul him out of the water quickly proved otherwise. Despite his age, he was hardly frail, and beneath the surface his six-foot frame was covered in several layers of water-logged clothing as well as a pair of heavy boots. To my surprise, I couldn't raise him more than a foot.

Compounding my dilemma, the Whaler had been outfitted with a metal railing extending some six inches above the gunwale, a safety feature clearly intended to prevent occupants from falling overboard. What the designers failed to consider, however, was that it presented an even more imposing obstacle for those who, having committed such a gaffe, might wish to come back aboard. Straining merely to hold the old man up, I found myself completely at a loss.

"Should've swum around to shore right off," commented Jack, weakly.

"It's all right. I'll get you out."

"Cold came on me too fast. —Couldn't move."

"Can you hang on here while I get a better hold?" I asked, bringing his hands up to the railing and thinking to grab him under the arms.

"Can't seem to..."

At this point his arms suddenly gave out, extending submissively while his head slumped over, cradling on a shoulder.

Now, barely able to keep his face above water, I started working my way aft, stepping over a thwart and various irregularities in the boat's flooring. At one point I slipped and fell heavily on a knee, cursing in pain and nearly letting go of my burden. As it was, Jack received a dunking, and came up sputtering miserably, his gaze far off.

"Let me go," he said, his resistance finally spent. "Just let me go, son."

"Don't start that!" I muttered irritably, if only to myself.

Continuing to work my way toward the transom, I got him to a point directly beside the engine, where I braced one foot against the top of the transom and with the leverage thus obtained, hauled his upper torso up and toward me, resting his weight on his chest and causing him to groan in pain. Next, reaching hand over hand along the back of his coat, I took a firm hold with both hands on his belt and heaved upward for all I was worth. And up he came, over the transom and directly on top of me, leaving us both sprawled on the floor amid an assortment of cushions and other gear.

He was out of the water, but hardly out of danger. Completely numb, his limbs utterly useless, he lay as still as a corpse, and as I attempted to sit him up on the floor, I feared he was about to become one. It was only a matter of time, for what little heat remained in his core was steadily draining away. Untying the Whaler, I started the engine and headed back across the channel, making straight for the small strip of beach in front of the cabin, where the boat was soon aground, and, hopping out, I pulled it firmly onto the sand.

So far, so good, but getting him out of the boat and up the shallow grade to the house was not going to be easy. Getting him out of the water had been one thing, but without the benefit of his buoyancy, I could scarcely budge him. First, I tried backing up to him and bringing his arms across my shoulders, but he remained so inflexible that I ended up falling back into his lap. Next, I tried grappling him about the waist and hoisting him onto a shoulder but succeeded only in tipping him over once more. Finally, I tried simply grabbing him about the chest and heaving him over the gunwale like a sack of concrete, but it was no use. Throughout these various maneuvers he remained mysteriously mute: a pale, seemingly bloodless Buddha for whom Nirvana was no doubt fast approaching.

Then, just when things seemed utterly hopeless, help arrived in the form of Janet and a female friend of hers who had stopped by her place soon after my departure. (It was to be a day of fortunate visits.) Growing concerned when I didn't return, they set out in the friend's outboard, cruising upriver and spotting me in the midst of what appeared to be a wrestling match on the beach.

"IT'S JACK," I shouted when they'd come within earshot. "HE'S BEEN IN THE WATER AND I CAN'T MOVE HIM!"

Landing nearby, they came on the run, and by dint of much pushing, pulling, guiding and carrying, the three of us eventually got him out of the boat and up to the cabin. Once inside, we steered him onto a chair directly in front of the wood stove, which, with the addition of an armful of kindling, was soon ablaze and pouring out heat. It remained only to rekindle the fire within him, and, stripping off his outer layers of clothing, we wrapped him in a number of dry towels. Before long, by dint of much rubbing, his limbs began to show signs of life in the form of violent shivering.

Next, putting a kettle on the kitchen stove, I made some tea, adding a large dollop of honey to the brew. After downing half a cup in short, convulsive sips, the old man uttered his first word since demanding that I let him drown.

"Whiskey!" he croaked hoarsely.

If only to cheer him up, I took a bottle of bourbon down from the shelf, and poured a single splash—a mere taste—into his tea.

By this time, twilight had begun to settle over the river, and leaving the women to attend to Jack, I went in search of the canoe I'd left drifting in the boathouse on the opposite shore. Re-crossing the channel in the Whaler, I found it floating quietly in the slip, and taking it in tow, soon had it back on the beach.

Meanwhile, Jack was doing much better, drinking his tea and describing the accident as his listeners responded with sympathetic concern. Soon, amid expressions of relief and gratitude for Jack's recovery, Janet and her friend got up and prepared to leave, anxious to get home before dark. Walking them to the door, I thanked them for their vigilance, and we all marveled at the good fortune of the day's events.

"Women," said Jack after they were gone, "...afraid of the dark. Hell, I've run this river at night more'n most people have by daylight."

He was recovering nicely, it seemed, though something in his voice was less than convincing. Clearly, he'd been badly shaken, and for several long moments he sat staring morosely into the fire, huddled weakly in a cocoon of towels.

"My wallet," he said suddenly. "Find it for me, will ya? There in my pants."

His clothes had been hung out in front of the fire to dry, and I found the wallet attached by a length of light chain to one of his belt loops.

"There's money inside. Spread it out there in front of the fire."

Opening the bill compartment, I discovered a thick, moist wad of Canadian currency, mostly tens and twenties, and began peeling off the bills one at a time. Soon they were spread out over a good portion of the floor in front of us, and Jack sat looking at them with the same distant gaze he had cast upon the fire.

"There's over five hundred dollars there," he said somberly. "If I can repay... ," he began, suddenly breaking down, his voice growing high-pitched with emotion.

It seemed the episode had been a blow to his pride as a riverman, and he was trying to buy it back.

"Don't be ridiculous," I said, dismissively. "You had an accident, that's all."

For a moment he looked chastened, then angry.

"Damn that old boathouse," he muttered in idle fury. "—And when the cold come on me there wasn't nothin' I could do. Don't know why I even bothered to call out. Wasn't a chance in a hundred anybody'd hear me."

"It was fate, I guess."

"Fate!" he barked in a voice full of scorn.

"How else could I have wound up in the right place at just the right time to hear you?"

"I don't know," he mused. "I saw the smoke from the chimney—figured somebody must be around."

"It was meant to be, I tell you."

"Now you're dreaming, son. —No, it was just a random thing, pure chance. That's the way the world is. One minute you're working—doing a job you've done a hundred times before—and the next. ..." With a slight wave of a hand he let the thought trail off.

"Well, you made it, anyway."

"That doesn't make any difference!" he insisted, sharply. "You gotta learn to look at things fair and square, not go putting 'em off on fate or anything else. There isn't any such thing as fate."

Recognizing that I wasn't going to be able to talk him into a better mood, I kept my mouth shut and he eventually calmed down.

"How long you planning to stay around?" he asked.

"Through the winter if I can."

"—By yourself?"

"'Fraid so," I laughed self-consciously.

"Do you have any idea what winters are like out here?"

"Not really."

"What are you going to do for a living?"

"I've got some work lined up. And some savings. Enough to get me through till spring."

"How about your water? —Aren't planning to keep the plumbing charged all winter with just this stove to heat the place, I hope."

"No. I figure I'll draw water from the river when the time comes."

"Alright, now listen. Once the ice sets in good, go out there and chop a hole about fifty feet from shore. Then get yourself a piece of plywood to set over it—with a frame and some hinges you could make yourself a trap door. The main thing is, as long as you keep the hole covered over, you'll have a permanent opening—won't have to chop ice again all winter. It's how I always did it."

"Sounds like a plan. I suppose I'll have to find another source for drinking, though."

"What for? Drink right out of the river! Once all the power boats aren't beatin' it to a froth anymore, the water'll be perfectly good. Besides, you're going to have enough to do without hauling drinking water. And don't go depending on fate or anyone else, 'cause there isn't going to be anybody out here. Get your head on straight about that. You'll just have to be careful, that's all."

With this the old man fell silent and the two of us sat looking into the fire.

"—You'll make out all right," he added at last.

"Think so?"

"Sure. You'll learn quick enough."

Later, his clothes having dried out, he started getting dressed, pulling on his shirt and pants and tucking his still-empty wallet into his back pocket. Meanwhile, having collected his money from the floor, I stood holding it out to him, but got no reaction. Affecting a preoccupation with the fit of his boots, he ignored me, and, folding the bills into a thick, compact wad, I stuffed it deep inside a pocket of his coat.

Soon he was all put together again and stood quietly in the middle of the cabin, nodding his head for a moment before abruptly starting for the door. Grabbing a flashlight, I followed him down to the beach.

By this time, full night had fallen, and the sky was clear and moonless. I waited for him to get into the Whaler, and, once he was aboard and settled, shoved the bow off the sand. Soon he had the engine started and, flipping a switch on the dashboard, he turned to watch the stern light flicker slightly and settle into a dim glow.

"See you around, Jack."

"Yep. See you around."

Soon he was on his way downriver, a solitary point of light slowly fading from sight within the surrounding darkness.

# Chapter 16

# North Country Narcosis

Shortly after Jack's close call, Janet left for her Paris apartment and the weather turned sharply colder, obliging me to shut off the water in the cabin lest the pipes freeze. This necessitated the construction of an outhouse, which I set about one chilly afternoon beneath lowering skies. Scavenging some lumber from a scrap pile, I knocked together a hut three feet square and outfitted it with a makeshift commode as well as a hatchway door that had formerly seen service on an old motor cruiser. Next, I started digging a septic pit in the woods adjoining the cabin, at one point looking up from my labors to see traces of snow drifting through the air. Racing to complete the job, I made the dirt fly in earnest, then ran back to the completed structure and carefully skidded it into place over the hole. By the time I was done, large flakes had filled the sky and were rapidly accumulating under foot as I fled for cover in the cabin. A month in advance of its onset as a calendar event, winter had arrived in the form of the first substantial snowstorm of the season.

For better or worse (the consensus of opinion inclines toward the latter), northern New York is famous for snow. Situated on the eastern margin of the Great Lakes Basin, the region lies immediately downwind of the largest volume of fresh water on Earth, and is subject to a meteorological phenomenon known as the "lake effect." In its purest form, this effect is not so much storm-related as it is a prevailing condition of the atmosphere, in which moisture-laden air cools as it rises over the Tug Hill Plateau. The resulting snow does not fall in the usual sense, but rather seems to materialize out of the air, swirling about in a thousand different directions, whipping up under eaves and overhangs, collecting in massive drifts, until the profusion of flakes seems to billow up from the ground itself as much as descend from above.

As a boy, I assumed that most everyone experienced winter in much the same way. Only later did I become aware that I was climate-impaired—that northern New York was well known to the rest of the world as a seasonal no-man's land. Even the elite soldiers of the fearless Tenth Mountain Division stationed at nearby Fort Drum considered the place tantamount to the Eastern Front during the Second World War. Another clue was to be found in the reaction of many newcomers to the area, who tended to respond to north country winters in the same way that dogs, tilting their heads in canine consternation, confront strange and unfathomable human behaviors. Why, they invariably asked, would anyone choose to live here? Such questions are not much appreciated by natives, of course, who tend to attribute strength of character as well as a number of fanciful health benefits to cold weather and regular snow-shoveling. Even local pride has its limits, however, and many otherwise well-adjusted local residents have been known to abandon the area with alacrity when given half a chance. Indeed, among those acquaintances I grew up with who subsequently moved south, the novelty of winters spent in balmy, snowless climes has never quite worn off, becoming a recurring theme of unseemly gloating suggestive of the abiding psychic trauma north country winters can inflict.

Snow and cold are not the only downsides of the area's climate, either; there's also its pervasive cloud cover to contend with. By late November the sky above the region typically becomes one vast, leaden arch, and for the next three months—the time it takes for the lakes to cool and freeze over—one can scarcely expect to glimpse the sun. The cumulative effect of such unremitting gloom is not easily reckoned, let alone endured. After several weeks, the desire to see blue sky becomes a kind of visceral craving based on one's sense of the fundamental benevolence and predictability of the natural world, and when such expectations are persistently thwarted, the results rarely contribute to a healthy outlook on life.

In my case, the relative normality of such seasonal deprivation no doubt insulated me to a degree from such ill effects. And yet, my experience of past winters had always been accompanied by the distractions of family, friends and school, whereas now, the arrival of the cloud coincided with long periods of profound isolation. With my car snowed in beyond all recovery, I found myself without any means of escape from my self-imposed exile apart from my own two feet, and before long the cloud came to seem the very substance of my solitude. Every morning, its featureless presence was there, and such was the uniformity of its gloom that all evidence of the sun's transit of the sky was lost, making the passage of time imperceptible. Going outside to engage in routine chores, I felt the presence of the cloud like a physical weight, an extra burden which, unlike the task before me, could not be put down or abandoned. Too soon the light of those brief afternoons grew dimmer, more diffuse, to be followed by the sudden descent of ever-lengthening nights, whose very darkness was smothered in cloud, starless, impenetrable.

In a few short weeks the cloud would change everything, turning the river itself dark and lifeless. Now as I went down to the shore on my daily rounds, its reflective surface no longer provided me with recourse to the happy associations of summer. Instead, the feeble, cloud-dimmed light was instantly absorbed into its depths and I was left to perform the purely mechanical function of drawing water. In went my bucket and out came a volume of water—not part of the River, just water.

Much of my growing anxiety during this period was related to a strange compulsion that had been inextricably bound up in my decision to winter over. It was a thing not to be spoken of, a desire whose promptings had been so subtle and gradual as to go unrecognized until it was beyond remedy; alas, I secretly longed to be a writer, an affliction that had first manifested itself during my abortive career as a journalist, a relatively innocuous and seemly outlet for such ambitions, and one which, had I stayed at it long enough, may well have cured the condition altogether. Now, however, my resistance weakened by solitude and a recent stint in academia, my muse began her siren's song in earnest. Like Ulysses bound to the mast, I strove to resist the haunting strains as best I could, trying to keep a grip on reality. But it was no use; I was a goner. And so, every morning after breakfast I sat at a makeshift desk I had fashioned from an irregular piece of plywood, and with standard Bic pen in hand and a series of legal pads before me, I wrote. Beneath the desk, secure in its plastic case, was my typewriter, a small electric model whose keys made revolting little spat, spat, spat sounds upon striking the paper—much too distracting for the delicate business of composition. I would use it only to prepare final drafts.

Very few of my efforts ever made it that far, however, the greater part failing to survive a humbling rereading the following day. Even so, I kept at it, struggling to assert meaning on the blank pages that awaited me each morning at my writing desk, and growing less and less sanguine about the results. Had I made allowance for the loftiness of such ambitions, transitioning to my aspirational profession might have been a bit easier, but as usual I had gone at the thing whole hog, trading my fixation with flying for a similarly reckless, do-or-die approach to writing, and in this context the moment of truth would last the whole winter long, with no relief beyond the daily chores by which I sustained myself. Indeed, the efforts of my morning hours soon spilled over into the rest of the day such that no sooner would I become engaged in purely physical tasks than the larger problem of the morning's work would obtrude, forcing me to convert each chore and ultimately every action into a kind of parable with some larger significance. A species of mental tic, such thinking eventually became reflexive, an unconscious effort to derive meaning from a thousand otherwise meaningless moments. So it was that, having in effect shifted my thinking into high gear, I couldn't seem to find neutral again, and the very ceaselessness of my thoughts became oppressive.

Once every two weeks or so, I journeyed to the mainland for groceries, first skiing to the other side of the island, where I had concealed a canoe along the shore, and then paddling across the main shipping channel to Alexandria Bay. Though the river's lesser channels were well on their way to freezing over by the middle of December, swift currents would keep the main channel ice-free for some time yet, allowing me to paddle as far as the town dock in the Bay. From there, I continued on foot to the local supermarket, where, mindful of the constraints of my budget and the need to carry all of my purchases on my back, I made a scrupulous selection of supplies and was soon started on the return trip.

While I was acquainted with a number of year-round residents in the village, I never thought to look them up or go visiting; inevitably they would want to know what I was up to, and the answer had become too involved and awkward to explain. Having thus avoided what few opportunities for human contact were available to me, I returned to the island feeling more isolated and freakishly alone than ever. And while exposure to new sights and surroundings offered a temporary respite from my obsessive imaginings, upon my return to the familiar scenes of the cabin and its environs, such thoughts came rushing back with a vengeance, as if to remind me of some hidden part of my nature that I could never disown. So it was that, one dark and oppressive evening, with snow falling thick and fast outside the cabin and a seemingly endless succession of grey days before me, I went over the edge.

I'd been reading in front of the stove, when all at once the words on the page before me became a blur and my heart started pounding in unaccountable panic. Though the cause of the attack remained unknown, it could scarcely have been more cataclysmic if the roof I'd taken the precaution to reinforce had indeed fallen upon my head. My brain seemed to shudder with apprehension, and for a moment I thought I was going to pass out. My face grew flushed, the blood forcing its way into my very eyes, until my entire field of vision was tinted red. It was as if two otherwise integral parts of my being had suddenly declared war on each other. One side, a violently angry one, had had quite enough of solitude, thank you very much, and wanted out, now, before the long weeks of isolation set in for good; while the other, more rational side—the side which had always been stronger and had the final say—continued to insist on staying put according to my original plan. So sudden and irreconcilable was the division between the two, that it seemed all but certain that I would go mad, and in the name of common decency drown myself at once in the river. After breaking out in a cold sweat, I regained a semblance of my normal equilibrium, yet I remained utterly shaken and for the rest of the evening my thoughts churned in a ceaseless effort to rationalize the cause of the fit. Eventually exhausted from the effort, I went to bed and succumbed gratefully to sleep.

If at any time during the interminable weeks that followed this initial attack I had been favored with an hour of sunshine or even a patch of blue sky, if I had been able to see the stars in a clear night sky, a boon granted even those who endure the winter-long darkness of the arctic, I might readily have restored myself to hope. And yet, it was not the absence of sunlight alone that threatened to unman me. No, it was the presence, rather, of a malevolent force intent on depriving me of all that was good in life. It was the cloud, I tell you, that cursed, diabolical cloud! Ever since its arrival, the world had been drained of color, the once-brilliant hues of autumn reduced to a few dull shades of ochre, then covered over with a featureless layer of white.

Above all, in concealing the larger cosmos, the cloud succeeded in taking from time itself all evidence of motion or progress, until each day, each hour, and ultimately every waking moment seemed to portend a lifetime of gloom and despair. That the sun was declining ever lower in the sky, I knew only too well from a strict accounting of daylight hours; that it would ever return again, however, was more than any clock or calendar could tell me. Was it really possible that I initially considered twelve weeks a mere interlude? Now every moment seemed to contain an eternity of dread.

Thus, the dwindling days of December bore me down to the bottom of the year, whose final week passed in one long, desperate bout of seasonal anxiety. Eventually becoming a creature of strict habit, I organized my life according to a deliberate plan that governed every waking moment. Clambering out of bed in the deep chill of the early morning, clad in an indispensable, double-layered union suit, I grabbed additional clothes and headed out to the main room, where the first order of business was to revive the fire with a fresh supply of wood from my drying box. Once the stove was crackling nicely and sending out a welcome wall of heat, I got dressed in its near proximity and moved into the kitchen to make breakfast: hot tea and banana pancakes (one of a few staple meals I adopted on the basis of cost, weight, nutrition, and personal preference—in that order). By the time the meal was prepared, the stove had pushed the cold half-way across the room and, moving back within the circle of warmth, I ate at a small table directly in front of the fire.

After breakfast I might spend twenty minutes or so skimming through such reading materials as I had collected about the place, after which I moved to my makeshift desk in the corner of the room. Tucked away in the hollows of the cinder blocks that supported the writing surface were my previous efforts, including the beginnings of a journal I eventually abandoned for lack of any note-worthy events to report (how many ways could one say it was cloudy and snowing?). Also tucked away were various correspondences from distant friends. In the absence of any other means of communication, I became a devoted letter-writer, savoring my return mail as the only tangible evidence of my connection to the outside world. Thus, throughout the morning hours I scribbled away at one thing or another, waiting for the muse to give shape to my inchoate longings.

By noon, I'd had enough, and, after a bite of lunch, I set about my daily chores. Venturing outside to the woodpile that lay covered with a tarp in the yard, I spent an hour or so cutting up logs with a chain saw, splitting the results with an axe, and carrying the stove wood inside to a drying box in a back room of the cabin. Next it was down to the river with a pair of buckets for water. Following Jack's advice, as soon as the ice became sufficiently strong, I chopped a hole some distance from shore and covered it with a trap door complete with hinges and a handle. The device worked as promised, and for much of the rest of the winter I was never obliged to chop more than a thin layer. More than this, the trap door provided me with a window on the river, and every day I peered through it as if to reassure myself that the warmer world of remembered summers was still available. Let the surface world be frozen over and buried in snow, I gloated insanely, let winter imprison everything in its terrible grip—I had a door through the ice!

After hauling water, I spent much of the remaining hours of daylight on skis, making regular trips to pick up mail or food or simply exploring my winter domain. My mail was delivered to a point a quarter mile from the cabin, where the island road came to an end at a series of mailboxes assigned to various summer cottages. Every day of postal service, I made my way to the spot by one of several routes, striding energetically along well-worn trails in hopes of receiving some communication from the outside world. More often than not the box would be empty, and the return trip would be accomplished with a heavier step, but when I drew back the small, galvanized door to find a letter, my mood soared, and on those rare occasions when two letters awaited me, I was suddenly transformed into an important personage whose ideas and opinions were much in demand. Skiing off with a will, I would retire to some secluded place to savor their contents.

Later, however, back in the cabin, the most difficult part of the day awaited me, for with the rapidly-fading light of evening I could feel the steady encroachment of the irrational fears associated with my panic attack. For much of the day, I managed to stay free of them, preoccupied by chores or simply distracted by my travels. But then, just when I thought to have shaken them, they would come creeping back into my mind like vermin from out of the woodwork, having waited for a moment of inactivity and mental stasis to renew their attack.

In order to stave them off, I was driven to read as much from anxiety as intellectual curiosity. I read everything I could find, from paperback thrillers to various historical tomes I had filched from my father's bookshelves in the main house. Gravitating toward the latter, I found it easier to lose myself in the great events of the past than making the effort required for more fanciful or esoteric narratives. As the evening wore on, however, I became increasingly aware of the need to make a smooth transition from reading to preparing my evening meal, allowing myself no idle moments in which the verminous thoughts might return. Moving into the kitchen, I clattered about amid the pots and pans, bustling around noisily as if to ward off their insidious encroachment.

Among the signs of my growing paranoia was an unaccountable insistence on locking all the doors of the cabin, as if anybody might be trying to get in. Also, having by now gone for long periods without seeing or speaking at any length with others, I began to grow increasingly apprehensive about those few encounters I could expect to have. While able to steel myself for occasional forays such as my weekly trips for groceries, the thought of spending extended periods of time in the company of other human beings nearly made me ill. Part of this apprehension stemmed from a growing conviction that the entire species was essentially depraved, yet it was not others I feared so much as myself. After such isolation, how would I behave when obliged to reenter society again? Such doubts eventually grew so pervasive that I found myself avoiding my reflection in the mirror, unwilling to confront any human image, including my own. Then one night with furtive self-consciousness, I took the mirrors down. It seemed the verminous thoughts were getting through, gnawing their way into my psyche.

No less tumultuous than my inner world was the one outside the cabin, for as it happened, that winter was an especially hard one. In late December and early January, three major blizzards arrived in rapid succession, each one dumping well over a foot of snow and knocking out power throughout the Northeast. It was one of those storm seasons that manages to win lasting fame on the basis of its sheer destructiveness, and for many years thereafter I would hear TV weather persons refer to the famous blizzards of 1977-78.

When the last one was over, I dug out and began exploring the world they had left in their wake. Already the surface of the snow reached halfway to the roof of the cabin and the shoveled area leading from the main door was suggestive of the small tunnel at the entrance to an igloo. Even walking the well-worn paths to the woodpile and down to the river meant slogging through knee-deep accumulations; step out of those paths and you were in over your waist. Meanwhile, the ski trails I had carefully laid down were repeatedly obliterated, with many fallen trees lying across the newly-buried roads leading to the other side of the island.

Shortly thereafter, with supplies running low, I set out on the long journey for groceries, first skiing across the island to where I had hidden the canoe. Nearly two weeks had passed since my last crossing, and in the meantime the river had frozen over considerably. Whereas previously I'd been able to paddle very nearly from one shore to the other, now some fifty yards of ice lay between the island and the open water of the channel. Digging the canoe out from under a deep drift, I tossed my backpack aboard and began pushing it ahead of me onto the ice, which became less reliable the farther I ventured from shore. To avoid breaking through at some isolated weak spot, I ended up straddling the canoe, using it to distribute my weight as I slid it a step at a time out toward open water. Arriving within several feet of the ice edge, I climbed aboard and used the paddle to shove my way across the remaining distance.

Soon I was safely afloat and paddling across the channel to the village, an experience rendered strange by the incongruous sights and sounds of the river in the middle of winter. How many times had I negotiated that channel when the wakes of all manner of boats had turned the surface into a fearsome chop of wave against wave, yet now the surface lay perfectly calm with not a boat or a soul to be seen. For some time, I sat drifting out in the middle, listening to the silence before continuing to the opposite shore. Here the ice floe was considerably thicker, and I was able to step from the canoe directly onto the frozen surface, pulling the craft up after me and skidding it all the way to the public dock, where force of habit led me to tie it nonsensically to a cleat.

Continuing on foot to the village supermarket, I wandered among the aisles of foodstuffs. By this time, I'd pared my grocery list down to bare essentials: a dozen cans of evaporated milk (I drank it straight from the tins), two pounds of butter (accept no substitutes), a half-pound of hamburger (more for flavoring than substance), three loaves of unsliced Italian bread (it keeps better that way), a box of pancake mix, a bunch of bananas, one large cylinder of oatmeal, two boxes of spaghetti, several cans of crushed tomatoes, two large onions, a couple of large rutabaga (at fifteen cents a pound I would acquire a taste for them), and a box of tea-bags.

Every now and then I caught a pike through my ice-door and made a large pot of fish chowder, but for the most part I was content with my staples. For twelve bucks, I could buy enough food to last about a week and a half, bringing my food expenses to little more than a dollar a day. However bland the fare, it was a diet that served me well, and apart from a diseased imagination I was never sick a day during the entire winter. Moreover, the very sameness of the menu became a source of reassurance far more important to me than the whims of my palate. After my selections had been made, I stood at the register and in response to the cashier's idle chatter found occasion to speak for the first time in weeks, my own voice seeming strangely unfamiliar.

Back on the snowy streets, I started for the docks feeling apprehensive about the return crossing. There was still the problem of regaining the opposite shore across the long stretch of thin ice, and I was anxious to get on with it. Placing my backpack in the middle of the boat, I dragged the canoe back out to the open water and slid it off the edge of the solid ice, stepping aboard as if launching from a dock. Conditions on the other side of the channel were not nearly so convenient, of course, and after crossing the open water I slid my backpack to the absolute stern and paddled hard for the edge of the ice, driving the unweighted bow as far as possible onto the floe. A first attempt succeeded in sending the canoe over the edge for perhaps a quarter of its length, but as soon as I tried to move forward, it slipped back down again. Reversing to give myself more room, I made a running start, paddling furiously up to and beyond the point of contact. Now the canoe stood nearly half out of the water, and with a last shove of the paddle I dove forward. For a moment there was an ominous cracking of ice as the canoe pivoted on the edge, then fell over on its bow as my weight made the difference, overbalancing the rest. Carefully working my way forward, I ice-paddled the hull further and was soon straddling the gunwales, shoving the canoe along beneath me all the way to shore.

Though precarious, the trip over and back had proven doable, giving me welcome assurance that neither ice nor thaw nor psychic dread could prevent me from escaping to the mainland. Though my car was now irretrievably buried, I was still mobile, still in touch with the rest of the world. Indeed, no sooner had I returned the canoe to its hiding place and put on my skis for the cross-island run, than I was surprised to discover a fellow islander digging his car out of the driveway of a small house near the resort where I had once worked as a busboy. Spotting me in return, he waved a greeting, and I skied over to say hello.

As it turned out, I knew him from my busboy days, when he and his family—English Canadians from Montreal—had been accustomed to spending part of their summers aboard a cruiser docked at the resort. Unfortunately, despite the fact that we were the same age and otherwise similarly inclined (he too was an avid water skier), we'd never been exactly friendly. His father, a regular patron of the resort with a lordly attitude toward the staff, had once gone so far as to order me about during a busy night in the dining room, an episode which so offended me that I was compelled to abandon altogether such service as I'd been providing. The incident had disposed me to mislike his son, Phil, who naturally returned the favor, and even now the dimly-remembered incident presented something of a barrier between us that required a careful, collaborative effort to dismantle. Having taken a job as manager of the resort, he was now my nearest neighbor, and in view of our mutual isolation, both of us were well disposed to let bygones be bygones. Indeed, when I prepared to continue on my way, he invited me to stop by of an evening for a drink, and I assured him I would.

Several days passed before I got around to acting on the invitation. With the light going down on another winter evening and a fresh squall of snow further darkening the western sky, I pulled on an old army ski parka (a garment I prized above all other articles of outer wear for its light weight and imperviousness to precipitation of all kinds), tucked a flashlight into its front pocket, and got started, following the tracks of my previous journeys across the fields behind the cabin and on through woods long familiar from my horseback riding days. Beyond the woods were more fields, across which lay a partially-buried barbed-wire fence, the exposed wire requiring me to pause briefly and side-step over. Having once reached the main island road, I followed it over a small wooden bridge spanning an old canal and continued on to the golf course of the Thousand Islands Club Resort. From there, I headed straight down the 18th fairway to Phil's house, where I was glad to see his lights on in the gathering dusk.

Arriving just as snowflakes were beginning to fill the air, I was ushered into my host's small living room, where he offered me a drink. As I had by this time sworn off alcohol, I asked if I might have some tea, whereupon he retired to the kitchen while I relaxed in a comfy chair and marveled at the modern conveniences of his snug winter abode. From the next room came the unfamiliar sound of tap water running in a sink, and down in the basement the dull hum of a furnace could be heard, dutifully pumping out heat at the turn of a thermostat. Compared to the cabin's perpetual chill, normal room temperature seemed nearly stifling.

In a moment he returned with my tea and a glass of Scotch for himself, and we started talking, somewhat haltingly at first, but with growing interest and animation, until there seemed to be no end of things worthy of discussion: the weather, the river, its history and something of our own. Under the circumstances, we were both starved of company and eager to remake an acquaintance that promised friendship. Thus, the time passed quickly, and some two hours later, not wanting to overstay my welcome, I prepared to head back. Meanwhile, however, the flurries that had only started falling upon my arrival had grown into a real storm and with the wind beginning to moan about the eaves and snow pelting the windows with an audible hiss, Phil invited me to stay for dinner in hopes of waiting out the worst of it. As I couldn't come up with a single, credible reason why I might need to get back to the cabin, I consented.

The evening thus graciously extended, we continued sharing stories, and by the time I got up to go it was after nine o'clock, at which point, peering out the window, Phil scoffed at the prospect of going outside.

"I can't even see as far as the driveway out there," he warned. "You better wait til morning. You can sleep on the couch."

"Nah, I'll be alright. I could find my way back blindfolded," I asserted, a boast I would soon be obliged to prove.

Reluctantly seeing me to the door, he invited me to stop by again whenever I liked, and I didn't doubt his sincerity. Whatever had led him to take such a lonely job (and I would discover his reason in time), the island seemed to be our mutual fate, and we could scarcely deny the solace of company of any kind under such isolated conditions.

Meanwhile, outside, the night was one mass of densely swirling flakes, and, stepping out into a howling gale, I put on my skis and started for home. By this time, my former track had long since been swept away, and after skiing a mere 25 yards, I turned to find the lights of Phil's house completely obliterated. Fortunately, the way home was very nearly straight into the wind, and as a point of reference the steady blast against my face became as invaluable as an airport beacon to a lost pilot. Out on the open fairway of the golf course the unimpeded force of the wind threatened to knock me off my feet, forcing me to lean far out over my skis, and after a long, half-conscious interval of plodding I ran into a tree. Suddenly it was just there, but the question was where was there? Which tree was it? Had I arrived at the end of the fairway, or was I off to one side? And if so which side? Though I knew that part of the island well, I had to admit that I didn't know it tree by tree. Close by was another tree, and another, then came an irregularity in the terrain—a large bump—and the snow underfoot was no longer as deep as before. I had found the main island road—or was it the loop leading back to the hotel? There was no way to be sure in all that swirling chaos.

Pushing on, I followed the snowy roadbed and eventually came upon the bridge; I had guessed right. Some fifty paces beyond, at a place where the road began to curve, I climbed over the snowbank and back into the deep drifts of the middle fields. To my right, the dark shadow of a nearby row of trees steered me part of the way across, but soon I was completely at sea, trudging along without any point of reference other than the wind. Then, stumbling upon some sort of obstruction, I fell headlong into the snow. It was the barbed wire fence. Catching me about the shins, it tumbled me forward, and I struggled to extract myself and get back on my feet.

Now completely disoriented but for the wind, I charged onward against the force of the blast, floundering across the field until I arrived at the edge of deep woods, where the wind-driven snow diminished and I found the horse trail leading through to the other side of the island. Once inside the protection of the trees, I rested, taking out my flashlight and shining it into the surrounding gloom. Continuing on, I passed through the woods to the edge of a broad open meadow and proceeding straight into the wind. Eventually stopping from simple fatigue, I looked up through the mass of wind-borne snow to detected a small, dim glow directly in front of me. It was the outer light of the cabin; I had skied to within thirty paces of the door.

Moments later I was inside, and stood reeling from the effects of the return journey. Feeling a certain rawness about my face, I was curious to see what kind of make-over the storm had wrought and, retrieving one of the mirrors I had previously put away, I had a look. Peering out of the opening of the parka's hood was a singularly frightening countenance covered by a layer of ice, creating an effect so bizarre that I began to laugh, at which point the ice-mask broke in pieces and fell away. Returning the mirror to its accustomed place on the wall, I took off my parka and began removing the snow that had collected on my clothing, eventually discovering a jagged tear in my pant leg. Upon closer inspection, the cloth was soaked with blood where the barbed wire fence had left a neat gash along my shinbone. In the cold I hadn't felt it, and the blood had quickly coagulated. Now it started to flow again, and I cheerfully cleaned and bandaged the wound, after which I put some more logs in the stove and set the draft for a slow burn. With the storm shrieking outside and small drifts of snow collecting along the interior of the windowsill, I went to bed. For once the dark thoughts that normally assailed me were nowhere to be found, and I fell readily asleep.

Two weeks later, once more in need of supplies, I made another trip to town, this time heading well downriver in hopes that the main channel would be frozen over. My earlier crossings by canoe had been made at one of the narrowest parts of the channel, where the swiftness of the current prevented ice from forming, but a mile downriver, off the head of Deer Island the channel was completely icebound. Skiing past the stone clubhouse of the Skull and Bones Society, the secret fraternity of Yale alumni, I reached a wide band of ice that stretched all the way to the mainland, and after casting a glance back along my track I started across.

By this time, I had grown familiar enough with the river ice that by pausing every few paces and jabbing it with a ski pole, I was quickly able to determine its thickness. The sound alone told much, the brief TUNK of a pole against solid ice being distinct from the queasy sort of KAH-WUNK to be heard when it began to grow dangerously thin and ping-y. Using this technique, I moved right along, eventually making my determinations on the fly. Kick, kick, TUNK—kick, kick, TUNK, and in this way made good time.

At a point a little more than halfway across, however, just when I was growing confident of a successful crossing, a disturbing new sound came to my ears: the frenzied, high-pitched barking of dogs. Looking up, I saw in the distance about a dozen of them making straight for me—farm dogs, mostly, accustomed to running deer in winter and otherwise reverting to the instinctual behavior of the pack. From the sound of their voices alone, I realized there would be no stopping them by word of command. By the time they got to me, they would be listening only to each other, and if they once knocked me down, I would be lucky to be left in one piece. The problem was that my hooded parka and backpack inevitably made me look like some strange amorphous beast, and the skis and poles didn't help matters.

Alone on the open ice, without easily recognizable tokens of humanness about me, I was just another animal they might kill for the sport of it.

I had only enough time to get out of my skis and shed the backpack before they closed in, at which point I held them off by swinging my poles first one way and then the other, causing the metal tips to make an ominous whistling sound. Brought up short, the lead dogs paused as the laggards came piling up behind them, each in its turn becoming confused by the sight and sound of the poles flashing by in quick succession. Even so, they kept looking for an opening, spreading out behind me such that one pole would not have been enough; they would have been on me before I could bring it around in a full circuit. Even with two, individual dogs took turns lunging in from different directions while the rest barked encouragement.

At some point I realized that I was yelling at the top of my lungs, an inarticulate bellow of protest and frustration, and only then did it occur to me to swipe off the hood of my parka so they might recognize me as human. At this, one dog after another seemed to come to its senses, and soon the barking quieted down. No longer the wild, moiling yap of the pack, the clamor broke into individual voices without the strident note of blood-lust. One by one, individual dogs reverted to being pets again and drifted off, back toward the village, and with the adrenalin passing out of my system, I got back into my skis and resumed my journey.

The incident stayed with me, however, and as I walked the aisles of the supermarket, I contrived to transform everyone I saw into the owners of those dogs. The careless bastards! This was a different sort of response than that of a few weeks earlier, when I had all but trembled at the thought of returning to human society. Now, instead of crippling self-doubt I was full of righteous anger. It was wonderful. I felt put-together again, and perfectly self-assured. As much as I resented them, those dogs had put the fight back in me.

Later, with supplies securely stowed in my backpack, I passed through the village and back across the ice-bridge to the head of Deer Island. Once safely across the channel, I started back upriver to the island, where all along the familiar trail from the mailboxes back to the cabin I sensed a change. Here was the same trail I had skied a hundred times, but suddenly everything appeared in a different light.

Overhead, the once solid layer of cloud had grown thinner and risen higher in the sky, and as I arrived in the open yard of the cabin, I could see a thin wedge of blue off to the southwest. After putting away my supplies, I ran back outside in time to see the sun descend into that narrow strip of blue and send its last rays streaming across the sky in a magnificent sunset. The everlasting cloud was finally clearing out.

Waking up shortly after sunrise the next morning, I scrambled out of the bedroom to find sunbeams pouring through the half-buried windows of the main room. Pulling on my clothes as I went, alternately hopping about on one foot while jamming the other into a boot, I lurched out the door, and there it was: Sunshine! Giver of life! Starlight with a purpose! It had been there all the time, of course, hidden behind that miserable, God-forsaken cloud, and now it filled the sky from one end to the other, glinting profusely from the surrounding drifts of snow. Tottering blindly about the yard, my face pointed skyward, I raced to intercept as many rays as possible as if to make up for the long weeks and months of waiting. Now the "lake effect" would work in reverse, and instead of generating a steady supply of water vapor, the ice-bound lakes would serve to stabilize the surrounding atmosphere, reinforcing the clear, high-pressure conditions of mid-winter.

For the space of some three weeks during the deepest cold spell of the season, much of the river's main channel was frozen over, and though large pools of open water remained on either side of the crossing point, I was able to ski into town in as little as half an hour. For once, my island hermitage seemed no more removed from the village than if I were living on one of its outer streets, yet by now my sense of isolation had become largely ingrained, and if not for the need to replenish my supplies I could scarcely imagine a reason to make the trip at all. Thus, I came and went much as I always had, the only difference being that whereas before I had remained aloof out of self-doubt, now my reserve found its source in a new willfulness. I was well on my way to becoming an irredeemable hermit, and if not for the occasional chats with my nearest neighbor, I might have lost all appreciation for human society.

Ever since the night of the blizzard, I made weekly visits to Phil's place, in the course of which we got to know each other quite well. At some point, I told him of my writing efforts, and in time he shared an even more personal secret of his own: the fact that he was suffering from kidney disease. The illness had overtaken him without warning several years earlier—a sudden failure of his renal system that sent him to the hospital and forced him to begin a bi-weekly regimen of dialysis. Eventually a transplant was performed in which his brother served as donor, and when this failed, his remaining kidney had started functioning once more. The recovery was not expected to last, however, and if and when the organ gave out again there would be little chance for a second transplant. I came to learn of this over time, for he spoke of it only rarely and always in the most casual way, as if it were happening to someone else. In any case, I continued to visit, he continued to welcome me, and our conversations seemed to do us both good.

Meanwhile, I continued my daily routine with the same dogged determination that had seen me through half the winter and would have to sustain me through the rest, working at my desk throughout the morning hours and then heading outdoors for wood, water, supplies and mail. With the return of regular weather patterns, my spirits improved considerably, but I was still pretty squirrelly and increasingly defensive of my territory. Few comings and goings within my snowy domain escaped my notice, and when, one sunny afternoon during an otherwise uneventful visit to the mailboxes, I discovered a pick-up truck and snowmobile trailer pulled over at the end of the plowed island road, and went over to investigate.

On the snow-covered road were two sets of footprints: the deliberate tread of a heavy-set man and those of a large dog. Nearby, a snowmobile track led down to the shore and out onto the ice. Following it across a narrow channel, I approached the foot of a prominent island, where I could see the snowmobile parked on the grounds of one of the area's more affluent summer estates. As I drew closer, the dog spotted me, and began barking loudly from the shoreline, whereupon a burly figure in snowmobile suit and pack boots appeared on the dock of a large boathouse and waved hello. Skiing over, I exchanged greetings with him, revealing an unaffected curiosity born of long months of solitude.

A caretaker who had come out to check on the place, he invited me to join him on a tour, and, stepping out of my skis, I climbed onto the dock, where we introduced ourselves and shook hands, at which point the dog became instantly friendly. After a quick look around the boathouse, we started up along the snowy path to the main dwelling, and were soon talking with the easy familiarity of old acquaintances, the surrounding desolate expanse of ice creating an immediate sense of comradeship.

 Situated on a broad shelf of rock connected to the island by a stone bridge, the place had formerly been owned by a family of considerable means, but was now the property of a company engaged in the manufacture of electrical components of some kind. Once inside, we made a brief tour of several well-appointed rooms in which the furniture had been carefully covered with sheets for the winter. Along one wall a large alcove overlooked a number of Canadian islands, while on the opposite side, a set of French doors led to a wide porch with panoramic views of the main shipping channel. Following along from one room to the next, I couldn't help comparing the grandeur of the place to the cramped austerity of the cabin, and had a hard time reconciling so extravagant a scene amid the otherwise familiar scenes of winter to which I'd become accustomed.

 Retiring at last to the kitchen, we sat at a table with bright sunlight flooding through the windows, and after disappearing down a stairway to the cellar, my host returned with two cans of beer.

 "I took the liberty," he said, handing me one.

 "Thanks, don't mind if I do." (The sun having returned; my recent bout of temperance suddenly seemed a rash and draconian measure.)

 "At least the beer didn't freeze, that's the important thing. I wasn't sure it would keep down there."

 "So, when will the company people start coming up?"

 "Not till June. The place is mainly used as a getaway for the weekends. They'll want to do some fishing, but mostly it's a place for socializing, entertaining business people and such. For a couple of months, I'm busy keeping the place stocked and running right—ferrying people over and taking them out on the river and such. But they treat me good, and I get plenty of time to do my own fishing and hunting in the spring and fall."

 "Sounds like a great deal."

 "Yeah, I don't kick much."

Just then the dog began whining outside, and when my host got up to open the door, it came bounding in with an abundance of energy, its tail wagging industriously.

"Sure is friendly," I said, "what's the breed?"

"She's a Chesapeake Retriever—named for the bay down south. They're terrific water dogs. Real good with kids, and they'll hunt all day long. This one loves nothing better than to come out here and run around on the ice."

"Ever worry about her going off somewhere and falling through?"

"Not with a female. If she goes through, she'll just hunker up over the edge and crawl back onto good ice. Now with a male it's different. Then you gotta worry, 'cause if a male goes through, chances are he won't be able to get out on his own."

"How so?"

"His pecker will get caught."

"Really?"

"Sure. You watch a male try to drag himself out, and he'll only get so far before he gets hung up."

"What a way to go," I lamented.

"Yeah, just shows ya how troublesome having a pecker can be."

"Amen," I said and, raising our cans in the sunlight, we drank (sarcastically, to be sure) to the long-suffering condition of maleness.

After finishing our beers, we headed back outside and, as he had chores to finish in the boathouse, I thanked him for his hospitality and started on my way. Soon I was skiing back across the ice, satisfied that my social skills with strangers remained reasonably intact despite very little practice.

Nevertheless, alone in the cabin once more, I found myself growing restless. Something about the image a dog stuck in the ice troubled me. What was I doing, holed up in arbitrary exile while the rest of the world was happily going about its business? And what was it going to be like when people started coming back, intruding upon my self-ordained solitude?

I would find out one cloudless, late-February afternoon when, while seated at my desk, I was surprised to hear the sound of voices immediately outside the cabin. Moments later, I opened the door to find an attractive young couple in their late twenties decked out in cross-country ski outfits. When I showed no immediate signs of recognition, the husband introduced himself, and I suddenly remembered him as a summer resident of one of the cottages toward the foot of the island, at which point I quickly invited them in.

"We were skiing by and saw the smoke from your chimney," he explained. "—Didn't want to sneak away without saying hello."

"I didn't recognize you at first with the beard. Good to see you, would you like some tea?"

"Sure, sounds like just the thing. We came out for the day to check on the cottage and do some skiing, and were surprised to find so many tracks."

"It's been my only means of transport ever since my car got snowed in. —So, how's everything at the cottage?"

"The place is in pretty good shape. I was worried about the boathouse with its flat roof, but I got it shoveled off alright. I've never seen so much snow."

"Yeah, it's been quite a winter," I admitted.

Soon, the tea was brewing, and I carried out mugs, spoons, sugar bowl and evaporated milk to the coffee table where they were seated in front of the stove.

"You must do a lot of skiing. It looks like a well-traveled trail down by us."

"I'm down that way every week-day for the mail and when I'm on the way to the Bay. I get onto the ice just past the end of the plowed road."

"You ski across the channel?" asked the husband.

"Have been for the past month, anyway."

"But, the ice... it can't be that strong. There are stretches of open water out there even now. We've seen 'em."

"You need to pick your spots, that's for sure. I've been crossing near the head of Deer Island with no problem."

"How do you know when it's good?"

"By the way it looks, and better still by the way it sounds. Good ice makes a certain sound when you tap it with your poles."

"So, what are the best trails for us," asked the wife.

"Would you like a tour?"

"Well, sure, if it's no trouble. We were thinking we'd head down toward the Lake of the Isles."

"No trouble at all."

Having finished our tea, we trundled out of the half-buried cabin into the bright afternoon, and were soon on our way across the back fields to the old farm. Continuing past the farmhouse, we followed a track through deep woods to one of the fairways of the golf course, then turned onto a trail leading to the top of a substantial cliff. Once on its crest, we stopped to rest at a place a high above the river with a long view to the west.

"There it is, the Lake of the Isles," I announced, making a proprietary gesture with a ski pole toward the icy expanse below.

"It looks so different in winter," the wife said, "—So empty."

"I know," responded the husband, giving her a hug. "It won't be long, though. Another couple of months and we'll have the boat in the water again."

Essentially a private conversation, the exchange had nothing to do with me, yet for some reason I found myself growing resentful, and stood trying to fathom the reason why.

"We should probably be heading back now," said the husband after a while.

"Yes," I agreed. "—It'll be faster if we go by ice."

Leading the way, I started down a section of trail leading to the base of the cliff and, turning off onto a narrow inlet at the bottom, stood waiting for them to come along. A spring ran out into the river at this point, leaving a soft spot in the ice, and while I waited, I jabbed at it with a pole, eventually breaking a hole through to the water below. Soon the others came along and stood nearby, wondering what I was doing.

"You see," I said, "the water's still there."

"But is the ice safe?" asked the wife.

"Absolutely. There's a spring just here, so we'll hug the shore for a bit, but you could run a herd of elephants out here this time of year."

Soon I was skiing again, kicking along through the lower outlet of the Lake and straight downriver. With the cabin in sight, I flew across the ice without so much as a backward glance, brooding inwardly as I went. —They would be coming back before long, all of them with their boats and dreams of summer. But where had they been during the solstice? Where had they been during the blizzards of January? Had they come visiting then, I would have forgiven them anything. But now, with the sun shining brightly in promise of the warm weather to come—who cared now? I was being perfectly churlish, but there was an element of self-preservation involved. After all, winter was not over yet, and as long as my solitude lasted, I needed to stay focused. Arriving back in the yard of the cabin, I started digging out logs from the woodpile, deliberately busying myself in order to avoid a formal leave-taking. No doubt recognizing this, my visitors kept to the shore-ice and, coming abreast of the cabin, called out their goodbyes from a distance. I stood staring at them for several moments, finally thrusting out my hand in a strange gesture comprised equally of farewell and defiance.

With the deep freeze of February giving way to the slow melt of March, I became aware of things I had otherwise taken for granted. By now the surface of the snow had become a kind of book whose subject matter was of the keenest interest to me. Each day as I skied about the woods and fields, I found signs of the wildlife that shared that small corner of the world with me; here the light-footed tracks of a fox crossing my ski tracks, there the wide smudge of a porcupine—the footprints all but obliterated by trailing quills—leading to the foot of a tall evergreen. And, sure enough, high in the branches was the prickly critter itself, rolled up in a ball and gone to sleep. More cryptic and dramatic were the signs of smaller rodents, their trails meandering across the snow to a point where a general depression and a few downy feathers marked an owl's kill, the sudden absence of footprints spelling out the fur-bearer's doom and a final parenthesis of wing-marks enclosing the scene (a brief aside in winter's story).

Beyond the evidence of animal life, there was a world of meaning in the snow itself. What an infinite variety of textures and consistencies it revealed! Every day it seemed to change by infinitesimal degrees, settling, melting, evaporating, its crystalline underpinnings breaking down molecule by molecule, until once-formidable drifts, exposed for long periods to the sun, were turned into a delicate latticework of ice that eventually shattered and collapsed of its own weight. Thus, the winter slowly disappeared, the ground emerging once again as if rising up from below.

Soon the advancing thaw obliged me to cross the channel again by canoe, and one day with the snow cover beginning to disappear, I skidded the narrow craft back across the fields while I was still able to, glad of the occasion to mark the end of that part of my island sojourn. This left me without a ready means to replenish my supplies, however, and one day in the latter part of March I made the journey to the village entirely on foot, hiking up-island to the suspension bridge, crossing to the mainland, and continuing down the opposite shore. It was a fine day, with winter in full retreat, and after gathering what I needed in the village I started on the return trip, lugging my loaded backpack along the same route I had come. Before I was through, I had walked some twenty miles, and looked forward to the day when I would be able to free my car at last.

It wouldn't be long now, and if nothing else my long winter's vigil had taught me to be patient—as patient as the massive oak tree whose branches overarched nearly the whole of the cabin and whose buds were beginning to show renewed signs of life. All winter long I had walked, worked, eaten, and slept beneath it without paying any notice. Then one sunny afternoon with the temperature soaring to 60 degrees and the snow all but gone, I suddenly became aware of it in its entirety, from the massive branches that towered above my head to the unseen network of roots beneath my feet—a living thing much older than I, whose wisdom consisted in waiting for just such a day as this to begin a new season of growth. I felt like calling out to it with some lunatic expression of fellowship, for we had survived the long cold season together and the warmth of spring came well-earned.

Chapter 17

# Re-entry

As harrowing, in its way, as my first winter on the island had been, it proved a successful exercise in survivalism and helped wean me away from my flying habit. While I still found myself reflexively assessing wind patterns and looking for take-off sites on every likely hillside, I came to accept that the sport didn't lend itself to sporadic practice; one either pursued it with single-minded devotion or left it alone, and only by means of self-imposed exile, it seemed, was I able to accept the latter. By providing its own existential distractions, my time on the island had served as a unique form of rehab, complete with the torments associated with detoxification.

Meanwhile, my wished-for transition to a writing career was clearly going to take longer than expected. Even so, the impulse persisted, and the profession itself seemed the more viable for a friendship I made after freeing my car from its snowy prison in early April. Restored to mobility once again, I began making regular trips to the Bay, where a local bar called the Gold Mine was one of the few establishments to open its doors in advance of the tourist season. It also happened to be a favored hangout of one of the village's better-known residents, Fred Exley, a writer whose first book, *A Fan's Notes*, had won the Faulkner Award as well as a nomination for the National Book Award. A second title, *Pages from a Cold Island*, had followed, and he was at work on a third, excerpts of which were being serialized in *Rolling Stone Magazine*.

## Near the Borderline

Then in his late forties, when not writing—which he did during isolated stints of sobriety—Fred could usually be found on a barstool at the Gold Mine, delivering running commentaries on the topics of the day for the general amusement of his fellow patrons. As irrepressible in him as the act of drinking itself, such performances could indeed be entertaining, yet after a certain hour of the evening the show tended to suffer from the effects of his prodigious consumption. In truth, he could easily have been mistaken for the town drunk, but then, Faulkner himself had acquired a similar reputation in his native Oxford, Mississippi.

Routinely visiting the place for an early dinner, I got to know Fred during his more lucid moments. A native of Watertown, he grew up in the shadow of a father who had achieved local notoriety as a semi-pro football player, and I admired the way his books depicted a place and circumstance not unfamiliar to me. In turn, Fred recognized in me a more than casual interest in his work, and, in view of my grad school experience and the weirdly reclusive life I'd been leading on the island, he encouraged me to apply for a job as a reader at Random House, going so far as to arrange a standing invitation for an interview with his editor.

While I didn't think much about the offer at the time, later that summer I mentioned it to a grad-school friend whose reaction made me reconsider.

"Are you serious?" he wailed. "–That's a major-league connection! I'd be there in a heartbeat."

When the same friend offered to put me up in his apartment in Brooklyn to facilitate the interview, I could hardly refuse. Thus, at the end of another round of coursework in Vermont, I drove to the city and made my way to an address on President Street, where he and his girlfriend lived in a comfortable brownstone not far from Prospect Park.

The next day, on a sweltering August afternoon, I spent the better part of an hour discussing the book business with as cordial and well-placed a professional as I could have hoped to find. As he explained, however, recent changes in the company's hiring practices dictated that, rather than entering the company as direct hires, readers were to be selected from the pool of existing employees. Accordingly, my next stop was the personnel office, where, after years of watching newcomers attain coveted editorial positions, the company's secretarial staff had asserted an effective countermeasure, insisting that all applicants be capable of typing at a rate of fifty words per minute—a rate that proved beyond my self-taught skills.

So ended my quest for a career in corporate publishing, though I was not exactly heartbroken by the result. In truth, I couldn't imagine a life for myself in the city, and riding the trains back to President Street in the suffocating summer heat only reinforced my disinclination to pursue such a scheme. Nevertheless, the outcome left me with few options. Returning to the River, I found a job working for an enterprising young contractor in Thousand Island Park, who was working on a series of projects that would last well into the fall. While the prospect of spending another winter on the island was chilling in every sense of the word, I was fresh out of ideas on the career front and once again slowly reconciled myself to such an eventuality—with plans for a number of logistical improvements to my living conditions.

This time, determined to remain mobile, I prepared for the coming cold season by clearing a small parking area in the woods abutting the island road about a half mile from the cabin, where the car could easily be shoveled free when needed. Another concession to my transportation needs involved restoring an old snowmobile that had long since fallen into disrepair. Tearing the engine down as far as the crankcase, I put the various parts in a bucket, carefully cleaned them and put them back together. Next, the original gas tank having been damaged beyond repair, I dug up an old, six-gallon outboard tank and, after removing a small storage bin at the rear of the snowmobile seat, attached the makeshift replacement tank in its stead. Finally, I removed the sled's broken windshield and affixed a narrow hardwood slat in an arc across the top of the cowling, forming a frame upon which to attach a sheet of transparent Lexan plastic. Though the results were decidedly non-standard, the resurrected machine proved all but indestructible and would serve me well throughout the ensuing winter.

Meanwhile, in the course of my regular visits to T.I. Park and Clayton I made a number of new friends who, for reasons no less obscure than my own, had chosen to remain on the island well into the fall. Included among these were a group of young women who, one weekend about the middle of November, invited me to join them on a planned boat trip to the village of Gananoque, Ontario.

We set off from the Park about noon in two outboards, a sixteen-foot Lyman whose owner, Annie, invited me to take the controls, and a somewhat longer, flat-bottomed Polar Kraft belonging to Alice. Heading upriver, we stopped at the town dock in Clayton, where Alice picked up two more friends, Betty and Charlotte, at which point we set out on the five-mile journey around the head of Grindstone and on to the Canadian mainland. Though the sky was overcast, the day was unseasonably mild, with light winds that produced little to no surface chop, ideal conditions for a trip that Annie described as one of her favorite summertime outings as a kid. At this point, of course, the advancing season had long since emptied the river of other boats, making the voyage a somewhat riskier proposition, which I suspect was at least partly why she'd invited me along.

After an uneventful crossing, we arrived at the custom dock in Gananoque only to find no one on hand to check us into the country, a discovery that inspired a good deal of satirical commentary on the rigors of international border control. Nothing daunted, we started for the center of town with no particular aim other than to have a good time, though even so modest a goal would prove a tall order in a place whose commercial life depended almost exclusively on the now-defunct tourist trade. We gave it a go just the same, stopping first at a local market for some Mackintosh toffee, a Canadian treat not available in the States and high on Annie's list of girlhood memories. In a nearby drugstore, we found a selection of picture postcards, providing yet another trip down memory lane with familiar scenes of the river in summertime. Eventually ending up in a bookstore, we poked around among the shelves for the better part of an hour, chatting and sampling the wares, before spilling back onto the sidewalk.

By this time, the sky had grown more somber and, making a final tour down the main drag, we decided to start back to Clayton, giving ourselves plenty of time to make happy-hour at O'Brien's, Clayton's roadhouse of record. Upon our return to the customs dock, a lone officer appeared—having returned, it seemed, from his lunch break—and we went through the motions of checking in immediately prior to our departure. More laughs at the expense of international formalities, and soon we were on our way, assuming the same boat assignments we had taken on the way over. Starting back across the Canadian Channel, we made our way through the Admiralty Islands and continued on toward Grindstone across a wide expanse of open water. As the two boats sped along, traveling abreast and in fairly close proximity, everyone became effectively mesmerized by the drone of the engines and the steady rush of water beneath the hulls.

When we reached the head of Grindstone, however, the mood changed, and with Clayton in sight, a sense of anticipation was coupled with the reassurance of being back in home waters once again. Emboldened by the rare stillness of such conditions (even in the balmy days of summer the weather end of the island seldom invited malingering), I thought to engage in a bit of boat-play. Angling in the direction of the Polar Kraft, I came within ten feet of it before turning somewhat abruptly away, sending a bit of spray toward our companions without putting anyone in danger of getting wet. The maneuver was a mere suggestion of mischief, nothing more, a harmless tease meant to enliven the end of an otherwise monotonous journey, and, thinking little of it, I resumed my course, scanning the distant shoreline for the docks of Clayton.

Moments later, however, I glanced over to see Alice speeding toward me at a sharp angle in the Polar Kraft, the thrill of retribution in her expression. It was easy enough to evade her by simply bearing away, but what happened next suddenly presented a whole new level of hazard. Jamming the engine's control arm hard over in an effort to spray us, she effected a turn so severe that the hull abruptly turned sideways, stopping short and sending its passengers flying over the low-slung gunwale like three sacks of grain from a careening truck. What she had failed to consider was that the boat's flat-bottomed configuration and ice-runners, while beneficial for use in winter conditions, made it uniquely resistant to skidding. When it came to the sport of spray-jousting, it was the worst boat in the world.

There was no time to mull the pros and cons of small-craft design, however; three people were in frigid water far from shore and, to make matters much worse, the Polar Kraft, having rid itself of its human cargo, quickly regained its momentum and continued on a broadly circular course.

"OH SHIT!" Annie wailed in alarm. And then, "—BETTY DOESN'T SWIM!"

Swinging back toward the scene of the mishap, I came to a stop amid the three victims, and Annie and I began helping get them aboard. While Alice and Charlotte were able to pull themselves out of the water with little help, Betty, who was managing to tread water wonderfully well for a beginner, was in such a state of shock as to be quite helpless when it came to reembarking. Working in unison, we hauled her over the side, and had no sooner got her aboard than I looked up to see the Polar Kraft bearing down on us like a big, goofy dog returning faithfully to its owner. I had often heard it said that an unmanned boat travelling at speed will inevitably return to the spot where it was abandoned, and while it made sense that anything other than a dead-ahead course would lead to a circular trajectory, I never quite believed in the legend until that moment. But sure enough, here it came, right on schedule, and I remember reading the boat's name, Rosie the Riveter, written along the bow as it loomed up before me, and thinking it a clever name for a metal workboat.

Luckily, the fugitive vessel was only running at half-throttle, and in the interval before it slammed into us the thought occurred to me that this was going to be as good an opportunity to recapture it as I was likely to get. Luckier still, it struck at a glancing angle, and in the brief interval of the rebound I was able to leap aboard, tumbling onto the floor between the seat thwarts, where I noticed three pairs of footwear scattered about me; all three girls had been thrown out of their shoes. Making my way aft, I grabbed the control tiller and brought the renegade craft back under control at last.

Next, returning to the now-overloaded Lyman, I pulled alongside and hustled all three sodden and shivering girls back into the Polar Kraft, thinking to make a bee-line for Clayton. At Alice's insistence, however, I headed instead for her family's place on nearby Grindstone, with Annie following close behind. Once at the dock, we tied up and started for the house, but not before Alice, in an act of contrition to the river gods, stripped and jumped back into the water. Like Jack a year earlier, she'd suffered a blow to her pride as a River Rat, and under the circumstances I felt obliged to confess my own bad judgment in triggering the whole sorry incident.

Once inside, the girls took turns taking hot showers, donning warm clothes from Alice's wardrobe and warming themselves before a hastily built fire. Soon, their spirits largely restored, we made the trip to Clayton to huddle over a few rounds at O'Brien's. Once again, it had been a lucky day, and a necessary reminder that the river in November bore little resemblance to the sun-glazed tourist mecca depicted on picture postcards.

Meanwhile, another fall continued to advance upon the increasingly abandoned islands, and it occurred to me to make one more improvement before winter set in. Calling the phone company from the main house, I arranged to have them run an extension line to the cabin, where I installed a new handset. The idea was born more of wishful thinking than any real need; given the limited number of acquaintances I might expect to contact, let alone hear from, the device promised to be little more than a safeguard in the event of emergencies, its presence a grim reminder, as if any were needed, of my impending isolation.

Thus, it came as a distinct surprise, one night in the latter part of December, to be awoken from the edge of sleep by its ringing. Staggering into the main room to answer it, I could scarcely imagine who might have learned of my new connection, let alone bothered to contact me. To my amazement, it was Sara.

Though the call seemed to come from out of nowhere, it was not without context. The previous winter, in the course of my various correspondences, I had written to her at last, acknowledging my long silence and hoping, however belatedly, that she was okay. She wrote back to assure me that she was fine and catch me up on her current situation. It turned out her marriage was still intact and she had given birth to another daughter within the year. At the time, her letter had been a ray of light within the overwhelming gloom of that first winter in the cabin.

Now, a full year later, using a number I had given her several summers past, she had taken a chance that I might still be on the river, and managed to reach me on a phone I had installed some few weeks earlier. Inspired, it seems, by a recent drive past the old fraternity house, she thought to check in and see how I was doing, which in truth was none too well, for with the approach of the solstice, cabin fever had set in once again, accompanied by its now-familiar demons. Even so, the call had the effect of snapping me out of it, and after a brief and restorative conversation I felt somehow transformed, as if the sound of her voice within my fortress of solitude had changed the place forever.

Shortly thereafter, eager to get off the island, however briefly, before the onset of blizzard season, I made the half-hour trip to Watertown to spend Christmas Eve with the family. Arriving about mid-afternoon, I spent some time catching up with the parents, and was relieved to find my older brother in a good mood and seemingly glad of the company. With the rest of the siblings due to arrive the next day, the two of us were obliged to revisit the less-than-halcyon circumstances in which we had slogged (and slugged) our way through high school, but at this point those days were nearly ten years in the past, a blessedly dim memory.

After settling into my old room, I returned downstairs to find him eager to play a game of backgammon in the living room, but by this time Dad had fallen asleep on a nearby sofa, and I begged off lest we awaken him.

"C'mon, he doesn't care," my brother assured me, distributing the playing pieces noisily about the board.

"Let's take it into the other room."

"No, this is where we play. He can move."

I conceded the point. It was either that or risk an argument likely to achieve the same unwanted result. Even so, his dismissiveness struck me as strangely discourteous, and before long Dad was indeed awoken by our playing, an eventuality my brother simply ignored.

Though a relatively small thing, the incident was nonetheless troubling, and I couldn't help thinking that a shift had taken place in otherwise familiar roles, a changing of the guard that left both parents correspondingly diminished. Given my brother's characteristic rigidity, such a change didn't bode well for either of them, let alone its implications for his own future. Six years after coming home from his abortive freshman year in college, what had begun as a stopgap until he could find a more viable existence now seemed a permanent solution. Whatever the near-term benefits of his prolonged home-stay might have been, its long-term prospects had only grown more ominous.

As to its underlying cause, the subject remained closed to discussion. At some point, I'd been given to understand that he was "seeing someone," presumably a counselor of some kind, but any details as to a diagnosis or treatment remained hidden within the mists of professional as well as parental confidences. Its relevance to the rest of his siblings was not part of the calculus. We, who had borne witness to our brother's emotional fragility ever since grade school and endured his many abusive melt-downs ever since, were to go about our business, which didn't include showing concern for his future.

The next day, after taking part in the holiday rituals, I returned to the cabin full of dark presentiments about my brother's future and a new resolve with respect to my own. Having endured my hermit/survivalist phase for one season and the beginnings of yet another, I was determined to make the coming winter's stay my last. At the very least, it was time to establish a new set of priorities. Accordingly, in the months that followed, I set about reconnecting with the world beyond my narrow corner of the island. Taking full advantage of continuous access to my car and makeshift snowmobile, I started looking up neglected friends in the area, went visiting, got back in circulation. And by the time spring arrived again, I was more than ready to leave, having had my fill of self-imposed exile.

*Near the Borderline*

# Chapter 18

# Family of Choice

At some point during my second winter on the island, I received a letter from the head of the grad-school in Vermont announcing a new satellite program to be conducted in England during the upcoming summer session. It seemed an enticing opportunity, but travel expenses were such that I scarcely gave the idea a second thought. My construction earnings notwithstanding, with the return of winter my chances of finding fresh employment were on the slim side of negligible, and thus the idea didn't pass muster with my internal accountant.

About the middle of January, however, in the course of a snowmobile visit to friends at the head of the island, I learned of a job offer that offered substantial pay for what promised to be easy work. For the past several months, two large parking lots had been constructed in the vicinity of the Thousand Islands Bridge, one on the American mainland and the other on the Canadian side. Over time, in compliance with tariff regulations, these lots had been filled with hundreds of new automobiles, and the import/export company involved in this operation was looking for drivers to move many of these cars from one lot to the other, a job that was to be performed in twelve-hour shifts over the course of two successive nights so as not to interfere with regular bridge traffic.

Despite the long hours, the job promised light duty, and some fifteen of us showed up at the company offices on a mid-winter evening, eager to take advantage of a rare opportunity. The only wrinkle involved the weather, for while the day had been clear and calm, the forecast called for temperatures in the teens and heavy snow squalls. Even so, a no-nonsense supervisor informed us of the routine to be followed, and we started on the first of many trips to the Canadian side, where a couple of vans were on hand to shuttle us back. For the first hour or so everything went smoothly enough, but rising winds eventually brought the expected snow, and road conditions deteriorated rapidly. Sometime after midnight, we were given a short break in a lunchroom at the American customs station, but then it was back to work in blizzard conditions. At this point, what had begun as a cakewalk turned into an icy demolition derby in which simply keeping the cars on the road, let alone maneuvering them through a maze of drift-filled lots became a considerable challenge.

It proved a long and wearing night, and by the time I got back to the cabin about mid-morning, I had just enough time to take an afternoon nap before setting out again. Nevertheless, we freelancers couldn't complain; as the supervisor sullenly explained, we were getting double overtime whereas, by the terms of his contract, he was only making standard pay. Anyway, the job proved a windfall, providing me with more than enough to cover the round-trip airfare and other travel expenses associated with the grad-school program in England. Thus, newly inspired about my prospects, I submitted an application, and some six weeks later was pleased to learn that I'd been accepted. If nothing else, my hermithood on the island had awakened in me a strong yearning for a dramatic change of scenery, and under the circumstances my new plans provided a much-needed boost, sustaining me through what remained of the cold season.

By the time summer arrived, I had finalized arrangements for a six-week stay in Oxford, plus an additional two weeks to be spent touring after the session. At this point, with everything in readiness, it would have been a good idea to avoid any hare-brained stunts in the interim, but this was asking a lot of my powers of self-restraint, and with the return of water-skiing weather I promptly broke my nose in a ramp-jumping accident.

The injury was such that the bridge of the broken appendage had to be pried back into place with a crowbar-like instrument in what promised to be a singularly unpleasant procedure, but the alternative meant spending the rest of my days looking like a woefully unlucky pugilist. Thus, following the application of a generous spritz of pharmaceutical cocaine, the nose was restored to its original shape with the sound of a snapping twig.

By the time I was ready to travel, however, I had been forced to reschedule my flight to England, thereby missing the first few days of classes. More inconvenient still, I arrived on the school's hallowed lawns with an aluminum nose-guard taped to my still-swollen face, creating a look that hardly bespoke the sort of intellectual depth and seriousness of purpose I hoped to convey. (Even in water-skiing circles, ramp jumping tends to be looked down upon, per a familiar saying: "The dumber you are, the farther you go.")

Nevertheless, I soon made the acquaintance a comely classmate named Donna, whose close ties to Maine provided us with an immediate sense of rapport. An English teacher at a boarding school in western Massachusetts, she had helped launch a wilderness camp for teenagers on an old farm complex on the upper Kennebec, and was a regular skier at Sugarloaf during the years since I was there. We started hanging around together, and one weekend, my face having healed sufficiently to dispense with the nose-guard, we took a bus to London and spent the day seeing the sights. Smart, funny and reliably upbeat, she was an experienced traveler, and, constrained by similarly limited budgets, we made the most of our time in the city, at one point racing through the National Gallery at a dead run, calling out attractions as we went: "Look, there's a Botticelli!" On another occasion, we chipped in on a shoebox of a rental car for a day-trip to the coast of Dorset, where we wandered the cliffs overlooking the English Channel and I told her everything she never wanted to know about hang-gliding.

One thing led to another. Before long we were taking turns hosting sleep-overs, and by the time the session was over we'd made tentative plans to get together upon our return to the States. Meanwhile, she had plans to tour Scotland with a girlfriend, while I, having learned of a hang-gliding club in Aberystwyth, took a bus to the coast of Wales, where I spent the last two weeks of my stay with a bunch of glider freaks on bank holiday, helping out at their launch site on a bluff overlooking the town, and watching enviously as they soared high above the shores of Cardigan Bay. Keen to hear about the sport's "early days" (all of five years in the past) they invited me to one of their gatherings in a local pub, where, over many rounds of ale, I regaled them with stories of Sugarloaf, Austria, and the fabled flying sites of California.

    A month or so after returning from England, following up on plans we made during the session, I invited Donna to come for a visit to the River, where I was once again working odd jobs on the island. She made the trip by car from western Massachusetts during an extended weekend break from her teaching job, arriving one balmy, Indian summer afternoon at the height of leaf season. Seeing her pull up to the cabin, I went out to greet her as she sat peering out her open car-window.
    "Is this the Midwest?" she wondered.
    "No, that would be Ohio, two states over."
    "It's so confusing. They should put up a sign on the interstate or something, let people know."
    "A sign? You mean like THIS ISN'T THE MIDWEST."
    "It's just a suggestion," she said with mock-defensiveness, "— if it wouldn't be too much trouble."
    "No, of course not. Good idea!"
    "Now you're being sarcastic."
    "Anyway, welcome to the River. C'mon in, I've got some interesting pictures you can look at. We call them maps."
    "Don't be rude, I'm a guest...."
    We spent the next few days getting reacquainted, hiking around, taking boat rides and making more plans.
    Accordingly, some five weeks later, at the outset of her Christmas break, I gathered up the bulk of my belongings, glider included, and headed off for a reciprocal visit to Northfield, where she lived in a three-room apartment in a girl's dormitory. With the student population away on vacation, we spent the holidays enjoying their absence, and after the start of the winter term I found a job manning a switchboard in nearby Brattleboro, Vermont, as well as a temporary apartment across the Connecticut in Hinsdale, New Hampshire. Meanwhile, I applied for a teaching internship at the prep-school and was hired in anticipation of a full-time position in the fall. During the intervening spring term, I started learning my

way around the front end of a classroom, and for the first time in years, found myself on something resembling a career track.

When summer vacation arrived, Donna and I spent a couple of weeks at the River before heading off to Vermont for another grad-school session, after which we continued east to Maine, spending the latter part of the season at the former wilderness camp she had helped run near the rustic town of Bingham. An ambitious project, the camp had hosted several dozen teen-agers, many of them inner-city kids, for each of a total of five summers, until insurance issues and health regulations became prohibitive. Located an hour east of Sugarloaf on the upper Kennebec, the setting was readily familiar, and I was glad of the chance to reconnect with scenes reminiscent of my flying days.

At the outset of the new school year, we moved back to the dormitory apartment and both began teaching full time, placing the school in the awkward position of turning a blind eye to our unmarried status. While nothing was said officially, we were made aware of general concerns and expectations in such matters, and eventually decided to forestall the eventuality of further inquiries. Thus, following a trip to Watertown to announce the news, we got married in a quiet ceremony in the school chapel toward the end of the Christmas break, no family attending and with honeymoon yet to be determined. Three days later, we were back at work.

For all of its expediency, the new arrangement proved entirely agreeable, and in view of my recent stint as a hermit, the teaching gig provided a compelling sort of contrast. Two years later we were living in a somewhat larger apartment, when, in a timely response to family planning efforts, a baby daughter was born, at which point the job of serving *in loco parentis* to a dorm full of prep-school girls grew old in a hurry. Happily, on the basis of Donna's seniority we were soon able to make another move, this time into a school-owned house on a quiet, tree-lined street near the campus, whereupon our lives became our own again, offering much improved opportunities to focus on the new member of the family.

More time passed and a second daughter was born, likewise a product of considered family planning. Having both grown up in litters of five siblings born in close succession, as parents we were keen to avoid sibling overcrowding in our own brood, ensuring that the newcomer arrived at a time when her sister, at three, was nearing school age. This proved particularly convenient when, a year and a half later, Donna received a school-teacher fellowship at the University of St. Andrews, prompting us to take an extended family trip to Scotland for the winter term.

Escaping another New England winter for the comparatively balmy environs of Fife, we settled into a comfortable apartment near the university and set about exploring our new surroundings, establishing a routine of morning walks to and from a local pre-school for our older daughter as well as stroller rides about town for her sister. When not thus engaged, we took advantage of the university facilities to pursue studies of our own—Donna researching the life and times of Elizabeth of York and I making daily trips to the school's computer center to begin work on what was to become a series of multi-media studies of military history.

On odd weekends we rented a car and went on various side-trips—across to the west coast, and as far south as the Lake District. And as time was beginning to run out on our stay, my parents showed up in response to an invitation we had proffered during the planning stages of the trip.

In truth, their visit would assume a remedial purpose, for our relations had been sorely strained by an incident involving my older brother some two years earlier. Prior to this, we were accustomed to spending much of our summers at the River, arriving soon after the end of the school year and staying in the main house. In those days, my brother stayed mostly in Watertown, and on occasions when he visited the island, we made every effort to be cordial, inviting him along on outings of one sort or another. Though he usually declined such offers, he nonetheless seemed to appreciate the gesture and we remained on reasonably good terms.

When our firstborn came along, however, our quarters in the main house became more cramped, leading to strained nerves, especially where my brother was concerned. Having assumed a role as care-taker of the property, he spent much of his time in a nearby workshop, but in practice the job proved too informal to accord him any real sense of purpose, and his habitual moodiness was never far from the surface, becoming a source of continual anxiety for my mother in particular.

One day, she and Donna decided to take our two-year-old to the Watertown house, where a tour of the attic turned up a long-forgotten rocking horse that had once been a favorite of mine as a child and proved an instant hit with our toddler. When Donna asked if she might have it to take back to Northfield with us, my mother was delighted to make a gift of it, and over the next several weeks Donna set about sanding and repainting it. By the end of the summer, she had restored it to like-new condition, never once suspecting that it might become a source of contention.

It was the morning of our departure for Northfield, and I was busy collecting gear in the house when I heard Donna call out in distress and ran outside to find her vying with my brother for possession of the rocking horse. Somehow, the thought of its departure had set him off, and he was trying to wrest it away from her as she was putting it in the car. My efforts to discover what he was doing only exasperated him further. He had no serviceable answer, and the fact that he'd resorted to force was plainly unacceptable. I made a move to secure the horse, and the resulting struggle inevitably came to blows, after which he left the scene, destination unknown. Meanwhile, drawn by the clamor, the rest of the family assembled in the yard, where, after a hasty and unsettled send-off, we started on our way back to Massachusetts.

In the weeks that followed we did our best to put the incident behind us, though not without considerable resentment. As we struggled to come to terms with what had happened, my father called to arrange a visit to Northfield for the purpose of discussing things. We found a place for him at a local B&B, and upon his arrival, he joined us for dinner, during which we carefully avoided any discussion of the recent incident. The next morning, we all went on a driving tour of the area, and after lunch my father and I got down to the business of the altercation, which he characterized as an unfortunate event requiring accommodation on all sides. Precisely what sort of accommodation he had in mind was not clear, however, and I couldn't help conveying a good deal of skepticism about the details. We went back and forth about it for a while, and in an effort to get to the heart of the matter, I uttered a simple statement: "One generation is enough."

The remark wasn't said in anger or accusation, but rather in an effort to clarify what was at stake. Even so, he bristled, clearly interpreting it as an indictment of his role as a parent when I had meant it rather as an appeal to his role as a grandparent. Under the circumstances, I was no more inclined to clarify myself than he was to seek clarification, and moments later, having accompanied him to his car, I thanked him for coming and we managed a curt handshake before he started on his return trip.

Now, two years later, during his visit to Scotland, the two of us had a chance to spend some time together, and the interposition of novel surroundings and experiences proved a balm to sore egos, helping us regain something of our former rapport. The strange incident with the rocking horse still lingered, however, and the issue of resuming our former visits to the River remained moot.

Chapter 19

# Three Days of the Canada Goose

In the movie *3 Days of the Condor* (1975), Robert Redford plays a CIA employee whose job is to read spy novels for clues about potential enemy schemes, a profile that lends the character all the intrigue of a spymaster with none of the culpability for what those in the business refer to as "tradecraft." Things go badly awry, however, when our hero steps away from the office for some coffee only to find, upon his return, that the place has been ransacked and all of his co-workers brutally murdered. Realizing that he's a marked man with no safe haven, he decides to kidnap Faye Dunaway and get her to hide him in her apartment with an unlikely story about how he's been targeted for assassination. Faye understandably doubts his motives and resents the intrusion, but when his claims are corroborated by evidence on ongoing mayhem, she decides that he's really a sweet guy who's gotten himself into some kind of jam at work. Thus, the two become romantically involved (who could have guessed?), and together manage to outwit a dastardly cabal of rogue CIA operatives.

  I suppose it was partly on the basis of thrillers such as this, with their nail-biting portrayal of Cold War paranoia, that I was inspired to visit Russian territory in the years immediately after the collapse of the Soviet Union. Even so, my interest in that part of the world went beyond such popular-culture portrayals, going back to my late teens, when, while perusing my father's collection of military histories, I came across a volume titled *With Napoleon in Russia*, a first-hand account of the disastrous 1812 campaign written by the

## Near the Borderline

emperor's Master of Horse, Armand de Caulaincourt. Upon first reading it, however, I was deeply skeptical of its veracity, unable to accept it as anything other than a work of fiction. Even more than the gruesome accounts of World War II battles, the story it told seemed too grotesque to be true, and I was inclined to chalk the whole thing up to the excitability of the French temperament. Only after a second, back-to-back reading did I come to accept it as a factual record, which forced me to conclude that actual history was vastly more interesting than the much-abridged version I was learning in school.

In any case, when my sabbatical year as a teacher arrived, making me eligible for a release-time grant to pursue a research project of my own, I took it into my head to make a solo tour through the newly-liberated Baltic States. Three years earlier, the Berlin Wall had been dismantled by freedom-loving Germans, a landmark event on the order of the moon landing, and with the "evil empire" now ostensibly defunct, I felt sufficiently emboldened to attempt a train journey around the Baltic, traveling east through Scandinavia, then south through Estonia, Latvia and Lithuania and west through Poland and Germany. How I thrilled at the scheme, fondly believing that the recently-declared New World Order would obviate many of the travel complications associated with the former Soviet empire. There were bound to be cultural hurdles, to be sure, but nothing a seasoned traveler to foreign lands couldn't handle. If only I could claim to be one.

Thus far, apart from my adventures in Munich, I'd spent all of three months en famille in Scotland, piggy backing on Donna's sabbatical. Now, five years later, my own sabbatical promised to be every bit as memorable, and Donna came up with a plan to take advantage of my trip just as I had hers. This time, with the girls aged ten and seven, we decided on a preliminary nine-day tour of Italy over spring break, Landing first in Brussels, we took a connecting flight to Rome, where we rented a car and drove north for an initial stay on an olive farm outside Sienna, our base for several day-trips in Tuscany. Next, we headed south on an extended ramble along the length and breadth of the Italian boot, the highlight of which (for me, anyway) was the discovery, through sheer guesswork and dead reckoning, of the ancient city of Cannae, scene of Hannibal's famous victory over the Roman Republic in the second century B.C.

Unable to find any reference to it on modern maps, I departed the main highway west of Barletta and continued east on a country road, eventually happening upon a sign in the middle of nowhere reading *Canne Della Battaglia*—Cannae of the battle. Nearby, atop a low ridge, a decrepit chain-link fence surrounded an area of exposed earth overlooking a broad plain dedicated to the cultivation of grapes. Then in the early stages of archeological exhumation, the "city" could easily have been mistaken for a minor landfill, and the small, empty parking area nearby suggested little, if any, public interest in the place. Even so, we got out and clambered around, examining the digs and climbing to the crest of the ridge to look out across a broad, vine-covered plain. With no one around and only a brief notice in Italian to provide context, the situation clearly called for one of Perfesser Dad's mini-lectures, a synopsis of the great battle fought there with particular reference to the classic military stratagem known as double-envelopment. The girls were underwhelmed.

After a brief stay in Bari, we returned north by way of the Amalfi Coast and Naples, eventually arriving back in Rome for our return flight to Brussels, where I spent a final night with the family before taking them to the airport for their flight home. At this point, purchasing a EURail pass, I set out on my sabbatical itinerary, passing through Hamburg and across the western end of the Baltic via train-ferry to Sweden. During a brief stay in Stockholm, I visited the 17th-century warship Wasa, King Gustavus Adolphus' would-be wonder weapon, which tipped over and sank shortly after leaving the dock on its maiden voyage. Perfectly preserved in the harbor mud, it was recovered and largely restored some 300 years later, complete with all sorts of period artifacts, and served as the centerpiece of a museum of its own. Magnificently ornamented, it was an artwork in itself, and if not for its lofty decks and over-abundance of heavy cannon, the ship might well have lived up to the king's high hopes of naval dominance.

As it happened, the story of the Wasa proved especially meaningful during the next leg of my journey, which consisted of an overnight trip across the Gulf of Bothnia on a cruise ship, a mode of travel that had never appealed to me. One look at the top-heavy vessel, with its Rubik's cube of cabins accessed by a maze of narrow passageways, only confirmed my opinion; in the event of a disaster at sea, the ship seemed a perfect deathtrap. After locating my berth and carefully memorizing my escape route, I retired to an onboard pub, where I spent the evening listening to an Irish trio with a mixed group of Laplanders (Sami), who were bound for the far northern regions of the country. As unimpressed with the basic seaworthiness of our boxy conveyance as I was, my newfound companions and I consoled ourselves with many rounds of ale before staggering back to our assigned cubicles in a condition that could scarcely have improved our chances of survival in the event of trouble.

Once ashore on the west coast of Finland, I boarded another well-appointed train and continued on my way to Helsinki, where I spent a couple of sunny days hiking around the town, enjoying the attractions of a bustling, yet accessible modern city emerging from the deep-freeze of a Scandinavian winter. Now roughly half-way through my circum-Baltic tour, I was well-pleased with my progress and confident of completing it as planned. Though my EURail pass didn't extend to the Eastern bloc countries, I was familiar enough with train travel by this time to be confident of my ability to carry on without it.

My first inkling that such optimism might be misplaced occurred while attempting to purchase a ferry ticket for passage to my next stop, Tallinn, Estonia. For some reason, the operators of the ferry seemed to know little and care less about matters of crowd-control, for instead of an orderly line in front of a stationary counter, would-be passengers were jammed together in a compact scrum in front of a lone ticketer, with no clear indication of who was to be served next. The result was an every-man-for-himself scenario with a good deal of subtle and not-so-subtle pushing and shoving.

The episode left me with a bad feeling. Thus far, my experience with public transportation had been trouble-free, and the sudden change didn't bode well for my entry into former Soviet territory. Equally troubling was the response of the other passengers, who put up with such treatment without protest or comment, as if it were standard operating procedure, a foretaste of what I could expect in the days ahead. Then too, I couldn't help noticing that my fellow travelers—for the most part Estonians on their way home from a visit to the Finnish capital—tended to be a good deal rougher in appearance than their Finnish neighbors, bearing scars and other indications of a hard life.

The next morning dawned windy and cold, and after lingering over breakfast at my B&B, I eventually made my way to a currency exchange for some Russian money. By the time I boarded the ferry a cloud front had moved in on a stiff west wind, and as we motored out of the harbor past a series of outlying islands, the Gulf of Finland revealed itself as an endless expanse of whitecapped rollers; we were clearly in for a pounding. Opting to make a tour of the interior of the passenger cabin, I missed the opportunity to claim a seat right away, an omission I came to regret upon discovering that there were none left, forcing me to join about a dozen others who would make the two-hour crossing as standees.

As it happened this proved something of a blessing, for as the ferry battered its way through the endless swells, it soon became apparent that the seated passengers were more susceptible to the pitching and rolling of the deck. Before long, one after another got up and started woozily for the bathrooms, looking none too happy. As their numbers increased, several were obliged to empty their stomachs along the way, which further aggravated the situation. Before long, the entire passenger cabin was full of the acrid reek of vomit, as various crew-members scurried about with pails of sawdust, pouring a scoopful on each new deposit. Under the circumstances, I was glad to be standing, the better to counteract many of the deck's convolutions. Taking a position near a window as far forward as I could get, I gazed steadfastly at the distant horizon and willed my hearty Finnish breakfast to stay where it belonged.

Somewhere along the way, I took note of the fact that I was crossing the Iron Curtain of Cold War fame, the ultimate borderline, and recalled something of my boyhood. Here I was again, flirting with the strictures of international boundaries, only on a more ominous scale. Already nervous about the prospect of negotiating the cultural divide, I started having particular concerns about my scant comprehension of Russian, a language whose alphabet alone seemed the essence of gobbledygook. Over the previous few months, I'd made halfhearted efforts to learn a few key phrases, fondly supposing that a vocabulary of perhaps fifty words would suffice. From the conversations I was privy to during the ferry-ride from hell, however, it soon became apparent that my comprehension was woefully inadequate.

Given my anxious state of mind and stomach, I cannot be held strictly accountable for my first impressions of Tallinn. Under more favorable circumstances, I might have been more receptive to its charms; however, my memory of the place on that bleak, raw day in the early spring of a year when the country's very future seemed to hang in the balance was hardly the stuff of glossy travel brochures. One impression that has stayed with me is of an extensive waterfront full of antiquated industrial cranes and the rusting hulks of salvage ships set against a backdrop of slag heaps and the wind-driven smoke of multiple, unseen fires. Helsinki had been a tidy, fairy-tale setting by comparison.

Even so, I was glad to reach land, if only for the chance to depart the good ship Barf Bucket, and my first encounter proved a pleasant surprise. Outside the ferry terminal, I was given an enthusiastic welcome and hustled into a curbside cab by a young Russian named Alex, who offered to give me a guided tour of the town, to which I readily agreed. Between his considerable command of English and my few words of his language, we were able to converse remarkably well, and, fresh from the unsettling circumstances of the ferry ride, I was eager to learn my way around the city in the relative comfort of his boxy but serviceable car, a much-used edition of the ubiquitous Russian Lada. As it was then lunchtime, he recommended that we visit his favorite eatery, a fast-food place on a well-traveled commercial strip, and though I would have preferred more traditional fare, I was curious to get a glimpse of his daily life and routines.

Over our meal, he had much to say about the rigors of the local taxi racket, which involved a constant struggle with local gangs for access to key locations. My greater concern was for the rail system, however, and when I told him about my planned train trip around the Baltic, he grew circumspect. For some reason the idea seemed strange to him, his expression conveying an unmistakable skepticism about its viability. Duly alarmed, I pressed him on it, seeking assurance that trains did indeed travel along my intended route, a fact he managed to confirm without endorsing. I was puzzled; what wasn't he telling me and why? Despite the relative fluency of our communication thus far, a more nuanced answer suddenly seemed beyond his ability or willingness to articulate, and in the end, he simply shrugged and made a strangely tepid comment: "You can try."

Try? I'd been riding trains all the way from Brussels with complete confidence; now suddenly the entire mode of transportation seemed an iffy proposition. In the absence of a better explanation, I could only assume that train travel was not something he was particularly familiar with, and on this basis, I let the subject drop.

Finishing our lunch, we got back in his car and drove to Tallinn's Old Town, a tourist destination offering me my first glimpse of onion-domes and other architectural novelties. Getting out to walk around, we came upon an attractive young woman selling miniature paintings at a small sidewalk stand. It turned out she was Alex's girlfriend, and, following introductions, I happily bought (and still possess) one of her compositions, a careful rendering of an historic public square. Taking out a small camera, I took a picture of the two of them smiling self-consciously in front of her stand, and was glad to have met so auspicious and enterprising a couple on such short notice. Any doubts I had entertained about the country's future for the moment seemed unfounded.

Eventually moving on, Alex and I returned to his car, where he revisited the subject of my ongoing travels. He had clearly given the matter some thought, and I was eager to hear what he had to say.

"I take you now to place where is right for you," he began. "You stay, maybe have drink, see teevee. Good place. You not leave, only to go to train. I show you way to station. You go, buy ticket, get on train. Everything okay."

The place he had in mind was a well-appointed yet essentially characterless hotel that served as a regular destination for Americans. Pulling up to the curb, he pointed in the general direction of the train station and, after settling up with him, I got out feeling reasonably comfortable in my new surroundings and prepared to go it alone from there.

Inside the hotel, I found my way to the bar, where I sat drinking Swedish beer and watching a wall-mounted television tuned to an English-speaking channel. The place was mostly empty, and in the wake of the morning's crowded events, I was content to enjoy some peace and quiet... but not for long. Something about Alex's carefully prescribed instructions had only piqued my interest in doing a bit of sight-seeing on my own, and, after killing an hour and a half, I decided to move on. By this time, it was going on four o'clock, and, determined to make the most of the remaining daylight, I set out to find the train station and do some exploring.

Walking in the direction Alex had pointed, I came upon a hilltop park, where I was able to identify the station from its prominent location on a major thoroughfare. Skittering along snow-covered paths, I made my way down the hill, and continued on a roundabout course through the area surrounding the station. Though the wind had abated, the evening was none the warmer for it, and I was starting to miss the cozy interior of the Hotel Americanski, or whatever they called it, when I suddenly came upon an elderly woman bundled in threadbare garments standing behind a small table upon which a single can of Coca-Cola was being offered for sale. Had I foreseen such an encounter, I might have simply averted my eyes and kept going, but her gaze was so full of pleading as to stop me in my tracks.

At once her circumstances seemed clear: a forlorn pensioner whose meager allowance had disappeared in the collapse of Soviet rule, leaving her to take to the streets in a desperate attempt to "do" capitalism. Digging out my wallet, I offered her a couple of rubles, to which she responded with a wan smile followed by a series of appreciative nods. This left me in a quandary, for I had no real interest in the product for sale. In fact, an atmospherically chilled can of Coke was the very last thing I had any use for, yet I felt compelled to take it, if only to bolster her confidence in the viability of free enterprise. Giving her a polite nod, I feigned satisfaction with the new purchase and continued on my way.

The incident haunted the rest of my walk; in a sad parody of commerce, I had purchased a product I didn't want from someone for whom the whole exchange had given the lie to a lifelong philosophy. Even so, I soon had occasion to be glad of the encounter, if only as a foretaste of what was in store for me at the train station. Darkness had fallen by the time I arrived in front of the bunker-like edifice, whose cavernous interior clearly did double-duty as a make-shift shelter for a considerable population of transients, many of whom were crippled or otherwise disfigured. Suddenly, Alex's otherwise cryptic instructions came clear, and, fixing my gaze on an imaginary destination, I made my way through the station's crowded concourse at a pace calculated to discourage any and all interruption. At one point, an unpleasant odor emanated from an alcove that I assumed must lead to a public toilet. Upon closer inspection, it proved the entrance to a cafeteria.

Eventually finding my way to the ticket booths, I paid for passage on an overnight train to Riga and made a point of visiting the corresponding platform for future reference. I was now in need a place to kill the two hours remaining before my departure, and, coming upon a broad flight of stairs, I instinctively started up them in an effort to escape the unsavory hordes that haunted the main concourse. Providentially, they led to a relatively well-appointed dining room blessedly out of earshot of the dull roar of the station below. Once inside, I checked my backpack in a side-room, and followed a maître d' to a small table in the middle of the dining area.

Glad to have found a haven of sorts in which to while away the time, I sat gratefully looking over the menu. It wasn't long, however, before I started having second thoughts about the place. My concerns had to do not so much with the setting or décor as with the clientele. Looking around at my fellow patrons, mostly middle-aged men, I couldn't help noticing the overtly proprietary attitude they conveyed toward their surroundings, returning my curious glances in their direction with a cool equanimity that gave me the creeps. As it happened, the maître d' had inquired about my nationality in the course of seeing me to my table, and, despite my muted response, managed in the course of an effusive welcome to broadcast the fact that I was an American.

During the planning stages of the trip, I had anticipated a certain amount of unsolicited attention on such occasions, and came up with the less-than-brilliant strategy of deflecting any anti-American sentiment by passing myself off as a Canadian. In the heat of the moment, however, I quickly realized that my passport would readily make a liar of me, thereby heightening any animus the locals might harbor toward proponents of the New World Order. After ordering the most innocuous item on the menu (some sort of cheese omelet), I struggled to maintain a sense of nonchalance amid what I could only interpret as unwelcoming, if not predatory, looks.

Just then, breaking in on my ruminations, a well-dressed, middle-aged man appeared at my table and asked, in English, if he might join me. Though the request came as a considerable surprise, he looked presentable enough, and, recovering my composure, I made a welcoming gesture toward the chair opposite. For several moments he sat smiling agreeably at me, then leaned forward in his chair and spoke confidentially.

"You should not be here."

At this point he had my complete attention, for he had spoken the very words my instincts had been shouting at me ever since sitting down.

"Tell me more," I fairly pleaded.

"This place," he said, tipping his head slightly toward our fellow patrons, "… it not safe for you alone."

It turned out he was an Estonian professional who, witnessing my arrival from across the room, had taken it upon himself to act the part of a pre-arranged in-country contact; hence his abbreviated introduction. Taking cues from his performance, I played along, and over a casual meal we spoke about his country, its history, and, incidentally, my current predicament.

"Ever since First World War, Estonia like tennis ball between Germans and Russians," he explained. "Back and forth. Now we have chance to be independent country again."

"It so happens, I was hoping I might have a chance to visit the First War battlefield at Tannenberg."

"Ah, you know about Tannenberg battle. What do you know about Estonian War?"

"Nothing, I'm sorry to say."

"After first war, Baltic states granted independence by treaty, but Russian revolutionaries invade anyway, taking Lithuania and Latvia, nearly Tallinn, too, but Estonians fight back, winning independence for all Baltic countries."

"Until the Second War."

"Yes, then they take over," he said, once again covertly indicating those nearby.

"Russians?"

He nodded. "—Like guests who overstay welcome."

"But they no longer hold public office, do they?"

"What is saying, 'possession is big part of law?'"
"Nine-tenths, very big part."
"Yes, now you see how big."
"I met a young Russian taxi-driver this morning, who was quite helpful," I mentioned.
"Young people willing to make change for sake of future. Older generation, no."
"I see. He wasn't very encouraging about my plans to travel by train. Is it safe?"
"Once on trains, yes," he said. "But not always in stations."
"Should I reconsider?"
"Not necessary, since you have ticket, but I show you where to wait for train to Riga."

For his trouble, I sprang for his meal, and after retrieving my gear, followed him downstairs, where he led the way to a police station not far from the train platforms. After introducing me to one of the officers, a fellow Estonian, he wished me luck and continued on the way to his train.

He'd been a big help, putting me wise to a reality I naively supposed had been rendered moot by the collapse of the Soviet system. Hardly. While the mother country underwent a name change and its former colonies were nominally independent states again, the Russian residents of those states weren't going anywhere. Instead, many were busy practicing their own style of capitalism, which happened to be indistinguishable from the methodologies of organized crime. The fact that I was obliged to wait for a train in the physical presence of security forces was but one manifestation of the country's ongoing difficulties, and under the circumstances I counted myself lucky to have met two "friendlies" in a single afternoon.

Meanwhile, when the time came to board my train, I was more than ready to call it a day, and looked forward to the relative privacy of a sleeping compartment. Here again, however, I was in for a disappointment, for the accommodations were not nearly as private or comfortable as I had hoped. Indeed, the train-car itself appeared to date back to the First War, if not the previous century. Ushered into a cramped space with several other passengers, I laid claim to a narrow bunk, while two young couples, college students from East Germany, chattered among themselves with an enthusiasm that didn't bode well for my beauty rest. When a concierge arrived and served us tea from an elaborate samovar, I felt as if I'd unwittingly been transported back in time, and could only wonder how much longer I would be obliged to listen to my bunkmates' incomprehensible blather.

Shortly after midnight, during a trip to the toilet, I discovered a whole new level of dismay. As the concierge had explained, the bathroom facilities were in a separate car; what she failed to mention was that getting there meant exiting the passenger compartment and crossing a dangerously exposed cat-walk over the coupling gear. Unaware of these details, I started on the trip half-dressed, my shoe-laces partly untied, and upon exiting the sleeping car suddenly found myself outside in the frigid night, violently swaying from side to side as the train shook and rattled its way across the snowy northern landscape. A single misstep on the cat-walk virtually guaranteed a speedy exit stage left or right, and in a brief, futuristic thought experiment I visualized being thrown from the train, only to be discovered weeks later as a frozen corpse during the spring thaw. I made it to the latrine and back alright, but the experience did nothing for my sleep-readiness or general sense of well-being.

The train arrived in Riga about eight in the morning, by which time I'd managed a total of perhaps a half-hour of sleep, and was not in peak condition. This in itself put a crimp in my far-from-meticulous planning, for the one attraction of an overnight train schedule had been the chance to avoid the expense of hotels. So much for that idea; now, my first order of business was to find a room and retire for some quality sack-time, and the earliest I would be able to check in was not until eleven. I spent the interim wandering around the city center, finding and making careful note of the American embassy. In view of recent experience, I was rapidly acquiring a new appreciation for the good old U.S. of A.

Later, after three hours of sleep in a pricey room, I was back out on the street feeling much restored. Riga was a bigger city than Tallinn with more to see and architecture on a grander scale. At one point, I found myself in a football-field-sized plaza dominated by a towering monument depicting a female figure holding aloft a crown of stars. No doubt it symbolized something—Mother Russia, perhaps, I couldn't tell. A couple of boys in their mid-teens came along just then, hoping to sell me a packet of color postcards—typical tourist fodder, but I played along, feigning interest and asking if they knew any English. When they nodded, I pointed to the monument: "The statue—What does it mean?"

They consulted each other for a moment, before one of them said, "It mean freedom."

"Ah, freedom is good, yes?"

"Yes."

"Where did you learn English?"

"We learn in school."

"It's your favorite subject, right?" I kidded them.

Speaking at the same time, one said no and the other a tentative yes, at which point I confronted the one who said yes: "Tell the truth, now, you're just saying that to make me happy."

The other one laughed and gave him a nudge.

"Okay, how much for the cards?" I asked, reaching into my pocket.

When they told me the price in Russian, I held out a handful of coins for them to sort through. One of them picked out a few of the larger denominations and I ended up giving the rest to the other.

"Now you two stand here while I take your picture," I said, motioning them to a spot in front of the monument.

Earlier, and indeed throughout the encounter, I'd noticed both of them making brief, surreptitious scans of the plaza, as if they might be planning a snatch-and-run operation. Now, as soon as I produced the camera, they suddenly grew agitated, waving their hands no and glancing behind them as if someone might be watching. Despite my protests they quickly drifted off, leaving me utterly baffled. Once again, my understanding of the local culture seemed sadly incomplete. I was missing something, and whatever it was, the knowledge of its absence was making me every bit as paranoid as my latest acquaintances.

Heading back toward the hotel, I decided to stop for a beer in a likely looking bar along my route, and, upon passing through a small foyer, I was met with a barrage of rock music emanating from a large and crowded room. Forging ahead, I found a place at the bar and ordered a draft by pointing the bartender to the appropriate tap. Due to the volume of the sound system, verbal communication was hardly possible, especially as the music was emanating from a television set tuned to the ubiquitous 90's rock-video purveyor, MTV. For the next twenty minutes, I stood in the midst of a mute, mostly younger crowd, listening to the likes of Aerosmith at Spinal-Tap volume eleven. In an unlit, live-music arena surrounded by head-banging stoners, there might have been a context for it, but in a well-lit bar during cocktail hour it was just weird. I couldn't decide who to feel sorrier for: the Latvians and their long-suppressed desire to embrace Western pop-culture, or the adherents of Western pop-culture themselves.

Later, back in the hotel room, I faced a quandary related to my master plan, which called for another overnight train trip, this time to Vilnius, Lithuania. By now, however, the night-train experience had lost much of its charm, and I was thinking seriously of staying the night in Riga. Though it would put me off my schedule, the room had already been paid for, and I hated to let it go. Then too, my stomach was not feeling tip top, a likely culprit being the fast-food lunch I had choked down in Tallinn. It seemed altogether possible, if not likely, that at some point I was going to throw up, which was not a pleasant prospect as I tend to do so with the raucous indelicacy of an alley cat ridding itself of a hairball. The thought of performing such a spectacle on a train in the course of another life-threatening dash between cars, proved decisive; I would stay the night in Riga in hopes that a good night's sleep would resolve my digestive woes. While this would mean waiting all day for the next train to Lithuania, it seemed the best option.

Unfortunately, I woke up the next morning still feeling ill, which called for some serious reconsideration. The idea of spending another day waiting on a hopelessly outmoded train system seemed crazy, yet the alternative of resorting to a five-hour bus ride on a bad stomach made even less sense. The only other option was to pull the plug on the whole circumnavigation thing and catch a flight back to the West, in which case the travel time would be reduced to little more than an hour and a half, after which I would be able to enjoy the comforts of modern civilization again.

By check-out time, I was only feeling sicker, and after settling up at the front desk, I took the opportunity to request a cab to the airport, having concluded that I had seen enough of the post-Soviet world for one trip. The wisdom of the plan would be confirmed by my ensuing experience with the cabbie, an older man with a perceptible aura of gangland about him (I could only hope my friend Alex would avoid such a fate). Upon our arrival at the airport, I proffered some ruble notes for the fare, but he wanted nothing to do with them.

"You pay American dollars," he said flatly.

With gear in hand and ready to walk, I responded, "No—I pay rubles."

At this, he gave me a look of more than malevolent disdain and said something in Russian that needed no translation. Eventually taking the money I proffered as if it were a grievous insult to his self-respect, he took off in a cloud of dust. The black market, it seemed, was alive and well in Riga.

Inside the air terminal, I bought a ticket on a Lufthansa flight to Denmark, and with an hour to go before boarding, made my way to a lounge not far from the gate. Sitting at the bar, I ordered a glass of ginger ale as a palliative for my stomach, and was soon feeling somewhat better, an improvement attributable in part to the prospect of my imminent departure. In any case, when the bar-tender presented me with a selection of hors d'oeuvres, I instinctively took him up on the offer, downing an innocuous-looking canape only to realize it was simply a chunk of lard garnished with a pimento. This time a ginger ale chaser was no help; once again, I was counting down the minutes until hairball time.

I got through the flight alright, but upon arrival in Copenhagen I was not feeling at all well, and I remember the near-hysterical gratitude I felt as I transited the terminal on a moving sidewalk with padded treadway underfoot; I was back in the world where personal comfort and convenience mattered again. Shortly thereafter, having gone through customs, I was sitting, utterly exhausted, in a small waiting area with a number of other passengers, when a young Danish woman, noting my hard-used appearance, asked if she could be of any help. I explained that I'd been through a few rough days, was new to Copenhagen and in need of a likely B&B, to which she responded by ushering me to a shuttle bus and accompanying me on a five-minute ride into the city, eventually pointing me to an entirely suitable place not far from Tivoli Gardens. Duly grateful, I was soon making my way to a clean, well-appointed room, where, after dropping my gear onto the bed, I proceeded to the bathroom and summarily emptied my stomach to the accompaniment of my usual, feline vocalizations. In all, I'd been in former Soviet territory for a mere three days, and was much relieved to have escaped.

    The next morning, back on the EURail system, I took a train to Paris and restored something of my cultural equilibrium amid the sights and sounds of spring in the city's green spaces. All in all, my travels of the previous three weeks had been a Tilt-a-Whirl carnival ride, complete with the resulting nausea.

Chapter 20

# A Near Thing

For the next few years, we spent our summers in Maine, visiting friends at the site of Donna's former wilderness camp on the upper Kennebec, a setting full of fond memories for us both. Meanwhile, in an effort to facilitate a return to the River at some point, I proposed to take up residence in the Little House, which had remained largely unoccupied ever since my hermit days. Though my older brother continued to spend his summers at the main house, his attitude had reportedly improved and the prospect of living under separate rooves promised to minimize contact and potential friction between us.

Having thus resolved to return within the orbit of my birth family, for several summers in a row we made the most of all the River had to offer, including regular contact with a variety of friends and cousins for the girls. Quickly embracing the area's social life, the two of them showed every sign of becoming confirmed River Rats in their own right. Indeed, their sense of Thousand Islands-inspired adventure would become the basis for a young adult novel written by their mother, who would go on to produce a definitive historical novel about the region: *Grindstone*.

Meanwhile, I had enlisted the aid of a number of teaching colleagues in the production of a multimedia study of the Civil War, a project that came as a particular surprise to my father, who had a keen interest in the subject and was warmly approving of the work I was able to show him. The study would serve as an opening for ongoing conversations about his experience as a Marine fighter pilot during World War II, in which he had flown the F4U-Corsair, an airplane instantly recognizable for its distinctive, bent-wing design. While I had long been aware of my father's special connection with the Corsair (plastic replicas of which had been a particular favorite during my model-making days), the particulars of his war years remained largely unknown to me, and became the subject of an active exchange of letters between us.

Later that year, both parents came to Northfield for a visit, during which I proposed that my father and I visit an air museum at Bradley International Airport in Connecticut. Though I'd never been there before, there was a good chance it might include a vintage warplane or two, and it came as a particular treat to discover that the pride of the collection was an impeccably restored Corsair. (I might have suspected as much, for the plane was designed and built in nearby Stratford.) We proceeded to make a careful study of it, my father with a proprietary sort of nonchalance, myself with unfeigned awe. Although by this time I had earned my own tags and would later take him for a flight from the airport in New Hampshire where I had done my training, the thought of flying that plane frankly terrified me. Even indoors on display, it was a fearsome looking machine, with an 18-cylinder, 2,000 horsepower radial engine behind which the pilot sat in a cockpit full of levers, switches and gauges—a rodeo-rider on a four-and-a-half-ton bull.

Inspired by the occasion, he proceeded to relate something of the plane's legendary history, explaining that for all of its exceptional flight performance, it was notoriously difficult to land on an aircraft carrier deck, where its long nose and tail-dragger configuration tended to block the pilot's view on approach, leading to numerous crashes and relegating it to land-based operations during the war. All of which detail was of particular interest to me, and in the course of our conversation, I encouraged him to put his memories into writing.

Among the pieces he sent me was the following:

## A Near Thing

### MANILA BAY—1944

*This one is not easy to write about or even remember.*

*We were flying out of the airstrip at Guinan on Leyte Gulf in the Philippines. It was a fighter sweep, which meant that we didn't have a specific target but were free to pick our own. We were sent to Laguna De Bay, a lake area south of Manila. The city itself was off limits because: 1) It was heavily defended by anti-aircraft guns, and 2) It was full of our friends, making it difficult to choose a target that would keep them safe. So, we were sweeping the area around the bay.*

*Our division was led, as usual, by the Major. His wingman, as always, was Nick Sigan. I was the section leader, and my wingman, as always, was Jim "Junior" Sturges. We, Jim and I, had been flying combat together for a long time, well over 50 missions, and were close friends. Of course, the Major was the Major and not an intimate.*

*During the sweep, I spotted a truck traveling along a road below and instantly recognized it as a military truck—there weren't any similar kinds of vehicles. I called the Major on the radio and told him of the potential target, he acknowledged and told me to go down and get it. He would stay aloft for cover.*

*So, I went down, circling around so as to come at the truck from the rear. Junior was on my wing, of course, but I was surprised to see that Nick Sigan had peeled off and come down with us, despite the fact that he didn't have authority to do so from the Major. I didn't say anything about it on the radio and he wasn't ordered back, so we all three went in. It was obviously going to be a strafing run and we couldn't go in abreast, so Junior and Nick lined up behind me.*

*We made an initial pass, each of us firing six .50 caliber machine guns. No one in the truck could possibly have survived; I had seen it stop dead in the road as soon as my bullets struck. For some reason it didn't smoke or catch fire, however, probably because it was powered by something other than gasoline. In any case, I took another pass, firing into the now-stationary target, the other two pilots following in line as before. Still no smoke, but it seemed to me a case of overkill and so I pulled up. Shortly thereafter, as I continued to gain altitude, I became aware that neither Junior nor Nick had pulled away, but were continuing to run at the target, at which point they were out of my control as well as out of touch with each other.*

*It happened so fast as I watched from above. Both of them were circling and strafing the truck—now a useless hulk—and flew head-on into each other. The collision tore the wings off both planes, and both went straight into the ground. It just happened so fast.*

*I circled, but there were no signs of life, and the Major and I flew home. I don't recall that either one of us talked on the radio. The Major never flew a combat mission again.*

This account, among several others, gave me some idea of why he had never been very forthcoming about his war experiences, a reticence I'd been inclined to attribute to a certain generational elitism. It also helped explain why he remained faithfully in touch with the surviving members of his squadron, with whom he took part in regular reunions, several of which had been held at our place at the River. Then too, it helped explain the otherwise mysterious presence of an old photograph he never failed to hang in a prominent place wherever his office might be. I first remember seeing it when I was perhaps five years old, during a visit to the downtown address where he first set up shop as a lawyer. A black-and-white enlargement, three feet by four, it featured a single Corsair flying at altitude, a bank of cumulus clouds visible in the background. Taken from another plane, the range was scarcely close enough to reveal the identity of the pilot, but self-promotion was not the point. The photo was a simple statement of fact, capturing a moment in time that had come to express something essential about him, and that was purpose and context enough.

As grateful as we both were for this new connection, however, it was not destined to last long, coming apart in a sudden and near-fatal recurrence of my brother's and my combative past. Having begun another summer more or less amicably, one morning in late June, with Dad in town and Donna and the girls away on a trip to Kingston, my brother and I agreed on a plan to renovate a run-down section of the family boathouse, and were soon caught up in the job, knocking down a weathered and essentially useless section of roof and preparing to clear away the debris. We had been at it for some twenty minutes, walking back and forth to a near-by workshop to retrieve or return various tools, and at one point while we were passing each other he suddenly stopped and confronted me. Something had set him off, though what it might be was a complete mystery. In his hand was a large screw-driver, in mine a hammer, and, recognizing his altered state from previous encounters going back many years, I tossed the hammer on the ground between us by way of precluding a fight. He responded by leveling the screw-driver at me.

"How would you like it if I stuck this in your guts?" he asked in a voice that channeled the very essence of his illness.

It was technically a rhetorical question, by which he could render himself blameless in the event I took him seriously, a stratagem I recognized with maddening familiarity from years past. Equally clear was the realization that the encounter had been carefully staged in advance. Lulled into believing that he had outgrown such treachery, I now found myself caught unawares once again. With no other witnesses to his behavior, he would be free to provoke a fight and it would be my word against his as to who was to blame, in which case he could depend on his mother's misplaced guilt to exonerate him. The undisguised malice of his treachery had been bad enough when we were in high school, the idea that he could make so bald an attempt now, with my own family in the offing, was beyond all reckoning, crossing a line he surely knew I could and would not tolerate.

For the moment, there was no way to know what he intended, and I was in no position to give him the benefit of the doubt. Accordingly, at the first sign of movement on his part I got the start of him, grabbing the shaft of the screw-driver with both hands, wrenching it away from him, and fending him off with it for good measure.

When he turned and ran, I was right on his heels, unwilling to let him escape the rage he had so deliberately called forth. Not this time. For once, rather than fight him to a standstill I was prepared to turn the tables, and for once he seemed truly terrified, as he had every reason to be. Cutting off his escape, I trapped him against the shoreline, and when he slowed down upon reaching the river bank, I barreled into him, grabbing him by the shoulders and riding him into the water. The next thing I knew, I was standing waist deep, holding him under as he struggled to free himself. The moment seemed to have a logic of its own, the culmination of many years of unavailing efforts to solve an intractable problem, and only when his struggles sent a sudden splash of water into my face, was the spell broken. Slowly relaxing my grip, I let him come up for air.

Back on his feet, he spluttered something about not wanting to go swimming, a feeble attempt to change the subject. Meanwhile, I was conscious only of the long history of such moments beginning many years earlier, when I had been hit by a stone some few feet away from where we were standing, an event that only seemed the more starkly unambiguous in hindsight. Though his voice no longer conveyed the menace of his darker self, I was taking no chances, and as he started making his way back up the riverbank, I followed him step for step. Reaching the deck of the boathouse, he backed up against one of its roof-posts as if defending the structure against any further depredations, a gesture that struck me as oddly similar to his equally strange unwillingness to part with the rocking horse years earlier. What was it about these disparate, seemingly unrelated incidents, that threatened him, triggering such plainly unaccountable and unacceptable reactions? I had no earthly idea, and in the absence of a recognizable motive, my only response, as ever, had been to mount a threat of violence equal to or greater than his own. With adrenalin still surging, I asked if he wanted to have another go, if only for the chance to revisit my decision to relent, whereupon he shook his head in answer.

So ended the fight, and with it all the many inducements that, over the years, had compelled me to ignore the long history of such episodes: parents, grandparents, River, Little House—everything. It was suddenly clear beyond all doubt that we could not stay there. Even if, as I continued to suspect, the entire episode had been a deliberate ploy on his part to force us to leave, so be it. None of it was worth the risk of another such confrontation.

Accordingly, upon Donna's return, I explained what had happened and we both agreed that we couldn't stay even another night. In an effort to cushion the shock of a sudden departure for the girls, we made arrangements to spend a couple of nights elsewhere on the island, where my younger brother made his home. Having had ample experience of similar incidents, the latter wasn't surprised to learn about the latest episode, and took the initiative to contact our father and set up a meeting for the next day to discuss the matter at his office. Though far from sanguine about the prospects of such an encounter, I agreed to take part, and the following morning we drove into town to make a case for some sort of concerted response to a long-standing yet ever-worsening problem.

Instead, we succeeded only in adding to our mutual frustration, for apart from making a tape-recording of my testimony as to what had happened—an experience I might gladly have spared myself—there was nothing my father was prepared to do about it. Though well aware of many such incidents in the course of the family's troubled history, he continued to argue against any legal recourse, the complexities of which he was far more competent to judge than we were. What was missing in his response, however, was any formal recognition on his part of the long history of my brother's threats and aggression, a history to which he had himself been a witness. Whatever its legal provenance, his omission showed precious little concern for those of us repeat victims, who at every fresh assault were inevitably obliged to build our cases from scratch.

Later, back on the island, Donna, the girls, and I packed up our stuff once again and with more than a month of summer vacation remaining, started back to Massachusetts. It remained only to await the foregone conclusion of my parents' non-response response, in which all hope of redress inevitably disappeared into the black hole that was my brother's malady, the inescapable gravity of which held sway over the family's entire moral and emotional universe.

Once back in Massachusetts, we made the best of things, finding places to hike and swim at a number of state parks in the vicinity of Northfield and in nearby New Hampshire. Such substitutes didn't bear comparison with the River, of course, and the memory of our abrupt departure lingered. The new housing arrangement that for several years seemed to have solved the problems associated with my brother's unpredictability had proven insufficient, and there could be no thought of returning. Even so, toward the end of the summer, in an effort to decouple the family troubles from the River at large, Donna decided to rent a cottage in Thousand Island Park, at the opposite end of the island. Offering a public beach, docks, store, movie theater and ice cream shop all within walking distance of the rental cottage, it seemed a likely place to facilitate our transition away from Laundry Point.

Though we had taken the place for two weeks, I stayed for only one before returning to Northfield to work on my history project. Meanwhile, Donna and the girls planned to enjoy the last of their summer vacations on their own, a decision they would have occasion to rethink when a line squall swept across the island one night toward the end of their stay, generating violent microbursts that brought down trees and utility poles alike, leaving a wide swath of destruction in its wake. In the midst of it all, our younger girl fell sick with a high fever, threatening to add a medical crisis to the drama taking place outside. Luckily, the cottage was spared, the fever broke, and in the morning they awoke to survey the damage, eventually proceeding outside to pick their way through a sodden tangle of downed trees and electrical lines.

It had been a summer of close calls.

# Chapter 21

# Any Landing You Walk Away From

Following our forced departure from the River, in a concerted effort to move on, we spent the latter part of the summer with our friends in Maine, who had recently bought a place on a wilderness lake at the edge of the unincorporated townships. In many ways, the lake was powerfully reminiscent of the River, with the dramatic peaks and ridges of the Hundred Mile Wilderness of the Appalachian Trail added as a backdrop. Over the course of the next two years, we rented places along its shore and began thinking seriously of buying a place of our own.

When a third summer of searching failed to turn up anything, we made the long drive back to Massachusetts for what we expected would be the last time. Within weeks of our return, however, our lake friends called to let us know of a new offering that had come on the market since our departure, and invited us to come back and stay with them to get a look at it. Though skeptical of what we might find, their kindness in the midst of an August heatwave proved irresistible, and, bringing along our bikes for the visit, we made the trip north for the second time in the space of a month.

The place they had in mind was a mile west of their cabin, in a cove on the western shore of the lake, and after settling in at their place we got up the next morning eager to explore the new listing. Having arranged an appointment with the realtor, we set off on our bikes along a dirt road following the shoreline, pedaling through sun-dappled forest as views of the lake flashed by through openings in the trees. Whatever might come of it, the outing itself provided a pleasant interlude, and, having crested a slight hill, we coasted down to a point where the main road met a lesser spur running back along the lakeshore. Nearby, a driveway led through a stand of towering pines to our destination: a log home of recent construction set in a sunny clearing. Even from the hyper-critical perspective of potential buyers, we couldn't find anything to dislike about either the structure or the setting—indeed, quite the opposite.

    We closed on the sale a month later, by which time the girls were immersed in their school lives and managed to arrange sleepovers with friends while Donna and I drove north once more to sign the paperwork and spend our first weekend. At once possessed of and by our new place, in the years that followed we settled in and made it our own, getting to know our neighbors and making a number of enduring friendships in the process. While the social scene for the girls couldn't match that at the River, they made the best of what the lake had to offer and before long started developing summer plans of their own. With a place now far removed from the complications of Laundry Point, we had indeed moved on.

    Meanwhile, contact with the grandparents fell into abeyance. In the immediate aftermath of the Great Unpleasantness, they had both attempted to restore relations over the phone, but such efforts only seemed to highlight their persistent silence over the long span of my brother's destructive history. I thought of all the times when efforts to address the situation on my part as well as that of the other siblings had been effectively stonewalled out of concern for his vulnerability, or worse, suspicions of our having unduly provoked him. In each case they had revealed a deep unwillingness to talk about the problem, providing little in the way of a model for our doing so.

    Not long after the blow-up, my father wrote a letter acknowledging that I had "borne the brunt of it," but absent a working definition of 'it,' I didn't know how to respond. Despite a long-standing desire to discuss the matter, without some basic language with which to begin, I was at a loss. Similarly, as much as I had hoped to pursue our former correspondence, when I sat down to write, the words wouldn't come, and as time went by the prospect of revisiting the subject seemed increasingly futile. It seemed we had simply reversed roles on the subject; when I had been willing to talk, he hadn't, and now that he was willing, I wasn't.

Two years later, in an effort to restore a semblance of former relations, Donna and I made plans to take the girls for a weekend visit to the River. The idea was to meet the grandparents for lunch in Thousand Island Park, a rendezvous Donna worked out with my mother and followed up by making reservations at a restaurant in the village. In the course of the long drive from Massachusetts, we decided to cross the border and stay in a river-side motel on the Canadian side, and the next morning, arriving in the Park, we revisited the scene of the big storm of recent memory, the effects of which were still much in evidence. Per our arrangement with the grandparents, we made our way to the restaurant only to wait for the better part of an hour without seeing any sign of them. Apparently, there had been a mix-up, which left us with little choice but to drive down-island in search of them. Though it meant risking an unwanted encounter with my brother, with any luck he wouldn't be around and we would get a chance to reconnect.

As it happened, we arrived to find my father alone in the house, and much pleased, if somewhat bewildered by our unanticipated appearance. My mother, it seemed, was on her way back from town, and as she was the one with whom Donna had made arrangements for the missed appointment, the assumption was that she had simply forgotten. My father, who had lost considerable ground since I'd seen him last, appeared to have no knowledge of it, and while aware of our estrangement, seemed unclear about the cause of our prolonged absence.

"You understand, we aren't able to come out for a visit the way we used to," he said.

"I'm aware of that," I responded. "And we aren't able to come here and visit you as we'd like, either."

When I ventured to explain why, his face fell in an expression of far-off recognition. "Isn't there something we could do?" he offered weakly.

"No, I'm afraid not."

At this point, my mother arrived, and from her strained reception I began to suspect that the missed appointment had not been due to a lapse in memory. It seemed more than likely that the omission was a message in hiding. In any case, she pretended to have forgotten, and I pretended to believe her.

Happily, there was no sign or further mention of my brother, though his presence in their lives was palpable. Having grown up with him, I didn't envy them the prospect of growing old under his influence, but there was nothing I could do about it, and in the end the visit only served to confirm our decision of three years earlier. We stayed and talked for a little more than an hour, and after a series of awkward good-byes, started for home. As we didn't get back on the road until the middle of the afternoon, we decided to take an alternate route through the Adirondacks, stopping for the night at a lakeside motel in a forlorn attempt to put a recreational spin on the trip. That night, in a fitting coda to the entire episode, the weird howling of coyotes in the nearby woods intruded upon our sleep.

The next spring, while Donna finished up another term of teaching in Northfield, I moved up to the lake house soon after the roads were clear of snow to begin work on a renovation project. By this time, having published my first multimedia title on CD-ROM and licensed it to a computer game company, I'd quit teaching to work full-time on two follow-on titles. Now freed from the academic calendar, I thought to get a jump on summer at the lake, and with plans to expand the upstairs bedroom area, I hired a local contractor to add some skylights and extend a shed roof over the mid-section of the house. Lending a hand, I helped with the prep work, removing the section of roof to be modified and clearing the way for the new construction. The contractor and his helper proved good company and I was glad of the chance to make a number of design decisions on the fly.

One day a truck arrived with a load of lumber for the addition, and I helped the driver unload it, making small talk in the process. It so happened he had grown up in a small town near Waterville, and I told him I used to know someone from that place. He asked for the name, and it turned out he had been a near neighbor of hers and knew of her still. Having divorced and remarried, she and her husband were now running a restaurant/sports-bar in the area.

Prior to this, having had no knowledge of Sara or where she might be, it never occurred to me to look her up, though I sometimes wondered about the possibility of running into her on the street somewhere, a prospect that seemed more than a little disquieting, like seeing a ghost. Now, knowing something of her circumstances and where to find her presented a chance to dispel the ghost once and for all. To ignore it would have been to reenact my long silence of years past, and I had gone through quite enough self-recrimination on that score. Still, getting in touch wasn't an easy thing to contemplate. For starters, I didn't want to cause either of us any trouble; then too, I was not at all sure she would welcome such a thing. Even so, it seemed to me that a statute of limitations ought to apply to one's past as it did to other criminal acts, and with the name of her business to go on, I found the phone number and made the call.

A hostess at the place answered, giving me the chance to give my name in advance of actually speaking to her, and when Sara came on the line, she sounded not displeased to hear from me. We chatted for a minute before I got around to the purpose of the call, which was to ask if I might stop by and see her in person. I tried to be breezy about it—an old friend who happened to be in the neighborhood (I was an hour away)—but it was clear that I had something to say that couldn't be said over the phone. In any case, she didn't object to the idea, and after setting up a meeting for the next day, I promised not to take up much of her time and abruptly rang off.

The next afternoon, I arrived at a one-story building whose modest facade belied a lively interior, with dining area on one side and bar on the other. Seeing no sign of Sara, I moved to the bar and ordered a beer from a young woman who, when told I was there to see the owner, smiled knowingly and nodded her head. A moment later, she went about her business, and, turning around on the barstool, I started checking out the clientele: mostly younger people with the easy familiarity of regulars. When I faced front again, Sara was standing expectantly on the other side of the bar, looking much the same as I remembered. Even so, it took me a moment to recall the sameness, at which point the stretch of years didn't seem so terribly long after all.

She had a few things to oversee before she could get away, and for the next several minutes we made small talk in the course of her comings and goings behind the bar. Then, with everything in order, she poured herself a glass of wine and led the way to a table in the middle of the dining room, where we began catching each other up on our current lives. Her family now included three grown children, and I was pleased to learn that her eldest, Tasha, was married with a daughter of her own. I kidded her about being a grandmother and told her she didn't look like one, which was verging on the overly familiar, I suppose. There were boundaries to such talk, and in the course of a brief account of my family and our new place up north, we both found occasion to suggest that we were happily married.

Eventually moving to the recent past, she spoke of her divorce, which had been far from amicable, with custody disputes and legal wrangling, "the whole deal," as she put it. It wasn't something either of us cared to dwell on, yet the topic pointed me in a direction I was determined to go. Even so, I hadn't planned what to say or how to bring it up, and when the moment arrived, the words came out without context or preamble.

"I need to tell you about a letter I got once upon a time in a newspaper office."

She nodded almost imperceptibly, and I continued, describing something of the circumstances under which I had received it; about the job and my crummy apartment in Nowheresville; about the evenings I had spent in front of the phone, wanting to help her out, but in the end being unable to decide what to do.

She responded with a matter-of-fact acknowledgement, as eager to put the matter behind us as I was to get through my confession, which wasn't as easy as I had hoped. When I finally shut up about it, the way was clear to talk about old times, and so we did, recalling some of the people we had known together and what had become of them. The list was by no means a long one, however, and we marveled at the shared sense of youthful idealism that had sustained us in those days, smiling at the memory, and shaking our heads before making our way back to the present.

Taking out a small photo album, she showed me various pictures, including one of herself and her granddaughter, the two of them bearing a strong resemblance to an old photo I once had of her and Tasha. It reminded me of my visit to her family home, and the adroit way she had managed the various relationships in her life: a single mom in a household where she herself was still a child. I studied the pictures and was proud of her all over again.

Before long, the better part of an hour had passed, and not wanting to overstay my welcome, I thanked her for indulging my spur-of-the-moment request, and got up to go. She was sitting with one arm resting on the table, and, unsure how to take my leave, I reached down and touched the back of her hand—a brief yet deliberate pat. There were the boundaries to consider, but the gesture seemed within acceptable limits.

Later, on the way back to the lake, I was relieved at having finally told her about my failure to respond to the letter, recognizing how much I had contrived to suppress the memory of it over the years. In the end, things had worked out well enough for us both, and seeing her again helped resolve things, restoring access to long-forbidden territory. As I thought back on our relationship, it seemed we had more in common than either of us fully appreciated at the time. Both of us, after all, had been dealing with complicated situations within our respective birth families, and if I had helped restore something of her confidence, she had likewise helped restore something of mine. And if, in the end, such transference had not been sustainable, she had been an important inspiration just the same. My flying adventures notwithstanding, I first learned how to defy gravity from her example.

Meanwhile, her story had been a key part of the narrative I had been trying to write ever since my sojourn on the island, and my silence about the letter had been a large part of why, in the years since, I'd been unable to complete it. Another impediment to my intermittent writing career had to do with my brother's ongoing difficulties. In the absence of any definitive understanding of a cause, let alone a solution, the family had been obliged to absorb the blows and hope for the best. In this respect, we siblings had done our duty, though not without cost to our own happiness and well-being. Nor would our parents be exempt. Increasingly isolated and exposed to my brother's combative presence, they would suffer consequences all the more regrettable. Late in my father's life, when a visiting public health official discovered suspicious bruises on his face, mandatory procedures were initiated whereby he was removed from the family home and placed in an extended care facility—a facility that my brother was legally forbidden to enter on his own.

In a series of visits during the last three years of his life, I witnessed my father's steady decline under a drug regimen that left him sluggish, bewildered and paranoid. By this time his circumstances, and my inability to do anything about them, had become a painful reality from which there was no escape or exoneration, and for a moment during one visit, no doubt recalling the vague outlines of our estrangement, he glared at me as if holding me responsible for his ending up in such a place. Without the heart to explain so complex a matter, I could only respond with an agonized expression of my own.

He died in early spring of the following year, and the funeral was held in the First Presbyterian Church, the same venue where, after downing a slug of scotch, I had staged my rebel-without-a-clue debut back in high school. I hadn't set foot in the place ever since those times, and the thought occurred to me—not unkindly—that in all likelihood neither had my father. It wasn't a moral failing that led to his sad ending, however; he was a good man caught in a parental catch-22. And the many friends and acquaintances among the area's legal and other professions in attendance testified to his long and successful public career.

Meanwhile, members of his immediate family performed the role of a Greek chorus, bearing solemn witness to his private tragedy.

Chapter 22

# Survivor Bias

During World War II, American military planners undertook a study designed to improve the survival rate of bomber aircraft. Upon returning from combat missions, planes were subjected to close examination to determine where they had received the most damage so that more armor could be added to those vulnerable areas. Because it was based solely on surviving aircraft, however, the study was inherently flawed. The subject planes, after all, had all made it back to base despite the evident damage. It was the planes that had not returned, but had been shot down, that could be useful in determining where more protection was needed. This revelation would give rise to the theory of survivor bias, calling attention to the possibility of reaching false conclusions due to sampling errors.

    I sometimes wonder if the theory might account for how, five years after buying our lake house and in an effort to be closer to it, we decided to pull up stakes in Massachusetts and become full-time residents of Maine. Despite ample experience of the relative harshness of the climate, we made the move largely on the basis of our recent experience of summers at the lake, which in itself represented a kind of sampling error.

    In any case, the decision was made with due deliberation. A year in advance of the move, in an effort to test the waters of year-round residency, I applied for a teaching job at a public high school not far from the lake in the town of Guilford. If I survived the winter there, I reasoned, living year-round in more temperate parts of the state would be a breeze. Prior to this, I'd been working at a daily newspaper in southern Vermont, which had been sufficiently receptive to my op-ed pieces to hire me as an editor. My tenure there had been little more than a year, however, when the paper's corporate owners abruptly fired the managing editor on the basis of her political views. As she had hired me and we had become close colleagues, the handwriting was on the wall, and partly in protest of her firing, I scared up the teaching job in Guilford and quit the paper to spend the latter part of the summer at the lake.

That fall, Donna returned to her teaching job in Massachusetts while I started commuting back and forth to Guilford High across a six-mile stretch of dirt road destined to become impassable to all but the occasional moose or bobcat as soon as the snow arrived. Somewhere in the back of my mind I was toying with the idea of reprising my "wintering over" days on the island, but by the middle of November sanity prevailed. Renting a farmhouse in Dover-Foxcroft, I closed up the lake house and moved into town, confining my commute to a well-maintained state highway. Even so, the coming winter loomed with an all-too-familiar oppressiveness.

My teaching assignment proved no less challenging. During orientation, those of us teachers new to the school were taken on a bus-ride into the more remote areas of the district, where we got a glimpse of the living conditions of some of the needier students we would be working with, a number of whom lived in houses with dirt floors where livestock was brought inside during the winter, a stark reminder of the economic realities of northernmost Appalachia. At this point, I'd been away from prep-school teaching for some seven years, which left me a bit uneasy about returning to the classroom in general. How I was going to get along with my new clientele and they with me added a whole new dimension of uncertainty.

Then too, from a curricular standpoint my understanding of the subject matter I'd been assigned to teach was limited. Charged with developing a course in Communications for students ranging in age from 14 to 19, I took the time to look over a couple of workbook-style texts, but found nothing upon which to base a year-long course. Indeed, confronted with classes involving a wide range of cognitive, developmental, disciplinary and motivational issues, I quickly abandoned any attempt at front-of-the-classroom pedagogy in favor of small-group work in pursuit of carefully-defined objectives. This was going to be one-room-schoolhouse-style teaching, and for all intents and purposes traditional book-learning would be irrelevant.

Happily, it was the dawn of the digital media age, and despite or because of its location on the outskirts of nowhere, the school had been selected to take part in an experimental state program in which every student was given a late-model Apple laptop. In fact, the one-to-one computer program was a big part of why I'd been interested in teaching there in the first place, if only as a means to discover how the new program might inform my software development work. When the Apple contract turned out to include a supply of digital media equipment, including multiple still and video cameras, the solution to my pedagogical dilemma suddenly became clear. I would make it my mission to turn the uncouth masses under my tutelage into articulate, intellectually curious journalists.

The moment of truth came during the third week of the fall term, when I presented my students with a novel game plan: to learn about modern communications we would engage in it, creating and publishing an electronic newspaper in which everyone would be responsible for developing content, and grades would be based on work received as well as commitment to the enterprise. It was to be a school newspaper, to be sure, but given the scarcity of local print periodicals in the region, our larger mission would be to tell stories relevant to the surrounding community as well. Not surprisingly, the idea met with a certain amount of grudging, teen-age resistance, and when I explained that their work would be published under bylines indicating their authorship, everyone grew momentarily silent, though whether from horror, anxiety or anticipation I couldn't tell.

In any case, the first thing to be decided upon was a name and logo for our publication.

"We could call it the Pirate Press," suggested a member of the football team, in recognition of the school mascot.

"A press normally indicates a book publisher," I told him. "How about the Pirate Post?"

"Yeah, that's what I meant."

Before long someone produced a photo-shopped digital facsimile of a crouching football lineman wearing an eye-patch and a tricorn hat. We were off and running, as it were.

As for my teaching responsibilities, from then on, I never gave a moment's thought to the tedious business of class preparation. In essence, ours was no longer a classroom so much as a newsroom. While I designed a suitable website template, the students worked in self-selected small groups, coming up with story ideas and deciding who would be responsible for what, all subject to my approval. Once the story ideas and assignments were established, the available cameras were signed out, and the writing would follow. Most of the legwork was done after school, and soon enough the material started coming in, delivered to me electronically for final editing and posting.

There were "hard news" stories about local construction projects, fires or other emergencies, features about persons of interest within and without the school community, and human-interest stuff of all kinds. One student did a write-up of his dad's car repair business, including a video clip of himself changing a tire while dad, an irrepressible raconteur, supplied hilarious commentary in a Maine accent thicker than the mid-winter snowpack. Two members of the cheerleading squad wanted to write an advice-for-the-lovelorn column (what could possibly go wrong there?), to which I initially said no. They kept after me about it, however, and in the end came up with a clever parody that put my doubts to shame.

On the whole, the quality of the work I received more than met my expectations and, just as surprisingly, its quantity more than filled the space I had allotted for our first edition, which observations I was only too happy to share with the classes. My praise was only part of the feedback they received, however, for as soon as the new publication went live, they started hearing about it from sources beyond the classroom. Indeed, several weeks later, a reporter from the Bangor-based "Piscataquis Observer" (The Voice of Rural Maine, according to their website) got in touch with me to ask if she might visit the classroom for the makings of a feature story. On the day she showed up, even the slackers were on their best behavior, and shortly thereafter the latest edition of the local weekly included a full-page story about our efforts, complete with a number of color photos of budding journalists in action.

The students were clearly pleased by the attention, which helped sustain their efforts for a second and third edition. By this time the search engines had found us, and one day, in an effort to illustrate the power of the new medium, I asked everyone to visit the Google homepage on their computers, type their names into the search widow, followed by 'Pirate Post,' and hit return. One by one, the searches called up links to our site and their particular stories, whereupon silence—the truest indicator of teenage edification—descended upon each of the classes in turn, the assembled student-authors revealing carefully-guarded glimmers of wonderment and pride. The idea that the world wide web extended to their own, ever-so-humble back yards seemed to put a whole new perspective on things for them.

All in all, the project was a hit, and when, sometime during the winter term, *The Pirate Post* won one of three web-development awards in a statewide competition judged by a panel of media professionals, its success transcended my rosiest expectations. The prizes consisting of school-wide licenses for the latest authoring software plus a certificate to be conferred in a special ceremony at Bowdoin College. When school officials determined that the honor warranted sending a bus on the two-hour drive to Brunswick, some 24 students signed up for the trip, several of whom had never been as far away from home in their lives. (Portland, another half hour south, was generally viewed as a sink-hole of big-city crime and corruption, a veritable Gomorrah to most of them.) Indeed, the staid surroundings of the Bowdoin campus were intimidating enough, and when it came time for them to receive their award from former governor and future senator Angus King, such was their trepidation that I was obliged to join them onstage, if only to provide moral support against any propensity to view them as rough-hewn curiosities from the northern frontier.

In truth, I was prouder of those kids than of any other group of students I could recall, and more satisfied with my efforts as instructor—with one notable exception. Early on in the school year, I had encountered an otherwise tractable student who simply wouldn't do any work. Complicating the matter was an issue I'd been having with a contentious character with well-known authority issues. Anxious to get the newspaper project off the ground, I was in hopes of getting both of them out of the group for my sake as well as that of the other students. In the case of the belligerent one, this was accomplished through back-channels on the basis of our mutual antipathy, but the other case was quite the opposite. The kid was as affable as could be; he just wouldn't do the work, and his presence in the classroom was a clear distraction to the rest, whom he insisted on engaging in conversation whenever the opportunity offered.

After confronting him several times about it, I finally took him aside and suggested that in future he report to the school library and use the time to some good purpose. Such reassignment was not standard operating procedure, but seemed the simplest and most expedient way to proceed, and he complied readily enough. That was the last I saw of him until one day some months later, in the middle of winter, when I caught a glimpse of him through a window as he arrived in the school parking lot, skittering across the ice-bound pavement on a beat-up bicycle three sizes too small for him. Moreover, he'd been riding in bitter cold through the teeth of a pelting snowstorm wearing nothing but a thin shell of a parka. No hat, no gloves, just a shock of unkempt hair to keep off the frostbite. It seemed more than likely that he lived on one of the hole-in-the-woods farmsteads I had seen during my orientation bus-trip.

In any case, he hadn't been under my direct supervision for many weeks; surely someone else was better informed about his situation than I, and better able to do something about it. Still, I couldn't help recalling his behavior in the classroom, and it dawned on me that what I had interpreted as stubborn non-compliance was most likely born of a terrible secret; in all likelihood, he was functionally illiterate. Even so, I couldn't summon the will to pursue the matter. Owning up to, or at least uncovering, an instance of educational malpractice, it seemed, required a more rigorous conscience than I possessed.

While the classes continued their work developing content for the website, I took each of them aside individually and sat them in front of a video camera in a small studio, where I recorded interviews with them. The idea was to give them some experience in front of the camera as well as behind it, and after a token amount of self-conscious resistance, they took to the sessions as if they were try-outs for roles in a remake of "Welcome Back, Kotter." After loosening them up with a few queries about their favorite sports and school subjects, I asked them about their futures and what they saw themselves doing in another ten years, questions that produced surprisingly earnest answers. While many of them had at least some notion of starting on a likely career path, a number of the girls planned to get married and have children, while an equal number of boys dreamed of moving to Alaska to get away from the "rat race."

Meanwhile, during her spring break from prep-school, Donna paid a visit to the farmhouse, making it her home base for a series of visits to various Maine private schools for the purpose of job interviews. When these eventually resulted in several offers, we hashed over her options and settled on an academy near Lewiston. It remained for us to finish out our respective assignments and prepare for the move, which occupied a good part of the ensuing summer. Once this was accomplished, we escaped to the lake for the balance of the season, glad for once to be a mere two hours away from our new winter home.

Having both malingered about the state of Maine for much of our adult lives, we were now year-round residents, and when the prep school offered us housing in a stately brick manse on a quiet byway, the accommodations proved sufficiently comfortable to encourage us to stay longer than we originally planned. Our larger goal had always been to find a place of our own for our "post-prime" years, and it turned out we would need the extra time. Our first thought was to find something in the country, but Maine real estate can be challenging on that score. One man's rusticity, after all, can be another man's squalor, and finding the right balance can be tricky. In our case, the issue was complicated by my interest in a variety of new-age construction methods. For some time, I'd been intrigued by the possibilities of berm (underground) and straw-bale homes. Donna, on the other hand, held more traditional views on the subject.

"Some choice," she scoffed. "We can either live like gophers or the dumbest of the three little pigs."

"How do you feel about shipping container homes?"

"—Sick to my stomach. How is it thinking outside the box to live inside one?"

Suffice it that my hippie dream of pursuing an unconventional lifestyle went the way of bell-bottomed jeans. In the end, we put the whole idea of a country house out to pasture for the simple reason that we already had such a place at the lake. It was time to get serious and widen our search to include the state's larger population centers, such as they were. Strangely enough, we'd never really considered such a thing before, and suddenly it seemed to make a lot of sense, the opportunity to walk into town for necessities, or just for the exercise, presenting a whole new outlook on life. At the same time, the shift in perspective had the effect of narrowing our search considerably, for this was Maine, after all, where urban settings were few and far between.

It came down to a Goldilocks sort of choice; on the one hand, the prep school was located in the Androscoggin watershed, a region of thin and rocky soil that abounds in hardscrabble farms, while on the other, the lake house was part of the Penobscot basin, much of which consists of a vast wilderness centered on Mount Katahdin. In between lay the happy medium of Kennebec country, the eponymous waters of which rise along a remote stretch of the Canadian border and drain southward through the region known as Midcoast.

There was a good deal of personal history involved as well, the Kennebec providing a water route to both of our pasts—from my college and Sugarloaf days to Donna's wilderness camp adventures. It remained only for us to find a suitable piece of property, and when, after a series of disappointments, we came upon a small, newly-restored brick house on a quiet, untrammeled lane, we underwent the same sort of acquisitive transformation we had experienced upon finding the lake house. Thus we became full-fledged Mainers at last, and over the course of the next two years we set about ferrying stuff from our school house to the new address, making a leisurely transition before moving in for good.

# Chapter 23

# Secrets of the Borderline

In the years following my father's death, my brother continued to live in the family's townhouse largely at the insistence of our mother, for whom he served as live-in caretaker. This arrangement continued until her death some seven years later, which brought about a major change in my brother's circumstances. Now in his sixties, he'd spent much of his life in the house, and fully expected to inherit it upon her passing. Instead, as stipulated in her will, the house was to be sold and modest accommodations provided for him elsewhere.

When the will was made known, my brother initially refused to leave the house, and such was his distress over the matter that he called me up for the first time in many years seeking support, though what he expected me to do about it was not clear. I went through the motions, making inquiries of those involved in the disposition of the property, but in the end the matter had been decided simply and emphatically on the basis of his having insufficient means to support himself in the house. Only when accommodations were made available for him on the outskirts of town, did he agree to vacate, but the process had certainly proved traumatic for him.

Then something happened that no one expected. Despite his initial efforts to characterize the move as a grievous injustice, in the weeks and months that followed, he made the transition with remarkable equanimity. According to my younger sister, who had visited him with at the new place, he showed every sign of being satisfied with the change, though she hadn't been invited inside and remained concerned about his general housekeeping habits. Nevertheless, considering his previous upset, the news that he was largely reconciled to his new circumstances was most welcome. Once vacated, the family home was duly renovated and sold, and for once it seemed the vexing uncertainty of our brother's future—an uncertainty that had driven his mother and father to distraction and the rest of us simply away—was settled. Indeed, the speed with which the issue was resolved begged questions as to why it couldn't have been accomplished many years earlier.

The answer was traceable in part to the prevailing prejudices of the conformist era in which we had grown up, when the stigma that attached to psychological disorders of all kinds helped create an industry in which "care" included electric and insulin shock treatments, stupefying drug regimens and all manner of physical restraints. Against such a backdrop, it was small wonder that all signs of such illnesses were routinely denied or ignored for fear of confirming a diagnosis. Further confusing the issue were popular notions of the influence of parenting on the origins of erratic and antisocial behavior, notions which—in keeping with a larger, cultural misogyny—tended to attach guilt to the mother's role in particular, which helped explain my mother's fierce defensiveness in the face of all attempts to hold my brother accountable for his bad behavior. Innately kind and generous to a fault, she was fighting for her own reputation as well as for the welfare of her troubled, eldest son.

Not long ago I received a phone call from my brother. It happened to be my birthday and he called to wish me a happy one, which came as something of a surprise. Such remembrances had hardly been standard operating procedure for us in the past, and the last I'd heard from him was some two years earlier, in the wake of my mother's death, on which occasion he'd been so overwrought that I was scarcely able to understand what he was saying. Now, however, in the absence of any hint of such upset, I was able to recognize the sunnier side of his personality, and his effort to restore a semblance of normality to our relations seemed genuine. Indeed, his tone was disarmingly upbeat, revealing a sense of humor I'd all but forgotten he possessed.

Among other things, he ventured to tell me about his new place, which on the whole had worked out far better than he expected. The only problem was that his limited living area had become hopelessly cluttered with various items he'd managed to accumulate. This was nothing new; I first became aware of his hoarding behavior during a visit to the family's townhouse shortly before our mother died, at which time her impeccably furnished living room—featuring a Baby Grand Steinway and rare 16th-century Venetian screen—had been rendered nearly unnavigable by an assortment of items he'd chosen to add to the collection. Apparently, this compulsion had followed him to the new place, where he was unable to summon the will or energy to rid himself of a jumble of random stuff.

As he seldom volunteered details about his personal life, I took the opportunity to press him on it.

"Here's an idea: stop collecting that stuff."

"Yeah, well... it's a hobby of sorts."

"Seems more like a bad habit."

"Could be."

"So why not break it? Get yourself some trash bags and start throwing stuff out."

No response.

"Really, how hard could that be?" I wondered, not a little frustrated at his silence on the subject.

For a moment it seemed I had crossed a line, entering upon long-forbidden territory, but soon enough he got past it and we carried on chatting about the latest news from Watertown and the rest of the family. Having caught each other up, we ended on a rare conciliatory note, agreeing to stay in better touch before eventually ringing off.

In hindsight, the call seemed something of a break-through. His willingness to reach out and carry on an amicable conversation was clearly a good sign, and his ability to speak, however guardedly, about his hoarding behavior was more encouraging still. In the past, such discussion had been effectively off-limits, according to an unspoken pledge of secrecy within the family. Initiated by parental example and with the best of intentions, our collective silence on the subject had been meant to protect him from the calumnies of the outside world, but in fact it only seemed to fuel his illness, helping normalize his aberrant behavior and confounding larger efforts to understand and deal with the problems he was having.

Ever since dropping out of college, he had apparently been getting professional counseling, but in the absence of any larger discussion of such treatment, the rest of us were left in the dark, the particulars of his illness remaining a terrible secret around which ever-more-elaborate defenses were constructed against the intrusions of the world. Due to prevailing attitudes about such things, he simply wasn't allowed to be ill, even within the confines of the family.

A still greater problem had to do with the lack of a distinct clinical descriptor for his condition. From the time he first began seeing someone about the problem, a decade would pass before his symptoms would receive an approved psychiatric diagnosis—borderline personality disorder—and even then, treatment regimens remained largely unformed and untested. The name itself was fraught with ambiguity, a catch-all coinage, it seemed, that originated as a means to identify patients whose symptoms refused to fall neatly into one of the two basic categories: neurosis (a lesser, stress-related illness) or psychosis (a disorder involving loss of touch with reality). Because these patients were routinely seen to cross over from one state to the other, they were thought to exist in a borderline condition.

Likewise, the origins of the illness seemed to occupy a grey area between the nature vs. nurture dichotomy, muddling the careful distinctions of psychiatric nomenclature and making treatment of the disorder all the more ambiguous. Originally thought to be a result of organic disease, a physical defect within the brain, BPD has since been shown to be closely associated with emotional trauma in infancy. According to the latter theory, its onset can be traced to the period of development when a child first begins to understand that he's an individual, separate from his mother or other caregivers. At this vulnerable stage, normally between the ages of one and a half to two years, the child comes to trust that when caregivers leave his immediate presence they are not gone forever, but can be counted on to come back and attend to him. If a traumatic event interferes with this crucial stage of development, it can leave an emotional scar, making him susceptible to persistent fears of rejection and abandonment.

Over the years since learning of this diagnosis, I made a point of reading up on the subject, in light of which his recent acknowledgement of compulsive hoarding rang a bell. Suddenly those episodes that had remained shrouded in mystery seemed to come into focus: his inexplicable reaction to a minor renovation of the boathouse, the notional loss of an old rocking horse, and many similar incidents, all of which seemed to provoke in him a kind of existential dread. Was it possible that the threatened disappearance of these things recalled unresolved infantile anxieties having to do with separation fears? The connection between these episodes and his difficulty in forming sustained and sustaining relationships suddenly seemed to make sense as well, the hoarded objects themselves serving as substitutes for the attachments he hadn't been able to form with people. Such psychiatric theorizing often seems a matter of mere speculation, and yet I had the feeling I was seeing, as if for the first time, the essence of his illness—an insight that had eluded me ever since childhood.

Then too, a potential trigger for such anxieties was not far to seek; I had only to count the number of months between his birthday and my own (15) to realize that my arrival in his world had likely caused or at least contributed to his disorder, placing added demands on our parents' time and affections just when his separation anxiety would have been most acute. Then too, this would help explain our habitual fighting, the source of which remained deeply embedded in our early history. In the absence of any clearer explanation, I had always attributed his combativeness to an innate character flaw, part of who he was, an ingrained malevolence ordained by fate. In light of these new insights, however, a clearer understanding of his developmental challenges—not to mention my own, inadvertent agency in creating them—changed the picture, opening the door to a more sympathetic and rational response.

Having formerly received little enlightenment from the abstract language of psychiatry, I'd always gravitated to the familiar definition of personality as an "unbroken series of successful gestures," attributing my brother's troubles to an inability to carry off the essential role-playing we all engage in. According to this formulation, he simply lacked confidence, and only needed greater support and encouragement to "get his act together." In the end, however, the theory had proven far too simplistic, placing much of the burden for his socialization on family members, and effectively discouraging efforts to seek other answers, let alone outside help.

If his affliction had been outwardly apparent, a physical handicap or some obvious impairment, he would surely have met with a very different response from the first. Instead, its essential obscurity and the well-intentioned tolerance that surrounded it, only served to normalize his bad behavior, bolstering his insistence on his own misguided rectitude. It came as no surprise to learn that a diagnosis of BPD tends to be as difficult for patients to accept as it is to define. In many ways its symptoms seem perfectly consistent with the human condition itself, for we are all the product of an incalculable mix of influences, genetic and experiential, whose infinitely various combinations are subject to forces as capricious as the wind. Accordingly, patients are apt to view their diagnosis as inherently subject to dispute, a matter of differences of opinion. Similarly, treatment regimens tend to be viewed as deeply suspect, and minor signs of progress routinely become invitations to abandon drug regimens or other protocols.

Even so, a growing body of knowledge has lent a crucial sense of legitimacy to the diagnosis as well as new hope for its treatment. One finding of such studies suggests that its symptoms diminish with age, and my brother's case would seem to confirm this. While it remains one of the most difficult mood disorders to treat, various drug regimens have proven useful, and a consensus has emerged around the effectiveness of one-on-one or small group counseling administered by therapists trained in the nuances of the disorder. While the descriptor itself has come under fire for its failure to reference any specific, identifying behavior, I came to appreciate its metaphorical significance, the sense in which it serves as a catch-all for a series of conflicting dualities: good/evil, nature/nurture, reason/emotion, male/female—borderlines we all confront as human beings.

Indeed, the name of his disorder would acquire a particular resonance for me. It explained things, enabling me to recognize the extent to which his affliction had been an integral part of my own history and development. Our enmity as brothers, after all, had been due in large part to a lack of language with which to explain what was happening to us, and much of what had gone wrong was traceable not to his illness so much as to a failure to speak truly and openly about its effects on everyone involved. In this respect, the diagnosis provided a key piece of the puzzle, giving shape and substance to an otherwise insoluble mystery. I came to see it as a good and useful concept, a name to be spoken out loud and explained in the plainest of language. No longer fraught with the stigma of psychological illness, it stood for a new understanding based on the kind of truth that sets one free.

    The other day, as promised, I called my brother on his birthday. His number I knew by heart, as he'd arranged to retain the one associated with the house we grew up in—another connection to the past that had become important to his sense of continuity and well-being. As with our earlier conversations, we found no shortage of things to talk about, and in the course of an animated exchange he proceeded to relate something of the family's history. Of special interest was the story of the first of our father's clan to arrive in the New World, a Hessian soldier who fought for the British Crown against the rebellious American colonists. For his military service, this forebear was granted a tract of land on a peninsula overlooking the Bay of Quinte, an arm of Lake Ontario some forty miles west of the city of Kingston. The existence of this Ur-Inglehart was news to me, and in the course of our conversation I proposed to do some research of my own, at which point we agreed to compare notes in a series of emails.
    I began my search with the possibility that our ancestor had arrived in America as part of the massive British build-up leading to the Battle of Long Island. If so, he would most likely have been part of the contingent of some 5,000 Hessians that went forward against the Patriot center on Gowanus Heights, driving the enemy back upon the village of Brooklyn and eventually helping capture New York City, then comprised of some 25,000 souls. Next, I followed a trail of speculation leading to Trenton, New Jersey, where a lesser force of Hessians—about a third of the original number—were serving garrison duty on the night of General Washington's famous crossing

of the ice-bound Delaware River and subsequent surprise attack. Among this smaller force, I hoped to have a better chance of finding an ancestor, and lo and behold, among the names I came across was one Johann Englehardt, an artillery officer who managed to escape capture in the ensuing action. Could this be the man I was after, the spelling of whose name had changed over time?

Apparently not, for shortly after I proposed such a thing, my brother wrote back to explain that the man who had been granted the homestead on Lake Ontario was Barnhart Inglehart, though the particulars of his subsequent history remained uncertain. In any case, by 1805 his son Ira had reconciled with his father's former enemies, crossing the river at Ogdensburg to settle in St. Lawrence County, New York, where he married a woman of Dutch extraction, one Elizabeth Van Waters. The couple eventually moved some fifty miles to the southwest, where they established a farmstead in the town of Hounsfield and raised three sons, one of whom, Cornelius, would become an outspoken abolitionist in the run-up to the Civil War as well as an early business leader, founding an insurance company in nearby Watertown.

Next in the line of hereditary succession was Cornelius' son, Hiram Foote Inglehart, who would build upon his father's entrepreneurial legacy, becoming the proprietor of several hotels in Alexandria Bay and Thousand Island Park, as well as a stockholder in the summer community at Westminster Park, where both his son and grandson would grow up. Hiram would also serve as the director of three banks and his father's insurance company, which his son George, my grandfather, headed for much of his life. This left my father, another George, whose service as a fighter pilot and a state supreme court judge served as crowning tributes to the industry and good works of his forebears.

In the end, such genealogical insights were my brother's particular gift, for prior to this, despite an abiding interest in the general contours of the past, the details of my forefathers' lives had never been of much interest to me. I knew them only as disembodied names that recurred in my father's often sardonic reference to our common heritage. For this reason, an overweening interest in bloodlines—however appropriate to the business of horse breeding— always struck me as a quaint affectation when applied to human beings. In the context of my brother's recent missives, however, the subject acquired a new relevance, redeeming something of our fraught kinship.

Our ancestors, after all, had survived the birth throes of a new nation and gone on to perform the hard work of reconciliation and assimilation within warring factions of their own countrymen. Likewise, as with every generation since the dawn of human history, they endured the no-less-formidable struggles of family life, giving rise to a more or less congenial clan of more or less well-adjusted members of society. Who was I to ignore their example? Accordingly, I came to a new reckoning with the past, resolving what remained of my ambivalence toward a part of the world I had grown up in, and away from.

Though opportunities to visit the River are few and far between these days, I make the trip every now and then, invariably choosing to take the northern route through the mountains, if only for the chance to recall something of the past, or what's left of it. A sleek new skyway has replaced the precarious piling structure over Lake Champlain, remnants of which can still be seen from the elevated deck of the new bridge, a sight that never fails to recall the first time I passed through that part of the world. So too, while traveling the long road through the cow country of the upper St. Lawrence valley, I inevitably keep an eye out for the weather-beaten church I remember coming upon during that first trip, though I suspect it has long since been torn down. All I remember about it with any clarity was the decrepit bulletin board out front and my fit of pique over the message it displayed: "To know all is to forgive all." Anyway, I have yet to confirm the sighting and can scarcely recall what it was that so offended me about the proverb.

—**END**—

www.ingramcontent.com/pod-product-compliance
Lightning Source LLC
Chambersburg PA
CBHW072047110526
44590CB00018B/3075